RUSSIA'S TRANSITION: INTERNATIONAL HELP OR MEDDLING?

RUSSIA'S TRANSITION: INTERNATIONAL HELP OR MEDDLING?

ALEXANDER KURA

Nova Science Publishers, Inc.
Huntington, New York

Senior Editors: Susan Boriotti and Donna Dennis
Office Manager: Annette Hellinger
Graphics: Wanda Serrano and Dorothy Marczak
Information Editor: Tatiana Shohov
Book Production: Cathy DeGregory, Matthew Kozlowski, Jonathan Rose, Jennifer Vogt and Lynette Van Helden
Circulation: Ave Maria Gonzalez, Mike Hedges, Ron Hedges and Andre Tillman

Library of Congress Cataloging-in-Publication Data
available upon request

ISBN 1-59033-022-6

227 Main Street, Suite 100
Huntington, New York 11743
Tele. 631-424-6682 Fax 631-425-5933
e-mail: Novascience@earthlink.net
Web Site: http://www.nexusworld.com/nova

Printed in the United States of America

CONTENTS

LIST OF TABLES AND FIGURES

TABLES

FIGURES

EXECUTIVE SUMMARY

PURPOSE

Since the breakup of the Soviet Union in 1991, multilateral organizations and bilateral donors, including the United States, have provided the Russian Federation (Russia) with tens of billions of dollars in economic assistance directed at helping Russia's transition to a market economy within a democratic state. The value of this assistance is difficult to assess, however, since Russia appears to be a long way from having a competitive, market economy, and its transition experience over the past decade has been more difficult than was expected. The approaches used to assist Russia, both in the past and for the future, continue to be debated. To help focus this debate, the Chairman and Ranking Minority Member of the Committee on Banking and Financial Services, House of Representatives, asked GAO to review the strategies of different lending institutions and donors in providing economic assistance to Russia with a view toward identifying lessons learned that might be valuable for making future decisions about assistance policies. Specifically, GAO examined (1) what types of assistance these institutions and donors have provided, what their program strategies were, and how the assistance has been coordinated; (2) how successful the institutions and donors have been in terms of meeting their assistance objectives and what factors have affected their success; and (3) what lessons can be learned that may have relevance for future policy decisions about Russia. The lending institutions GAO included in this review are the International Monetary Fund, the World Bank's International Bank for Reconstruction and Development,[1] and the European Bank for Reconstruction and Development. The other programs are U.S. bilateral assistance under the 1992 Freedom Support Act[2] and the European Union's Technical Assistance to the Commonwealth of Independent States program. From 1992 until September 2000, these five programs have provided about $36

[1] GAO examined the lending made to Russia by the International Bank for Reconstruction and Development because it has provided the vast majority of the World Bank Group's funding to Russia. Two other parts of the World Bank Group that have provided funding to Russia are the International Finance Corporation and the Multilateral Investment Guarantee Agency in Russia.

[2] "Freedom" in the name of this act stands for Freedom for Russia and Emerging Eurasian Democracies and Open Markets (P.L. 102-511). Throughout this report, GAO refers to the act as the "Freedom Support Act."

billion in assistance to Russia, with U.S. bilateral assistance under the Freedom Support Act of $2.3 billion. To meet its objectives, GAO analyzed a wide range of documents and interviewed current and former officials from each of the five lending institutions and donors as well as Russia experts from think tanks, academic institutions, and nongovernmental organizations. GAO traveled to Russia and interviewed current and former Russian government officials, in-country donor representatives and experts, and also project beneficiaries. GAO obtained access to International Monetary Fund, World Bank, and European Bank for Reconstruction and Development officials and documents through the Department of the Treasury and through the U.S. member of each institution's executive board.

Results in Brief

The international community generally agreed on some fundamental principles concerning Russia's economic transition, but it did not have a comprehensive strategy regarding the level, timing, and priorities of assistance and how assistance would be coordinated. The leaders of the major industrial nations, including the United States, chose early on not to commit substantial bilateral resources to Russia, leaving the International Monetary Fund and the World Bank to provide the bulk of financial assistance. The strategies and means for providing assistance of the international institutions and donors have reflected their different missions. For example, the International Monetary Fund has provided loans to Russia's central government, tied to reforms aimed particularly at controlling inflation and achieving macroeconomic stability, while the much more limited U.S. bilateral program has targeted primarily market reforms, but also democracy and humanitarian needs, largely through providing technical assistance. Over the transition period, institutions and donors themselves and the Russian government have created various forums for coordination of assistance. This coordination has improved in some areas over time, but it is still a challenge to the institutions and donors and to the Russian government.

While there have been successes across individual program objectives for the institutions and donors GAO reviewed, officials have acknowledged that in many respects, there has been limited progress in reaching their broad program goals. While the worst fears of the early transition period, such as anarchy or return to communist rule, have not been realized, Russia's economic decline has been more severe and its recovery slower than anticipated. At the individual project level, the success of assistance of these institutions and donors has been mixed, according to their own evaluations and the views of officials and analysts GAO interviewed. Limitations in program success are due to obstacles encountered in Russia, including the lack of domestic political consensus behind reform and emergence of powerful vested interests; sometimes poorly designed or implemented programs; and the scale and complexities of the challenges. These factors can be interrelated. Assistance efforts in four key policy areas—macroeconomic stabilization, social safety net protection, privatization, and banking sector reform—

illustrate barriers to success and how limited reforms in some areas have undermined progress in other areas. Institutions and donors have modified their strategies and programs in Russia in different ways over the decade, but remaining engaged in Russia has been a common goal.

A number of conclusions and lessons learned can be drawn from assistance efforts in Russia that have implications for looking ahead. The overarching lesson is that without some degree of consensus and political commitment within Russia, the impact of assistance programs on political and economic reforms is limited. The immense challenge of Russia's transition to a market economy and democratic society was underestimated by the international community and by Russians, and the transition will clearly take longer than initially expected. The transition involves developing effective laws and institutions and restructuring many enterprises. It requires broad, grassroots support and calls for greater means to cushion social impacts on vulnerable groups. The Russian government's recent development of a long-term economic program demonstrates that the government has the capacity to seriously evaluate and debate the economic policy choices the country faces and that those choices remain difficult ones for Russia. International assistance efforts need to be structured for the possibility of long-term involvement.

BACKGROUND

The common assumption among western leaders was that Russia's conversion from a Communist state to a market economy within a democratic state would bring long-term stability within Russia and between Russia and the West. This transformation required fundamental changes throughout the Russian economy, government, and society. Unlike other transition countries such as Poland and Hungary, Russia had no vestige of a democracy or competitive market economy and almost nothing in the way of supporting institutions or economic relationships with western partners.

Many bilateral donors and international institutions implemented programs to assist Russia's transition process. According to one U.S. government estimate, the total value of international assistance disbursed to Russia through September 1998 was $66 billion,[3] excluding food aid loans, trade credits, and debt rollovers. The five institutions and donors that GAO reviewed have provided loans, grants, and technical assistance to aid Russia's economic transition. The International Monetary Fund (IMF) lent Russia more than $22.2 billion to help stabilize the economy. The World Bank targeted reforms in various sectors of the economy, disbursing $7.5 billion in loans. The European Bank for Reconstruction and Development aided the development of the private sector in Russia, disbursing $2.2 billion in loans and investments in Russian firms. Under the Freedom

[3] Although there are important limitations to the comparisons, for purposes of context, this can be compared to the more than $500 billion the German government has spent since 1989 to support the economic transition in eastern Germany, and international assistance to Poland of about $36 billion from 1989 through 1994.

Support Act, the United States has expended $2.3 billion in grants for technical assistance, exchanges, and other programs to address humanitarian needs and support economic and democratic reform. The European Union's Technical Assistance to the Commonwealth of Independent States program has spent $1.6 billion to provide grantfinanced technical assistance to support the development of a market economy and a democratic society (see fig. 1 for an illustration of donor assistance to Russia, 1991-September 2000).

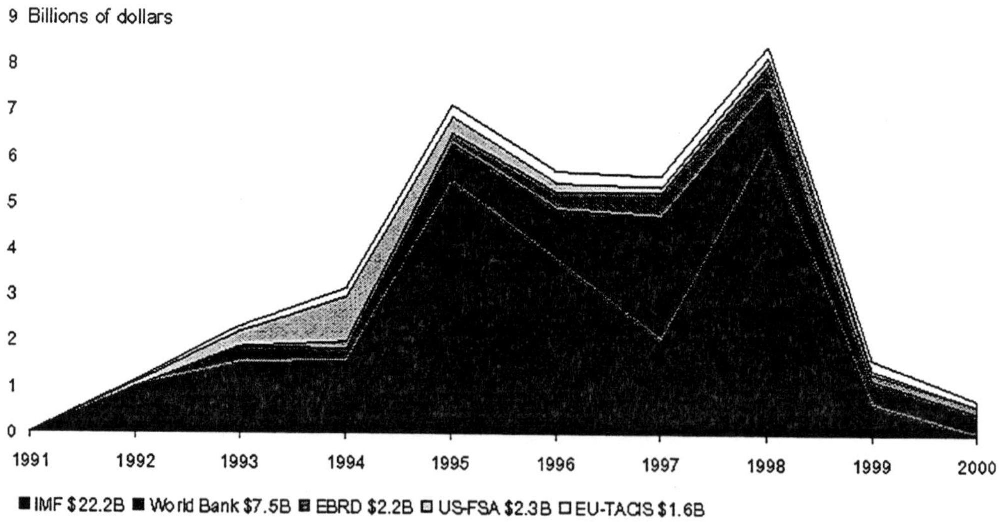

Figure 1: Disbursements to Russia by Five Institutions and Donors, 1991-September 2000

Legend: EU-TACIS=European Union's Technical Assistance to the Commonwealth of Independent States
EBRD=European Bank for Reconstruction and Development
FSA=Freedom Support Act
Note 1: These figures have not been adjusted for inflation.
Note 2: Figures for the IMF, World Bank, and EBRD do not include disbursements for technical assistance programs.
Sources: GAO analysis of information from the IMF, the World Bank, the European Bank for Reconstruction and Development, the U.S. Department of State, and the European Union.

PRINCIPAL FINDINGS

Donors Have Adopted Different Strategies and Means for Providing Assistance

In its early efforts to assist Russia's economic transition, the international community generally agreed on some fundamental principles concerning the transition, but it did not have a comprehensive strategy for the assistance it would provide and how its efforts would be coordinated. With other foreign policy concerns and domestic political constraints, the major industrial countries chose early on not to commit substantial bilateral resources to Russia. Instead, primary responsibility for providing assistance fell to multilateral organizations such as the IMF and the World Bank. Western leaders, and a key group of Russian officials, shared several basic assumptions. They believed, for example, that controls on prices and trade needed to be removed right away and inflation controlled and that state enterprises should be privatized quickly, with the assumption that the institutions needed to support the new market economy would develop over time. Beyond those basic principles, however, many aspects of overall assistance policy were not laid out, such as interrelationships among different aspects of transition and how well assistance needs fit the traditional instruments of the international financial institutions. Effective coordination of assistance proved difficult.

The institutions and donors GAO reviewed have pursued the similar broad objectives of helping Russia make the transition to a market-based economy, but their individual strategies and means for providing assistance have differed, reflecting their different roles. The primary objective of the IMF's involvement with Russia has been to achieve macroeconomic stabilization, largely defined by low inflation. The IMF has provided loans to Russia's Ministry of Finance and central bank; it has given technical assistance and engaged in high-level dialogue with Russian officials. IMF financing has been tied to Russia's meeting certain economic conditions, often measured by quantitative indicators, such as budget deficit and revenue targets. Over time, the IMF's strategy in Russia has shifted to emphasize structural reforms, such as changes in Russia's tax system and financial sector, to improve the environment for economic growth. The World Bank has used both lending and nonlending services to pursue its objectives of supporting Russia's transition to a market economy based on initiatives in the private sector, protection of poor and vulnerable groups, and the development and strengthening of Russian institutions. Implementation of World Bank programs in Russia began slowly. From 1992 through 1995, the World Bank approved $3.4 billion for investment projects across several Russian sectors, but by the end of 1995, only $278 million in investment lending had been disbursed.[4] The World Bank's strategy has shifted during the transition away from financing a variety of investment projects across Russia toward providing large loans aimed at federal-level reforms, ranging from policies for specific sectors, such as coal, to tax and pension policies. The European Bank for Reconstruction and

[4] The World Bank disbursed a $600-million adjustment loan for balance-of-payments support to the Russian government in 1993.

Development's strategy has focused on financing commercial projects in Russia's private sector while having a "transition impact," not competing with private sources of funding and, at the same time, making a small profit. Over time, the strategy has become more focused on promoting restructuring in large companies and developing small- and medium-sized businesses.

The objectives of the U.S. Freedom Support Act bilateral program have been to promote market reform and democracy and to address urgent human needs related to Russia's transition to a market economy. The United States has pursued these objectives through a variety of instruments including technical assistance, exchanges and training, grants, trade promotion, and enterprise funds. The U.S. program has generally emphasized the objective of promoting market reforms, although recent budgets have placed more relative emphasis on democracy and rule of law programs. In 1996, the U.S. program began shifting resources from work at the federal level to a few reform-minded regions. The strategy of the EU's Technical Assistance program has been to finance the provision of technical assistance in Russia by consultants and European institutions, with the objectives of assisting and accelerating the socioeconomic and democratic reform process. Over time, its strategy has shifted from providing small, quick projects in close collaboration with the Russian government to emphasizing larger projects with a greater focus on developing civil society, removing structural barriers to reform, and carrying out efforts that more closely link Russia and the European Union.

Initial attempts to coordinate these institutions' and donors' efforts were impeded by the lack of a clear western strategy. At the same time, it was not clear to those providing assistance whether the Russian government wanted coordinated assistance efforts. Early formal coordination bodies, such as a group set up by the Group of Seven industrialized countries (G-7), proved cumbersome and were disbanded in 1997.[5] Donor officials told us they prefer the informal mechanisms that have developed over time to share information and discuss approaches. In selected sectors, such as health and banking sector reform, for example, donors have formed informal working groups. Donor programs sometimes lay the groundwork, through grants and technical assistance, for World Bank and European Bank for Reconstruction and Development loans in specific areas, including housing, tax, the financial sector, and legal reform.

The Russian government is not totally satisfied with the coordination of this assistance, and officials told GAO that one ministry is not always aware of donor efforts in other ministries. Representatives of the donor community in Russia also told GAO that although some improvements have been made, coordination with the Russian government continues to be a challenge, often complicated by difficulties in coordinating within the Russian government. Russia's 1998 financial crisis demonstrated the need for more formal coordination in banking sector reform and, in the aftermath of the crisis, the Central Bank of Russia set up a coordinating committee composed of donor and government representatives. Donor officials told us that progress to date has been mixed.

---

[5] The G-7 consists of the United States, the United Kingdom, Germany, Japan, France, Italy, and Canada. It has been very involved in the international community's efforts to assist Russia in its transition to a market economy.

The Impact of Assistance Programs Has Been Mixed, With Broad Results Limited in Many Respects

While there have been a number of individual successes of assistance programs in Russia, officials have acknowledged that progress toward reaching broad program goals has been limited. According to a number of indicators, the performance of the Russian economy over the past decade has been poor, with Russia's economic decline among the most severe and its recovery among the most limited among transition countries in Eastern Europe and the former Soviet Union. For example, measured economic output in 1995 was about 65 percent of 1991 levels and remained stagnant through 1998 before showing some improvement. Obstacles to economic growth continue to exist in many areas where the international community has focused its efforts; these obstacles include the absence of effective competition in many sectors and the continuing lack of social services to adequately protect poor and vulnerable groups.

The success of the individual projects and other elements of the Russia programs of the institutions and donors GAO reviewed has been mixed, according to their own evaluations and the views of officials and analysts GAO interviewed. While the IMF has not comprehensively evaluated its Russia program, GAO identified a range of views on the success of IMF programs in Russia. A number of U.S. and Russian government officials as well as economists and Russia analysts at think tanks have taken issue with aspects of IMF programs, ranging from the exchange rate policies it supported to whether the IMF was "too soft" in enforcing the conditions of its lending program. However, a number of analysts and U.S. and Russian officials told us that the policy advice and high-level dialogue provided by the IMF has been of value to Russia's transition in several important respects. World Bank officials, in their December 1999 Russia strategy paper, characterized the success of World Bank programs in Russia as mixed but overall disappointing relative to their expectations. According to World Bank assessments, the percentage of loans in its Russia portfolio meeting development and implementation objectives has ranged from 33 percent to 82 percent over the period, showing improvement in 1996 and 1997, falling sharply after the 1998 financial crisis, and then improving after post-crisis loan restructurings. According to World Bank officials, the value of its large adjustment loans directed at central government reforms remains to be seen, but some indicators of success have become more apparent in recent months.

The European Bank for Reconstruction and Development has also rated the success of its projects in Russia as mixed. According to European Bank for Reconstruction and Development officials, their efforts have been most successful in areas of small business development and other projects entailing work with smaller firms. They acknowledged that the financial turmoil in 1998 damaged many European Bank for Reconstruction and Development efforts, especially in the financial sector, and it has had limited success in promoting restructuring in large Russian firms. Russian officials and analysts had differing perspectives on European Bank for Reconstruction and Development efforts in Russia, with some generally positive but others stating that the Bank's role duplicates lending and investment functions provided by the private sector.

With respect to the U.S. Freedom Support Act programs in Russia, based on GAO's analysis of available evaluations, discussions with officials, and prior GAO work, the programs have had mixed results. GAO's past reviews of U.S. assistance projects in Russia found that while some met their objectives and were seen as valuable by Russian recipients, others were viewed as having limited impact.

The general assessment of the European Union's Technical Assistance programs in Russia is also mixed, based on the EU's own evaluations and on discussions with European Union and Russian officials and other analysts. For example, a March 2000 European Union report on its Technical Assistance program for Russia gave it high marks for education and training efforts and lower marks for enterprise restructuring and building the framework for a market economy.

Obstacles to Assistance

GAO identified three main interrelated obstacles to assistance programs in Russia attaining project and program objectives: (1) difficult conditions in Russia, including the lack of domestic political consensus behind reforms, the constant change in government officials, and the presence of vested interests and corruption; (2) limitations in how programs were designed and implemented; and (3) the vastness of the challenge and the interdependent nature of Russia's transition needs.

GAO found that a common frustration among the lending institutions and donors, with the IMF an exception to some degree, has been the difficulty of establishing and maintaining effective working relationships with Russian government officials. This situation has been due, in part, to rapid turnover in officials and a distrust of or disinterest in some donor programs. It has also been due to a lack of effective consensus between the executive and legislative branches of the Russian government and among the broader public regarding a reform agenda. The increasing concentration of economic power in Russia and the rise of politically powerful interest groups are widely viewed as impeding progress in meeting economic reform objectives. For example, powerful vested interests have been able to block several efforts to reform the tax system. In addition, according to analysts, donor officials, and documents, corruption at different levels of government has undermined reform efforts and also efforts to spur private sector economic activity.

Limitations in the design and implementation of assistance programs also impeded program effectiveness. Some of these limitations were directly related to the mandates and traditional roles of the institutions and donors GAO reviewed. Others stemmed from limited institutional and program capabilities and decisions about what strategies to pursue and how to implement them. Beginning in 1992, for example, international institutions faced pressures to lend money to Russia quickly. A tension thus resulted between taking time to study conditions and needs in Russia and adequately design programs, on the one hand, and trying to disburse funds quickly in order to have a role in the reform process, on the other. In addition, international institutions, particularly the World Bank, were concerned about Russia's ability to repay the loans. The international institutions that were expected to assume the lead in providing assistance had never before worked in the Soviet Union and lacked staff familiar with Russia. Similarly, the U.S. government faced substantial pressure to disburse Freedom Support Act funds quickly beginning in 1993, when funding for bilateral assistance directed at economic transition increased.

According to officials from the World Bank, the European Bank for Reconstruction and Development, the United States, and the European Union, the effectiveness of assistance programs often suffered from being too broad and inadequately focused. Assistance resources were spread broadly for a number of reasons, ranging from a belief that wide-ranging involvement was called for to pressure to respond to different constituencies, such as U.S. government agencies or European Union member countries. Donor program and Russian officials and other analysts also cited not having adequate personnel on the ground in Russia and unevenness in the quality of consultants as limiting program impact. GAO found that the success of assistance programs has also been limited by the interdependencies across Russia's needs and by the relatively small scale of assistance programs in relation to the extent of Russia's needs. Building a market economy and democratic society in Russia involves change on an immense scale and, in many instances, even very successful donor projects cannot have more than a limited impact.

Based on its assessment of key issues in Russia's transition over the past 8 years and through discussions with Russia experts, GAO selected four policy areas—macroeconomic stabilization, social safety net protection, privatization, and banking sector reform—that illustrate both the range of challenges faced and the degree to which the amount of progress in one area has affected reforms in other areas. For example, while inflation was finally brought under control in late 1995, serious macroeconomic imbalances remained, which contributed to the financial crisis of 1998. These imbalances, including the need to finance large government deficits through paying very high interest rates on government securities, were due in part to structural problems in the economy, especially the inability of the government to collect taxes. With respect to macroeconomic policy choices, while a highly valued ruble may have helped in controlling inflation during part of the mid-1990s, it is likely also to have hindered economic growth through making it more difficult for Russian producers to compete with imported goods, according to many officials and experts. While privatization of state-owned enterprises was an essential element of Russia's transition, the ways in which some of the largest enterprises were privatized increased the concentration of economic power and made achieving reforms in areas such as tax collection more difficult.

The international community strongly encouraged Russia's decision to privatize firms quickly and was significantly involved in the design and implementation of the voucher privatization program. While the program was carried out quickly and efficiently, assessments of its ultimate impact are mixed. The "insider" nature of the privatization process undermined its economic benefits, according to many officials and analysts. The loans-for-shares privatization program, carried out in late 1995, is one of the most controversial aspects of Russia's transition.[6] Through the program, a handful of

[6] The loans-for-shares program was a mechanism the Russian government used in 1995 to privatize certain government enterprises in order to raise money. The auctions were not transparent, and the government fell far short of its revenue targets.

financial-industrial groups in Russia became controlling shareholders in some of the country's most valuable enterprises, in return for providing about $1 billion in revenues for Russia to meet its budgetary financing needs for that year. While the international community did not directly support the loan-for-shares program, it did not strongly object, according to evidence GAO reviewed.

Russia's banking sector was targeted early on in donor assistance efforts; however, progress in strengthening Russia's banking sector has been limited. The 1998 financial crisis decimated Russia's banks and revealed how unsound their financial condition was. It also illustrated the need for better coordination between the Russian authorities and the institutions and donors on banking reform efforts. Views of analysts and officials GAO met with in Russia on the priority of banking sector restructuring efforts were mixed. Although there is still little bank lending to small- and medium-sized businesses, many experts felt that the demand for such loans was limited and that the lack of bank financing was not the most important impediment to the growth of such enterprises in Russia.

The evolution of international assistance efforts in Russia reflects institutions' and donors' continued commitment to remain engaged in Russia largely because of the country's strategic importance. In some cases, institutions and donors have responded to similar frustrations in Russia by changing their programs in different ways, with shifts reflecting differences in the nature, mandate, and political context of the institutions. For example, the United States and the World Bank modified their Russia programs in very different ways. In response to the difficulty in implementing projects and in an attempt to exert greater leverage, the World Bank shifted beginning in 1996 from attempting numerous projects across multiple sectors and Russia's regions to lending to and dealing more with the central government. In contrast, the United States shifted in 1996-97 from trying to influence policy changes within the central government to concentrating its efforts in several regions. Substantial reductions in U.S. funding limiting the ability to obtain nationwide results, the heightened importance of demonstrating assistance results, and growing resistance from the Duma and federal government to enacting meaningful reform encouraged the U.S. shift to the regions.

Political considerations have also affected program implementation in Russia. For example, despite concerns regarding poor implementation of the first program, the IMF executive board approved disbursement of $1.5 billion in March 1994 to show support for the Russian government. In 1996, the IMF frequently reviewed the Russia program and modified target requirements for additional disbursements. According to the IMF, weak macroeconomic performance was felt to reflect instability related to the upcoming presidential elections, and the board wanted to show continued support for the Russian government.

Over time, explicit anticorruption efforts have represented a relatively small share of international assistance to Russia. However, many programs have indirect anticorruption elements. For example, funding for democracy and rule of law programs have represented about 24 percent of U.S. assistance under the Freedom Support Act. The World Bank first explicitly addressed corruption in its 1999 country assistance strategy for Russia, although, according to Bank officials, several aspects of its Russia program over time have had an anticorruption dimension. The World Bank cited its coal sector lending as one area in which limiting opportunities for corruption has had an increasing focus in the Bank's program. The programs GAO reviewed have implemented specific procedures to increase protection of their program funds from corruption and theft. These institutions and donors have reported either that they have not suffered any theft, or have not suffered major theft, of funds in Russia. GAO did not independently evaluate the issue of whether there has been theft or diversion of program funds.

Conclusions and Lessons Learned

At the end of nearly a decade of involvement in Russia's economic transition, institutions and donors have drawn a number of conclusions about what has and has not worked, and lessons from the experience (see apps. I-V for donor-specific lessons). The institutions and donors are generally in the process of reevaluating, with the Russian government, the level and design of their assistance programs. Based on GAO's work, the following conclusions and lessons learned may have relevance for future assistance efforts.

Conclusions

- The challenge of Russia's transition was enormous and greater than generally appreciated by the West. In hindsight, expectations within Russia and among institutions and donors of achieving quick results were unrealistic.
- Some aspects of transition assistance that the international community identified early on as important proved difficult to provide, for several reasons, and have continued to be obstacles to needed reforms. In particular, the lack of social support to ease the cost of economic restructuring has increased the impact of the transition on poor and vulnerable groups, decreased Russian public support for reform, and been a limiting factor in economic restructuring.
- Russia's transition path has been made harder by the concentration of power and income in the hands of a few, a process that had begun prior to the transition and that was accelerated by the privatization of the most valuable sectors of Russian enterprise in 1994 and 1995.
- The degree to which the international community, with different policies and levels of involvement, could have influenced a different path remains the subject of substantial debate. The question cannot be fully answered, because what would have happened under alternative policies remains unknown. However, many officials and analysts have stated that, in hindsight, they would have made different choices in some cases. These include the push to privatize the largest firms quickly and the failure of the international community to strongly object to the loans-for-shares privatization program in 1995.

- The donors' and institutions' initial expectations and hopes that Russians would accept and quickly implement advice proved unfounded. The transition to a market economy and democratic society in Russia required grassroots support and the development of effective institutions, laws, and enforcement processes. These changes have profound implications for Russian society and politics and thus required a degree of political consensus within Russia that did not exist for much of the decade.
- Little progress has been made in achieving reforms in areas where there has not been ownership and support from the Russian government, including the individuals and institutions with the authority to influence outcomes. Working to achieve adequate ownership, and even identify when it exists, has proved difficult for donors.
- The unexpectedly strong performance of Russia's economy since the August 1998 financial collapse, due only in part to high export earnings from oil, has underscored the limitations of how well the Russians and the international community have understood the evolution and functioning of the Russian economy, and have caused a reexamination of some policy choices.
- The Russian government's recent development of a long-term economic program demonstrates its capacity to seriously evaluate and debate the economic policy choices the country faces. Donors can take some credit for helping develop this capacity. The program also demonstrates that the policy choices facing the Russian government remain very hard ones.

Lessons Learned

When taken together, these conclusions about past efforts to assist the transition in Russia have some important implications for future assistance efforts. Although there are no easy prescriptions for how to best support reform in Russia, the following lessons can be of value.

- In light of the realization that Russia's transition to a market economy will take longer than anyone initially thought, to have the ability to make a significant impact, donor programs should be structured for the possibility of long-term involvement in Russia. For example, donors can help build grassroots support for the development of institutions in Russia to underlie a competitive market economy within a democratic society. This is likely to require involvement over many years.
- In light of the fact that Russian political will is so important to the success of reform efforts, donors may have a bigger impact if they concentrate their assistance efforts on the areas in which the Russians are open to making reforms. Working to develop ownership as widely and deeply as possible within the Russian government and across society is likely to pay off in terms of assistance having the greatest benefit.

- Because progress on the path to democracy and a market economy is not a smooth one, donors need to maintain flexibility in their programs to the extent possible, so that they can respond to changing conditions and windows of opportunity.

Chapter 1

INTRODUCTION

Since 1991, the international community has faced an uncertain political and economic environment first in the Soviet Union and then in the Russian Federation (Russia). Russia's transformation to a market economy within a democratic state required fundamental changes throughout the Russian economy, government, and society. The transformation process has presented both opportunities and challenges to the Russians and to the institutions and donors that chose to provide economic assistance. From 1991 through September 2000, the assistance from the five institutions and donors in our review amounted to nearly $35.8 billion for programs in Russia.

THE POLITICAL AND ECONOMIC ENVIRONMENT IN WHICH INSTITUTIONS AND DONORS HAVE PROVIDED ASSISTANCE

The official end of the Soviet Union in December 1991 was the culmination of several years of growing economic and political instability. The collapse presented the Soviet Union's former Cold War adversaries with opportunities and challenges. The major organized threat to the West vanished, but thousands of nuclear warheads and also aging nuclear power plants remained in a region characterized by political uncertainty and economic turmoil. In addition, the international community faced the challenge of trying to support economic and democratic reform in a country that had for many years closely guarded information about its economy and political institutions. While Russia experienced difficult economic times throughout most of the 1990s, the financial crisis that occurred in 1998 spurred the international community to reevaluate both the Russian economy and the role of economic assistance.

The Collapse of the Soviet Union

The final years of the Soviet Union were marked by political turmoil and economic chaos. When Mikhail Gorbachev was named to head the Communist Party of the Soviet

Union in 1985, he inherited a stagnant political system and a slowly declining economy. Recognizing the need for change, Gorbachev launched a series of reforms designed to bring more openness to the political system and to restructure the economy. However, the partial dismantling of systems of control within the existing Soviet state led to further economic decline. At the same time, the increasing political openness was evolving from guarded criticism to calls for rebellion against the system. In a series of unprecedented elections in 1989 and 1990, many high-ranking Soviet officials were swept from power as the general public overwhelmingly voted for reformers, nationalists, and anti-Communists. By the beginning of 1991, the economic crisis in the Soviet Union had reached an acute phase. Spontaneously, firms began to privatize, and exports to Central Europe, Russia's primary market, collapsed, as Central European countries went through their own economic transitions. In addition, to maintain increasingly costly imports of food and consumer goods, the Soviet government undertook substantial borrowing from the West.

In August 1991, after a failed coup attempt by Communist hard-liners, Boris Yeltsin, recently elected President of the Russian republic, was thrust into a position of political prominence. He openly called for Russia's independence and, in conjunction with leaders of other Soviet republics, thwarted the efforts of an increasingly weakened Gorbachev to maintain a sense of unity within the rapidly dissolving Soviet Union. On Christmas Day 1991, Gorbachev officially declared the Soviet Union dissolved—replaced by 12 independent states.[1] By the beginning of 1992, a newly independent Russia was in the midst of a severe economic recession. Some analysts openly questioned whether Russia would be able to feed its population through the winter. In response, Yeltsin appointed a new team of reformers, committed to furthering a rapid transition from a state-run, centrally planned economy to a private market system. They turned to western donors and lending institutions for financial and technical help.

Western Assistance in An Uncertain Environment

The first joint official reaction of western governments to Soviet requests for assistance with economic transition came during the July 1990 Houston Economic Summit of the Group of Seven countries (G-7).[2] Although the West had spent decades carefully analyzing the Soviet Union, western economists knew very little about how it actually functioned. The G-7 countries commissioned a detailed study of the Soviet economy in an attempt to inform assistance efforts.[3] Donors had begun providing economic assistance to the Soviet Union in late 1990—largely in the form of loans or

[1] Estonia, Latvia, and Lithuania had already declared independence by this time.

[2] The G-7 is an informal group of seven leading industrialized nations including the United States, the United Kingdom, Germany, Japan, France, Italy, and Canada. Representatives from these countries meet periodically to discuss economic and political issues of common concern.

[3] The report, "A Study of the Soviet Economy," known as the "joint study" was done by the International Monetary Fund, the World Bank, the European Bank for Reconstruction and Development, and the Organization for Economic Cooperation and Development and was issued in February 1991.

trade credits. Some limited technical assistance and financing from the European Union (EU), the European Bank for Reconstruction and Development, the International Monetary Fund, and the World Bank began in 1991, but efforts were hampered by the Soviet Union's political upheaval. U.S. assistance prior to the Soviet breakup primarily consisted of guarantees for Soviet loans to buy U.S. agricultural goods. In late 1991, the United States provided some grant food aid, as famine conditions threatened. European governments also provided some support. The largest amount of bilateral assistance through 1991 was from Germany, much of which came under a program to build housing in Russia for Soviet troops who were withdrawing from the former East Germany.

The political context of this assistance was complex. The overriding political goal in the West was to promote national security by maintaining stability in Russia. Western leaders were particularly concerned that instability in Russia called into question who controlled access to nuclear weapons. Leaders in Europe were also concerned that poor economic conditions in Russia, combined with political turmoil, could lead to large refugee flows and raised questions about Russia's ability to safely operate and maintain its nuclear power plants. These concerns created political pressure for institutions and donors to implement programs to assist Russia as soon as possible.

Russia Faced Significant Challenges

The common assumption among western leaders was that the conversion of Russia from a Communist state to a market economy within a democratic state would bring long-term stability within Russia and between Russia and the West. This transformation required fundamental changes throughout the Russian economy, government, and society. Unlike other transition countries such as Poland and Hungary, Russia had no vestige of a democracy or competitive market economy and almost nothing in the way of supporting institutions, or economic relationships with western partners. Thus, Communist-era institutions that controlled the economy had to adapt to very different roles of oversight, mediation, and regulation.

Moreover, a government bureaucracy that had been responsible to the Communist Party now had to reorient itself to respond to the will of the people; work with an elected legislature; and determine relationships among the federal, regional, and local governments. At a broader level, mindsets developed over 70 years of Communist rule were required to adapt to a new system based on self-initiative and competition. Although new government institutions were in place and elections had occurred, the supporting framework for a democratic society did not exist. With almost no independent media, few public interest groups, weak political parties, and little legacy of pursuing grievances with the government, Russian society lacked the basic foundations of civil society.

The 1998 Financial Crisis Caused a Reevaluation of Assistance Programs

While Russia had experienced severe economic decline and a series of economic and political crises during the 1990s, its financial collapse of August 1998 spurred a serious reevaluation within the international community about how far the Russian economy had come and the role of economic assistance.

In late 1997, Russia's economic and financial environment was deteriorating due, in part, to reduced investor confidence in emerging markets in the wake of a financial crisis in Asia and, also, to lower oil prices that reduced Russia's export prices. Domestically, the Russian government was financing its deficit by issuing government securities. As investor confidence deteriorated in 1998, these had to be issued at very high interest rates. Russian banks had invested heavily in these securities, whose prices were falling rapidly, and also entered into large sales of dollars in forward exchange contracts, which made them vulnerable to ruble devaluation.[4]

Russia received a multilateral support package in July 1998, designed to try to restore investor confidence and to give the Russian government an opportunity to work out its financial difficulties, but this effort was not successful. The Central Bank of Russia used the financing to support the exchange rate while investors were taking their money out of Russia.[5] Faced with dwindling international reserves, in mid-August the Russian government announced a series of emergency measures, essentially placing the Russian government in default, which further reduced investor confidence and increased the outflow of capital.[6] These actions led to a collapse in the domestic banking sector and, as a result, there was a severe contraction in Russia's output and trade. The crisis had serious social consequences, effectively depriving many Russians of their savings and undermining any trust in financial institutions.

Five Major Lending Institutions and Donors

Many bilateral and multilateral international donors implemented programs to help Russia's transition process. According to one estimate from the Central Intelligence Agency, the total value of disbursed international assistance to Russia from 1989 to September 1998, without food aid loans, trade credits, and debt rollovers, came to $66 billion. We looked at five major institutions and donors that provided assistance to Russia since its independence in late 1991: the IMF, the World Bank, the EBRD, U.S. bilateral

[4] A forward exchange contract is an agreement between two parties to exchange one currency for another at a forward or future date. In the case of Russia, foreign investors who had wished to hedge (to reduce risk by taking a position that offsets existing or anticipated exposure to a change in market prices) against possible ruble (the ruble is Russia's currency) devaluation had bought dollar forward exchange contracts from Russian banks.

[5] International, or foreign exchange, reserves are the stock of liquid assets denominated in foreign currencies held by the central bank.

[6] These measures included declaring a de facto default on government debt, a de facto ruble devaluation, and a 90-day moratorium on commercial debt payments for the banking sector.

support provided under the 1992 Freedom Support Act,[7] and the European Union's Technical Assistance to the Commonwealth of Independent States (TACIS) program. From 1991 through September 2000, these institutions disbursed nearly $35.8 billion for programs in Russia: $31.3 billion, or 88 percent, have been loans from the IMF, the World Bank,[8] and the EBRD.[9] Much of the remaining $30.2 billion in assistance came from the German government, which contributed several billion dollars for the relocation of Russian troops from eastern Germany. Other major donors we did not review include France, Italy, Japan, the Organization for Economic Cooperation and Development, and the United Kingdom who all contributed substantially less grant assistance than the United States or the EU.

The levels of economic assistance to Russia can be compared to other recent transition assistance programs. For example, the German government has spent over $500 billion since 1989 to support the transition from Communism to a market economy in eastern Germany. International assistance to Poland from 1989 through 1994 alone was about $36 billion.

The IMF

The IMF helps countries stabilize their economies and work out balance-of-payments problems.[10] Its role in Russia was to provide loans and advice to the Russian government to help bring inflation under control, stabilize its economy, and address structural issues, such as bank and industrial restructuring, tax policies, and trade policies. As of August 31, 2000, the IMF had disbursed more than $22 billion in loans for Russia, of which more than $8 billion had been repaid (see fig. 2). For the past 2 years, Russia has paid more to the IMF than it has received. Russia has not missed a scheduled repayment of its IMF debt.

---

[7] "Freedom" in the name of this act stands for Freedom for Russia and Emerging Eurasian Democracies and Open Markets. Throughout this report, we refer to it as the "Freedom Support Act."

[8] The International Bank for Reconstruction and Development is the only World Bank Group member included in this review. In addition, the International Finance Corporation of the World Bank has provided $458 million in financing for 46 projects in Russia, and has a disbursed and outstanding portfolio in Russia of $256 million. The Multilateral Investment Guarantee Agency has a total gross exposure of $269 million for 10 contracts of guarantee in Russia. Throughout this report, references to World Bank lending refer to lending by the International Bank for Reconstruction and Development.

[9] Figures for the IMF, World Bank, and EBRD do not include their spending for technical assistance.

[10] A country's balance-of-payments accounts summarize its dealings with the outside world. A balance-of-payments problem occurs when its normal receipts from external transactions (e.g., export earnings, grants, loans, foreign direct investment and other financial inflows) are less than its payments (e.g., imports, interest and amortization). This external deficit may be financed by drawing down the country's international reserves and/or seeking exceptional financing, for example, IMF loans and debt relief.

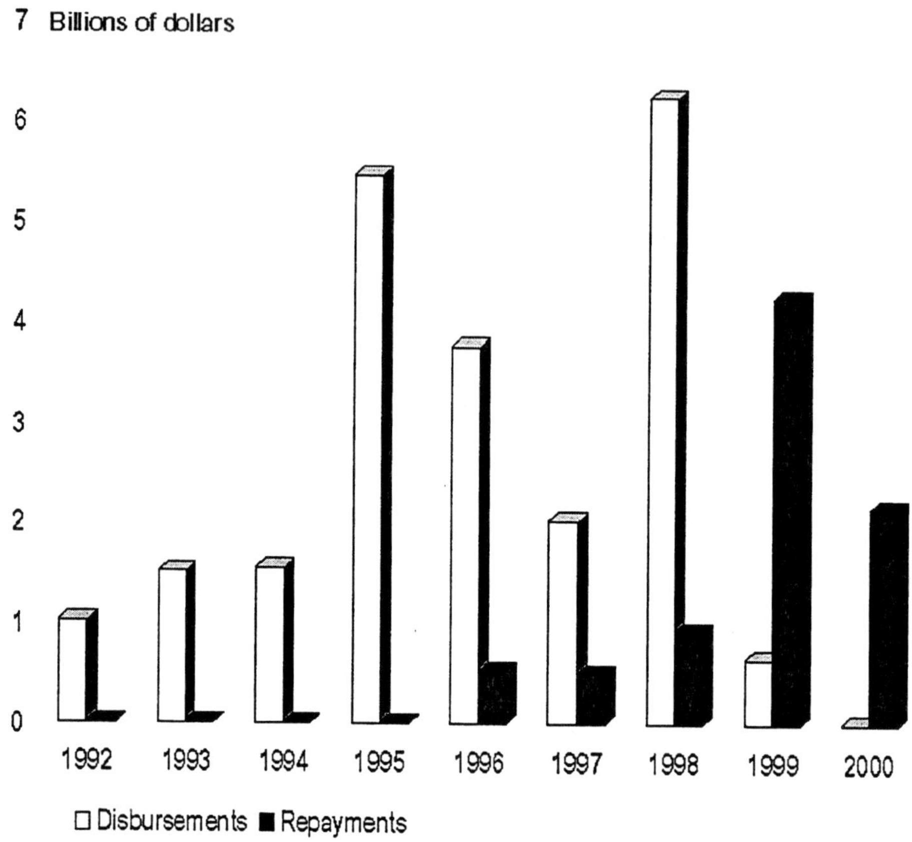

Figure 2: IMF Disbursements and Russian Repayments, 1992-2000

Source: IMF.

The World Bank

The World Bank's overall mission is to alleviate poverty and improve living standards in the developing world. In Russia, it provided loans and advice to the Russian government in a variety of economic sectors, with the general goal of promoting economic reform, alleviating poverty, and developing and strengthening institutions. Since 1992, the World Bank has approved more than $12.1 billion, and disbursed more than $7.5 billion, in loans for 46 projects in Russia. (see fig. 3).[11]

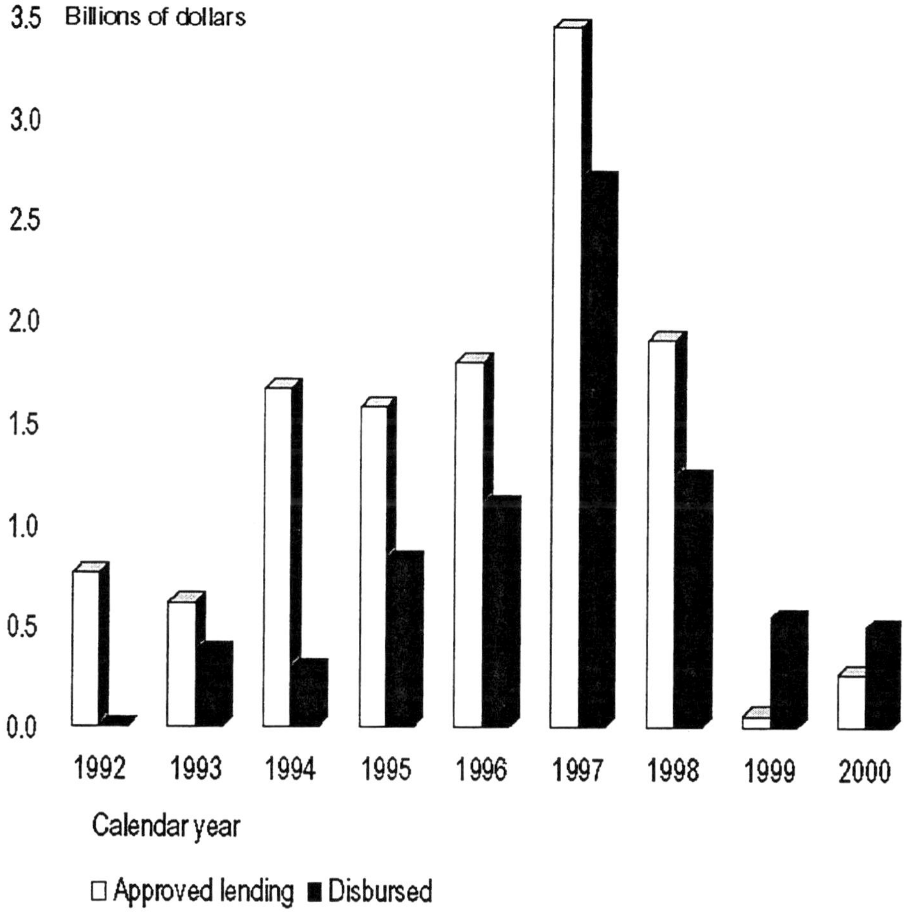

Figure 3: World Bank Approved Lending and Disbursements to Russia, 1992-2000
Source: World Bank.

The EBRD

The EBRD is a regional multilateral bank specifically created in 1990 to foster economic transition and support the development of the private sector in the countries of Central Europe and the former Soviet Union. In Russia, it lent money primarily to the private sector, invested in companies, and provided technical assistance to encourage development of the private sector and enhance the transition to a market economy. Since 1991, the EBRD has signed $4.4 billion worth of projects for Russia. As of August 31, 2000, the EBRD had disbursed $2.2 billion of these funds (see fig. 4).

[11] Commitments later canceled amounted to $2.4 billion, including $1.1 billion from the recent cancellation of the third structural adjustment loan.

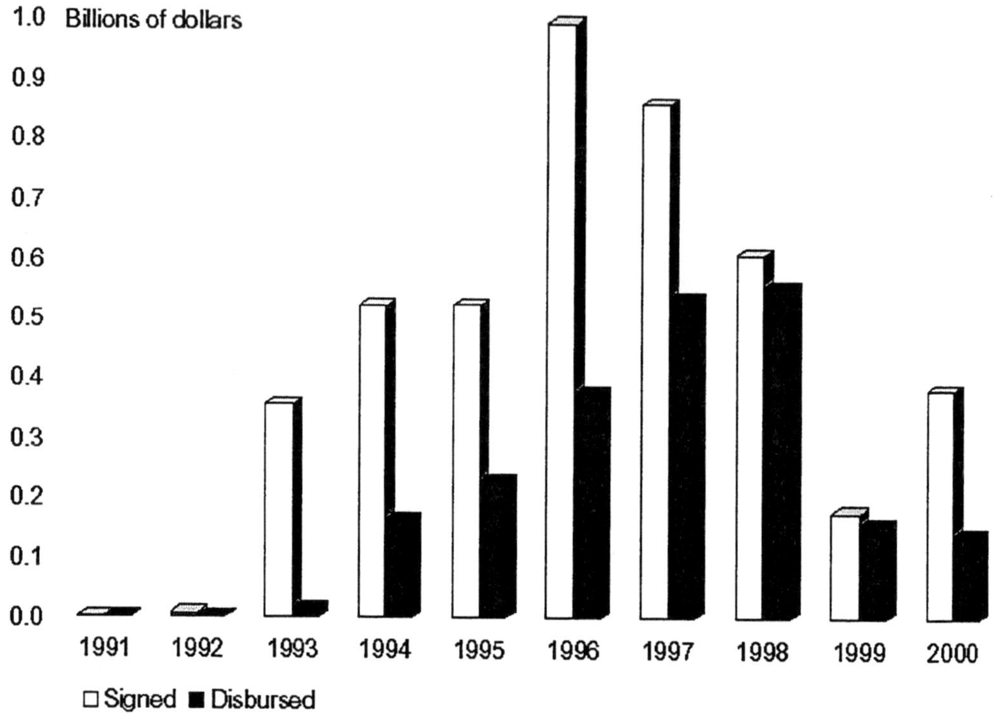

Figure 4: EBRD Annual Funding for Russia Projects, 1991-2000
Source: EBRD.

The U.S. Program

The United States has used a variety of programs to assist Russia and the other countries of the former Soviet Union. The programs include (1) the Cooperative Threat Reduction program to dismantle nuclear weapons and increase security over the remaining stockpile of weapons of mass destruction, (2) food aid, and (3) provision of assistance under the Freedom Support Act[12] (see app. IV for a summary of assistance for Russia from these programs).[13] Enacted in 1992, the Freedom Support Act is the primary vehicle for U.S. assistance to market reform and democracy building in the countries of the former Soviet Union. The United States has pursued three general goals in Russia with its Freedom Support Act assistance: (1) promote market reform, (2) support the creation of a democratic state, and (3) help alleviate the social costs of the transition process. Freedom Support Act programs have been implemented primarily through the provision of technical assistance. Since 1992, the United States has appropriated $2.7 billion in Freedom Support Act funds for Russia and disbursed $2.3 billion (see fig. 5).

---

[12] 22 U.S.C. 5801 et seq.

[13] Several U.S. departments and agencies have also implemented commercial, scientific, and cooperative programs with Russia under a wide variety of authorizations since 1992.

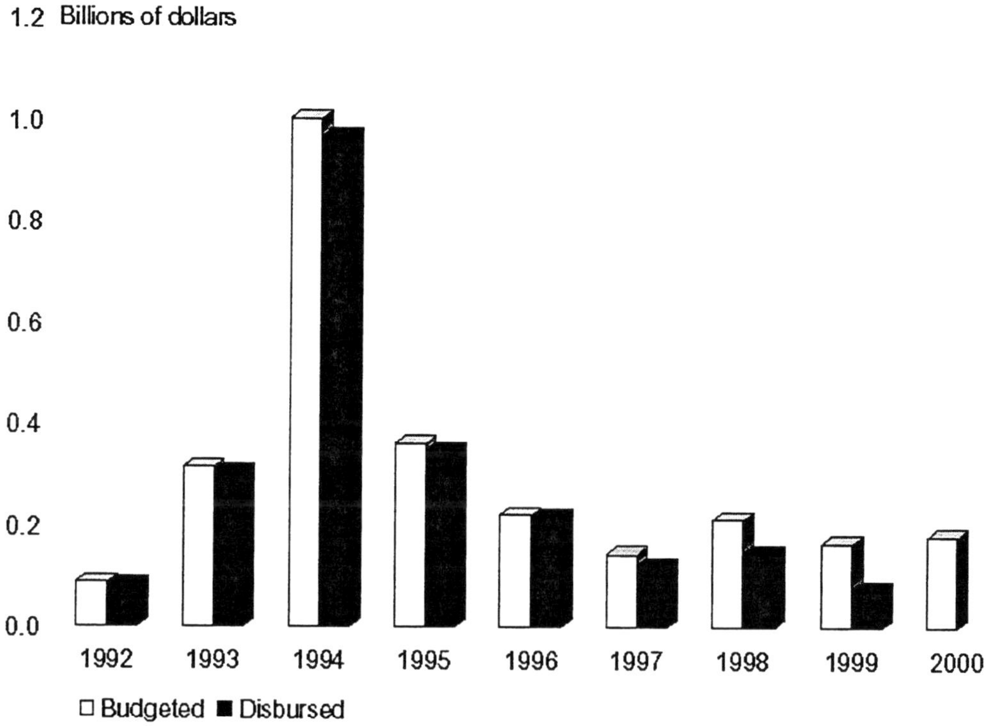

Figure 5: U.S. Freedom Support Act Annual Funding for Russia, 1992-2000[14]
Note: U.S. disbursement data for 2000 is not available. Source: State Department.

The EU's TACIS Program

In 1991, the European Union created the TACIS program to provide grant-financed technical assistance to support the process of transition to market economies and democratic societies in the former Soviet Union. Since then, TACIS efforts in Russia have focused on several sectors including human resource development, enterprise restructuring, agriculture, and energy. Since 1991, TACIS has committed $2.7 billion and disbursed $1.6 billion for programs in Russia (see fig. 6).

[14] Congress appropriates Freedom Support Act funds for the former Soviet Union in a lump sum. The State Department then creates budgets for individual countries.

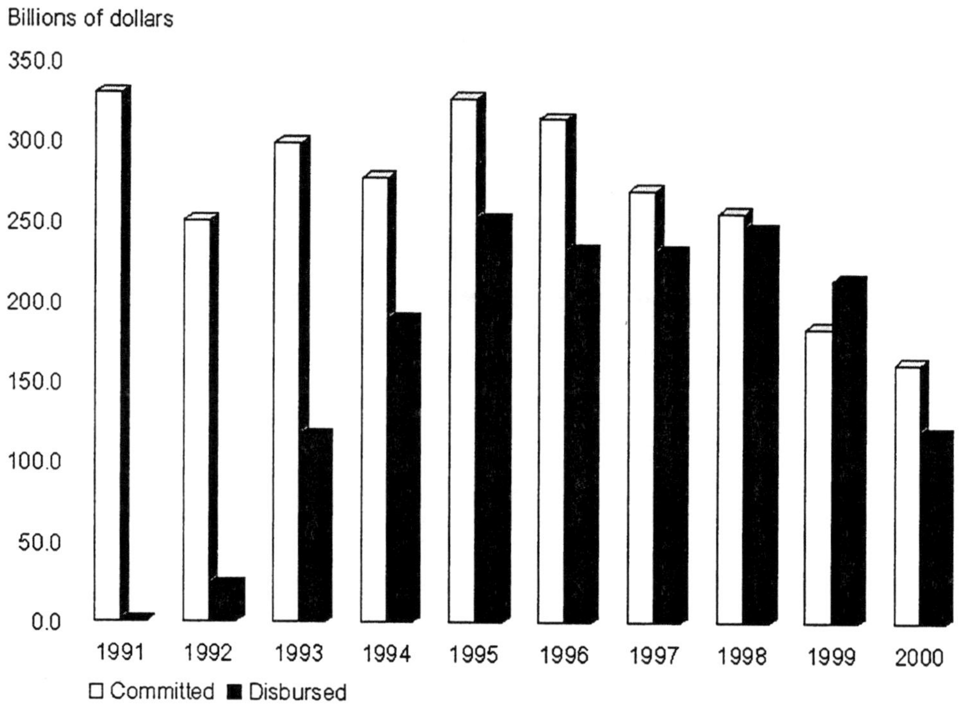

Figure 6: TACIS Annual Funding for Russia, 1991-2000

Source: European Commission.

Objectives, Scope, and Methodology

To help inform the continuing debate about international assistance to Russia, the Chairman and the Ranking Member of the House Banking and Financial Services Committee asked the GAO to review the strategies of different donors and lending institutions in providing economic assistance to Russia with a view toward identifying lessons learned from this experience. Specifically examined were: (1) what types of assistance lending institutions and donors have provided, what their program strategies were, and how this assistance has been coordinated, (2) how successful the institutions and donors have been in terms of meeting their assistance objectives and what factors have affected their success, and (3) what lessons can be learned that may have relevance for future policy decisions about Russia.

The GAO examined programs implemented by the IMF, the World Bank's International Bank for Reconstruction and Development, the EBRD, the U.S. under the Freedom Support Act, and TACIS because they represented a significant portion of assistance funds disbursed for Russia to date. These institutions and the U.S. also offered several types of assistance, including technical assistance and loans, and represented a mixture of international financial institutions and bilateral organizations. The GAO looked at the programs these institutions and the U.S. implemented in Russia from 1992 through September 2000. Access was granted to IMF, World Bank, and EBRD officials and documents through the U.S. Department of the Treasury and through the staff of the U.S. member of each institution's executive board. Only documents from these institutions that were also provided to their executive boards were examined. Some of the key strategy documents we reviewed included:

- IMF staff papers and program review documents, the Russian government's Letters of Intent and Memoranda of Economic Policies;[15]
- World Bank country assistance strategies;
- EBRD country strategies and transition reports;
- State Department annual reports and U. S. Agency for International Development annual country strategies; and
- TACIS indicative and action programs for Russia.[16]

Also reviewed were a variety of public and internal documents related to specific aspects of the operations and implementation of programs by all five donors and lending institutions.

To help understand the strategies used, actions taken, and lessons learned by the five donors in the review, the GAO identified four key policy areas that have affected the course of the Russian reform process, making a selection based on discussions with several experts and our assessment of key issues in the process of Russia's transition to a market economy over the past 8 years. The four areas are:

- Macroeconomic stabilization. Throughout the 1990s, lending institutions and donors tried to help the Russian government bring inflation under control, develop an effective monetary policy, and reduce the budget deficit.
- Social safety net protection. Many analysts in the early 1990s believed that Russia needed to maintain a suitable social safety net to mitigate social hardships during the transition process and to facilitate the restructuring of inefficient enterprises.
- Privatization. Donors played an important role in supporting the implementation of Russia's rapid, mass voucher privatization program in 1992-94. Although not supported by the donors, the "loans-for-shares" privatization conducted by the Russian government in late 1995 was a critical event in the transition process.
- Banking sector reform. All five donors in our review provided assistance to support the development of a viable private banking sector in Russia only to see most of the banking sector wiped out in the 1998 financial crisis.

[15] Letters of Intent and Memoranda of Economic Policies are documents prepared by IMF member countries that describe the policies that a country intends to implement in the context of its request for financial support from the IMF.

Provision and Coordination of Assistance

To determine the level of assistance provided, the strategies used, and the coordination of assistance among donors and with the Russian government, the GAO reviewed documents obtained from all five institutions and donors and supplemented analysis with discussions with officials from these institutions. The authors also met with officials from the Russian government, private think tanks, and universities, assessing coordination by examining the extent to which donors exchanged information, worked together to develop common goals and objectives, avoided duplication, and implemented projects that complemented each other's efforts.

Factors Affecting Success

To determine the factors that affected the success of donors in meeting their broad objectives, the GAO identified the donors' overarching objectives from documents and discussions and analyzed the relative success in meeting donors' overarching objectives by comparing the general objectives with current conditions in Russia. The review of the success of individual projects is based on the donors' own evaluations and discussions with officials from the donors, the Russian government, and other analysts. Also relied on were the results of our past work for assessing selected portions of the U.S. bilateral programs. The GAO did not independently verify the findings presented in others' reports or assess the effectiveness of individual programs as part of this review. With the exception of GAO past work, the comments on project success represent a synthesis of others' views. To determine the factors that affected success, the GAO synthesized the information we obtained from evaluation reports, other documentation, and discussions with officials.

Lessons Learned

To develop lessons learned, the GAO reviewed documents obtained from the lending institutions and donors to identify lessons they had formally identified. The GAO supplemented this review with discussions with program officials, Russian officials, and representatives from think tanks, universities, and nongovernmental organizations.

During efforts on all three objectives, GAO researchers worked in Washington, D.C.; Boston, Massachusetts; London, United Kingdom; Brussels, Belgium; and Moscow, Novgorod, and Samara, Russia. During these visits, researchers met with senior officials from the lending institutions and donors in the review, including:

---

[16] Indicative programs are TACIS multiyear plans that lay out basic objectives and strategies. Action programs are prepared annually and spell out the specific projects that will be implemented to support the objectives in the indicative program.

- the IMF's Director of the European II Department, the former heads of the Russia program from 1992 through the present, and the current IMF Resident Representative in Moscow;
- the World Bank's current and former vice presidents for Europe and Central Asia, the country director for Russia, current and former managing directors, and Bank staff responsible for developing and overseeing projects in several different sectors;
- the President of the EBRD, the First Vice President, two deputy vice presidents, the current Russia Country Director, and other staff;
- the current Coordinator for U.S. assistance to the former Soviet Union, former Coordinators, the current and former U.S. Agency for International Development mission directors, former National Security Council staff responsible for developing Russia policy, former Central Intelligence Agency staff, former senior Treasury officials, the current and former directors of the Russian desk at the Department of the Treasury, and the U.S. Executive Directors at the IMF, World Bank, and EBRD; and
- the head of the TACIS office in Moscow, the Russia Administrator in Brussels, the head of the TACIS evaluation unit, the former EU Ambassador to Russia, and officials from the U.S. Mission to the EU and the European Parliament.

Also met with were several current and former Russian government officials, including officials from the Ministries of Finance, Economy, and Tax; sector heads of Russia's Gref Commission;[17] a former Acting Prime Minister; the Chairman of the Banking Committee of the Duma; Russian executive directors of the World Bank, the IMF, and the EBRD; regional officials from Novgorod and Samara; and several project beneficiaries.

Finally, the GAO met with analysts from a number of universities, think tanks, private firms, and international organizations, including in part the Brookings Institution, the Heritage Foundation, the Carnegie Endowment for International Peace, PlanEcon, Inc., the London School for Economics, the Center for European Policy Studies, Harvard University, the University of Maryland, and the University of Pittsburgh.

This work occurred from September 1999 through September 2000 in accordance with generally accepted government auditing standards.

---

[17] The Gref Commission was established by then-Acting President Putin in February 2000 to develop a comprehensive 10-year economic strategy for the country, which was adopted in July.

Chapter 2

Donors Have Adopted Different Strategies and Means for Providing Assistance

In its early efforts to assist Russia's economic transition, the international community generally agreed on some fundamental principles concerning the transition, but it did not have a comprehensive strategy for the assistance it would provide and how its efforts would be coordinated. The overarching goal of the programs we reviewed has been to help Russia make the transition to a market-based economy. Donors have pursued similar objectives in their economic assistance efforts in Russia, but their strategies and means for providing the assistance have differed. The majority of the assistance has been provided through loans, while other funding has been given through technical assistance and grants. Over the decade, the institutions and donors themselves and the Russian government have instituted various forums for the coordination of donor assistance. This coordination has improved in some areas over time, but it is still a challenge to the institutions and donors and the Russian government.

The International Community Agreed on Fundamentals Regarding Russia's Economic Transition but Lacked a Comprehensive Strategy for Assistance

The international community's early efforts to assist Russia's economic transition were characterized by general agreement on some fundamental principles concerning the transition, but international leaders did not lay out a comprehensive strategy regarding what types of assistance would be provided and how the assistance would be coordinated.

In their summary of the joint study of the Soviet economy issued in December 1990, the international financial institutions recommended a program of comprehensive reforms. These reforms included decontrol of prices, privatization of enterprises, and liberalization of trade and investment, consistent with what have been termed

"Washington Consensus" principles.[1] The study also recommended creation of a social safety net to cushion the impact of transition on vulnerable groups and individuals. According to officials involved in writing the study, because it was carried out during a time of uncertainty about the future political organization of the Soviet Union, its authors were limited in their ability to analyze questions regarding how the Russian economy would be operating independently from other republics. They did not know, for example, how legislative and executive powers would be divided between different levels of government and what specific kinds of financial support the government would need.

During this time, some experts within the academic and policy community argued against elements of rapid economic transition, but they were in a minority. On the need to remove price controls and barriers to international trade, there was little debate, but some scholars and analysts were skeptical of the consequences of rapidly privatizing state enterprises. They argued that a viable private sector required the existence of new laws and institutions, such as banks and courts, and questioned the assumption that these laws and institutions would come about relatively quickly in response to demand from new business owners.[2] Some analysts also pointed out that the way in which social services were provided under the communist system could result in severe social hardship and also limit the ability of firms to restructure and become more efficient. However, by mid-1991, western support for rapid economic transition in Russia was strengthened by early evidence from the transition experience of Central European countries. Poland, for example, had implemented a major stabilization program in 1989 that became the foundation for its later economic recovery and restructuring. Many aspects of the reforms already implemented or underway in Poland, including tightening fiscal and monetary policy, liberalizing prices, and privatizing enterprises, were prescribed for Russia.[3]

Soviet Union's Collapse and Western Response

The speed of the breakup of the Soviet Union at the end of 1991 caught the international community by surprise, according to many officials and analysts we interviewed. Western response to this "window of opportunity" has been the subject of considerable controversy. It was a period of fundamental ambivalence about the

[1] The "Washington Consensus" is a term that economist John Williamson introduced in articles beginning in 1990. Williamson's original definition involved ten different aspects of economic policy toward developing countries. The term, however, has become associated more generally with the view that economic development is best served by a commitment to free markets, private property, and individual incentives, and with calls for specific measures such as freeing prices, removing trade barriers, and privatizing enterprises. The consensus grew out of the observation of the experience of several Latin American countries during the 1980s, and the term results from its link to the U.S. government and the international financial institutions headquartered in Washington.

[2] The joint study, while it advocated immediate privatization of small firms, stated that the privatization of larger firms would take longer and that the large firms should be commercialized and operated as joint stock companies while they continued under public sector ownership.

[3] In fact, the lessons from the transition experience of Central European countries have become complicated over time. While Poland pursued stabilization, it also moved slowly in efforts to privatize its economy and reform its banking system, which some analysts maintain worked to its advantage.

appropriate level and types of U.S. and international assistance. One of the first official acts of G-7 leaders following an October 1991 speech by Yeltsin asking for western assistance and cooperation was to send a delegation of deputy finance ministers to Moscow to secure claims to the Soviet foreign debt.[4] In January 1992, the United States convened a conference of foreign ministers and representatives of international institutions to coordinate assistance. Its focus was primarily on humanitarian assistance and not economic transition policies.

In April 1992, President George Bush and German Chancellor Helmut Kohl announced a G-7 assistance package for Russia of $24 billion. The components of the package—$4.5 billion from the World Bank, the IMF, and the EBRD, $6 billion for a fund to support the value of Russia's currency, $2.5 billion for debt relief, and $11 billion in bilateral assistance— primarily credits to buy food—turned out to include potential transfers that had already been promised and others that were not forthcoming. The package depended, at least in part, on agreement on a set of reforms between Russia and the IMF, which Russia formally joined that June. In their Munich summit in July of 1992, G-7 leaders issued an economic declaration calling for cooperation between Russia and the IMF.

From the perspective of hindsight, many analysts and officials have observed that the early western response to the newly independent Russia did not constitute a strategy for action. Russia was encouraged to work with the IMF and World Bank and meet their criteria for assistance, but there was little direction regarding how different aspects of assistance would relate to and support each other. Donors and other analysts have attributed this to several causes. Leaders in the United States and Germany were at the time focused on other concerns. The United States, for example, engaged in a war with Iraq in 1991, and in 1992 President Bush was looking toward reelection in November. Germany was in the midst of an extremely costly undertaking to bring about the economic unification of the former East Germany with the West. Also, some western leaders were initially ambivalent about the ability of the Yeltsin government to provide effective leadership, according to some analysts we interviewed, and also whether the situation in Russia was too chaotic, for example, for additional financial support to have made a difference.

The ultimate effect of the relatively slow western response in providing assistance for Russia's economic transition, and the expectations of assistance in 1992 that went beyond what was provided, has also been widely debated. One argument of potential effect, made by a number of analysts and current and former officials, is that the lack of visible support from the international community may have undermined Russian reformers at a key point in 1992. For example, whatever actual use might have been made of the funds, Acting Russian Prime Minister Yegor Gaidar, a key reformer under President Yeltsin, had announced they would be forthcoming, staking personal political credibility in Russia on the expectations. Some officials and analysts believe that the lack of support from the

[4] This action resulted in Russia's agreeing to jointly assume responsibility for all Soviet debts owed to western creditors in return for obtaining control over all Soviet overseas assets.

international community undermined Gaidar's credibility and contributed to his removal from office by the end of 1992.

Assistance for Russia and the other countries of the former Soviet Union figured prominently in the agenda of G-7 matters at the Tokyo Summit in July 1993. During the summit, the G-7 called for the creation of several programs for Russia, including efforts to accelerate the pace of economic restructuring, promote the development of small- and medium- sized enterprises, and improve the coordination of donor assistance. This detail on specific aspects of assistance was unusual and not repeated at later summits. Since 1993, the G-7 has periodically provided general, political guidance for donor assistance efforts but has not offered detailed plans or prioritization. After Russia began attending portions of the G-7 summits in 1994, the summits themselves became a forum for directly lobbying Russian leaders on the need for reform in specific areas. In April 2000, a draft strategy for G-7 economic support for Russia, that laid out broad goals and roles of different international institutions and donors, was circulated by some members but not adopted.

Assistance Programs Have Pursued Similar Objectives With Different Instruments and Strategies

The institutions and donors in our review have pursued similar broad objectives in their economic assistance efforts in Russia, while their instruments and strategies for providing the assistance have differed. The common, broad goal of assistance efforts has been to help Russia make the transition to a market-based economy. IMF, World Bank, and EBRD funds have been provided as loans to Russia, which need to be repaid. The U.S. Freedom Support Act and TACIS programs have provided mostly technical assistance and grants. The operations of the EBRD, activities carried out under the U.S. Freedom Support Act, and TACIS are generally project based, while the IMF works with member governments to develop economic reform goals and monitor progress and provides financing to member central governments and central banks. The World Bank program has been a mix of project lending and adjustment lending tied to specific reform goals.

The IMF Has Concentrated on Macroeconomic Stability in Russia

As shown in table 1, the evolution of the IMF's involvement with Russia can be broken down into five periods (see app. I for more information on the IMF's programs).

The primary objective of the IMF's involvement with Russia has been to achieve macroeconomic stabilization, largely defined by low inflation, and increase economic output to facilitate Russia's economic transition. The IMF's involvement with Russia began before Russia was an IMF member through the provision of technical, but not financial, assistance. Once Russia joined the IMF in June 1992, it was entitled to obtain financing for balance-of-payments problems through various IMF facilities. The IMF has used a number of interrelated instruments in its dealings with Russia: financing provided to the Ministry of Finance and the Central Bank of Russia, technical assistance and high-level dialogue with Russian officials, and conditionality such as quantitative criteria to monitor macroeconomic performance and benchmarks for structural reform.[5] Conditionality is generally defined as the economic policies that IMF members intend to follow as a condition for the use of IMF resources.

The IMF's strategy for achieving macroeconomic stability in Russia has consistently focused on reducing and then controlling inflation. The IMF programs with Russia from 1992 to 1995 contained primarily macroeconomic conditions with limited structural reform requirements. As economic conditions in Russia changed, the IMF modified its strategy and used different mechanisms to deal with inflation, while increasing its emphasis on the importance of structural reforms to facilitate economic growth. In 1992, Russia received its first IMF disbursement under a 5-month program with limited conditionality. In 1993, the IMF created a new facility, called the Systemic Transformation Facility,[6] because it recognized that some transition countries, including Russia, were not ready for the full conditionality requirements under its regular facilities. Although Russia's performance in meeting the 1993 macroeconomic targets was poor, it did receive its second IMF disbursement in 1994. Despite Russia's continuing weak performance in meeting conditions, in 1995 the IMF determined Russia was ready for a Stand-by Arrangement—a traditional short-term program with more extensive conditionality requirements— with monthly monitoring. This was based on the IMF's assessment that the chances of implementing the agreed-upon program were better than they had been in the past due, in part, to an improved political situation.[7] While Russia's performance in meeting the conditions of this program was mixed,[8] Russia did succeed in bringing inflation under control in 1995 in part due to the government's adoption of an exchange rate band.[9]

---

[5] Structural reforms relate to policies across the economy, including, for example, tax and banking sector policies.

[6] The Systemic Transformation Facility is a temporary means of providing financial assistance to members facing balance-of-payments difficulties arising from shocks to their economy due to a shift from a centrally planned economy to a market-based economy.

[7] The Stand-by Arrangement provides short-term assistance for problems of a temporary nature, usually 1 to 2 years, provided the IMF member observes the conditions in the supporting arrangement.

[8] Although the IMF initially believed that Russia had met all of its targets, a 1999 PriceWaterhouseCoopers audit showed that Russia missed 2 of its targets. In addition, Russia met the budget deficit targets by accumulating massive wage and pension arrears because budget outlays, not obligations, were used to define the deficit. Beginning in 1997, expenditure arrears were incorporated in definition of the deficit.

[9] A mechanism in which the Central Bank of Russia undertook supporting measures and policies that attempted to maintain the exchange rate within a preannounced upper and lower range.

Table 1: Highlights of the IMF's Assistance Strategy for Russia, 1991-2000

Time period	Highlights of the strategy
Early involvement (1991)	• October moratorium on Russia debt payments calls for IMF program. • The IMF provided technical, but not financial, assistance to the Soviet Union. • Relationship continued de facto with Russia after Soviet Union disbanded.
Efforts to control inflation (1992-95)	1992-1994
	• Russia becomes an IMF member (June 1992). • $1 billion disbursed in first agreement (August 1992), with limited macroeconomic conditions. • $1.5 billion disbursed under new facility the IMF created for transition economies (June 1993). • Program went off track (September 1993). • New program agreed to despite concerns over weak Russian performance (March 1994); $1.5 billion disbursed; program failed to meet objectives. 1995 • Russia signs agreement for $6.8 billion under first standard IMF program (April); monthly monitoring of performance instituted. • The IMF concurs with Russia's adoption of a managed exchange rate system (exchange rate band) as basis for monetary program. • Inflation is brought under control for the first time. • Russia appears to meet all of the program requirements; however, 1999 audits show that it missed 2 targets.
Continued emphasis on controlling inflation: increased stress on structural reforms: (Mid-1996-mid-1998)	• The IMF and Russia agree to a 3-year arrangement that contains more structural reform requirements (March 1996). • Russia's performance in meeting requirements in 1996 was weak; tax collection requirements continually not met. • Continuing government budget deficits financed largely with securities issuance and IMF/World Bank funds. • The IMF continued to make disbursements, in part, because the IMF felt Russia's weak performance reflected instability related to the upcoming presidential elections. • 1997 began with increased growth; Asian financial crisis affected investor confidence toward the end of the year. • Agreement for 1998 program requirements not reached until June.
Financial crisis (July-September 1998):	• A worsening financial crisis leads to interim IMF package of $11.2 billion (July); initial disbursement of $4.8 billion. • No further disbursements are made under this program.
Post-crisis era (1999-2000)	• Russia and the IMF agree to a new $4.5 billion arrangement (July). One disbursement of $640 million made. • Scheduled December program review not completed; failure to meet structural requirements cited; no further disbursements made. • Russian economy grows due to increased demand for domestic production and higher oil prices. • The IMF continues its involvement, including through technical assistance.

Source: GAO analysis of IMF documents and discussions with IMF officials.

In 1996, Russia and the IMF agreed to a 3-year program under an IMF facility—called an Extended Fund Facility—designed to emphasize structural reforms because of the IMF belief that although Russia had made progress in stabilization, structural reform was also required.[10] The conditions Russia was to meet were agreed to annually. The program focused on several structural areas including banking sector reform, privatization and restructuring of large enterprises, and the energy sector. Throughout this program, Russia's performance was mixed, resulting in the IMF 's delaying or reducing disbursements on several occasions. However, the IMF frequently modified targets in the leadup to Russia's presidential elections in June 1996. According to the IMF, these target modifications were made because of unexpected events, especially the large capital outflow in advance of the presidential elections that made those targets unattainable. Also, in late 1996, the IMF made revenue collection a program priority in an effort to reduce the budget deficit; however, Russia generally missed these targets.

Although in 1997 Russia began to experience economic growth for the first time in 6 years, the Asian financial crisis led to massive capital outflows at the end of the year due to a loss of investor confidence. Russia responded by raising interest rates and selling more domestic government securities, called GKOs, in order to reduce capital outflows. The IMF advised Russia to continue raising interest rates further, but against IMF advice, the government expended substantial foreign exchange to support the ruble, before finally raising interest rates sufficiently to stabilize the situation.

In the leadup to Russia's financial crisis, in July 1998, the IMF's strategy was to try to increase investor confidence by providing Russia with a large, $11.2-billion emergency financing package, containing strengthened program conditions.[11] Only one disbursement was made under this program, and it was reduced from $5.6 billion to $4.8 billion due to the unwillingness of Russia's legislature to pass pieces of legislation that were conditions of the program. The investor community's restored confidence was short-lived and massive capital outflows followed. The Russian government announced that it would (1) widen the exchange rate band, (2) implement a 90-day moratorium on commercial and banking sector external debt repayment, and (3) announce restructuring of the government's ruble-denominated securities (GKOs). Although the Russian government immediately implemented the 90-day moratorium on external commercial debt repayment for the banking sector, it did not initially announce a clear plan to restructure government securities. This delay added to market uncertainty. At the same time, despite intervention in the currency market by the Central Bank of Russia,[12] the ruble continued to depreciate within the exchange rate band until the Russian government allowed it to float, resulting in a sharp ruble devaluation. Russia formally terminated this IMF program in March 1999.

---

[10] The Extended Fund Facility provides longer-term (generally for a 3-year period) balance-of payments assistance aimed at overcoming balance-of-payments difficulties resulting from macroeconomic and structural problems.

[11] An overall assistance package of $22 billion announced at that time also included potential financing from the World Bank and Japan.

[12] The central bank intervened by purchasing rubles using U.S. dollar reserves in order to decrease the supply of rubles in the economy, thereby raising its value against the U.S. dollar.

In the aftermath of the crisis, the IMF's strategy has been to continue to support the Russian government through policy dialogue and technical assistance, with little financing provided. The IMF and Russia agreed to a new \$4.5-billion Stand-by Arrangement in July 1999 in order to focus on fiscal improvements and structural reforms in the difficult, post-crisis economic environment. Russia received the first \$640 million disbursement; however, no additional disbursements have been made. Although Russia had met the macroeconomic conditions of the program, the IMF withheld further disbursements due to poor performance in meeting structural requirements. The IMF has continued to engage in policy dialogue, program discussions, and its usual surveillance activities for members with Russia. It has also provided technical assistance, particularly on banking sector reform, in the 1999-2000 period.

The World Bank Has Targeted Private Sector Development and Social Protection

The evolution of the World Bank's program of assistance to Russia can be broken down into five stages, as depicted in table 2: The World Bank's involvement in Russia began before Russia became a member of the World Bank in June 1992. In 1991, the executive board established a \$30-million trust fund to provide technical assistance grants to the republics of the Soviet Union. Following Russia's independence at the end of 1991, the World Bank was under pressure to deliver a program of assistance as soon as possible. On August 6, 1992, the first World Bank loan to Russia was approved, a \$600-million rehabilitation loan that was essentially for balance-of-payments support. However, the loan did not become effective for another 5 months. This loan was tied to the IMF's initial lending program for Russia to support macroeconomic stabilization. Although World Bank officials supported the World Bank's involvement in Russia's economic transition, the best strategy for engagement was not obvious, according to Bank officials. According to these officials, there was a tension between the World Bank's having a development impact in Russia and the financial risks that it could prudently assume. The World Bank's expertise regarding the Russian economy and institutions was limited, and there was very little institutional capacity within the Russian government to implement World Bank-financed projects. In addition, there was substantial debate about the proper mix, composition, and funding level of projects. Former senior World Bank officials characterized the situation during this period, both in Russia and with respect to developing the Bank's program, as chaotic.

Table 2: Highlights of the World Bank's Assistance Strategy for Russia, 1991-Present

Time period	Highlights of the strategy
The initial years (1991-92): Establishing the Russia program	• $30 million trust fund established for the former Soviet Union republics (Aug. 1991) and work program for Russia issued (Feb. 1992). • Resident mission set up (fall 1991). • Russia became a World Bank member (June 1992). • First $600-million rehabilitation loan approved (Aug.1992).
The early years (1993-94): Seeking areas for rapid buildup of the portfolio	• G-7 pressure to develop and implement projects quickly. • Early debate on adjustment vs. investment lending. • Approved about $2.3 billion for 9 investment loans in several sectors. • Start-up delays in project implementation resulted in slow disbursements.
The transition years (1995-96): Addressing project effectiveness and reassessing the strategy	• Project implementation is fraught with difficulties; only $278.4 million of $3.4 billion in approved investment lending had been disbursed (as of Dec. 1995). • World Bank President's Moscow visit makes project effectiveness a priority (1995). • High-level review of projects to identify and address implementation problems (1996). • World Bank views post-1996 election period as opportunity for comprehensive structural reforms and moves toward adjustment lending
The later years (1997-98): Shifting the strategic focus to Federal structural reform	• Country director named, and authority decentralized to the Moscow office (1997). • World Bank/government dialogue rises to a higher level. • Emphasis shifts from investment projects at the regional and local level to adjustment lending at the federal level. • Financial crisis adversely impacts World Bank projects (Aug. 1998).
Post-financial crisis (1999-present): Focusing on long-term efforts	• Russia becomes the weakest country in World Bank portfolio due to the financial crisis, but intensive efforts significantly improve project performance. • Strategy focuses on addressing systemic weaknesses that financial crisis highlighted. • More modest funding levels.

Source: GAO analysis of World Bank documents and discussions with World Bank officials.

From 1992 through 1995, the World Bank approved $4.6 billion for 20 projects across several sectors, including energy, agriculture, and infrastructure. Although social protection was an explicit focus of the World Bank's initial strategy for Russia, the social sector accounted for a small fraction of actual projects. (See app. II for a listing and status of all World Bank loans to Russia.) The projects were to be implemented largely at the regional and local level. This broad scope of early Bank efforts in Russia was driven, in part, by the belief that, given Russia's size, the World Bank needed broad involvement to have a meaningful impact on the reform process. It was also dictated to a large extent by the World Bank's limited access to high-level officials in Russia and thus the need to move into areas where the doors for World Bank involvement were open.

At first, World Bank officials were reluctant to make adjustment loans beyond the initial rehabilitation loans, because they did not think that there was sufficient consensus in Russia to carry out and sustain reforms, and thus they believed that substantial adjustment lending would constitute too great a financial risk for the Bank. However, by 1994, serious problems with disbursing funds and implementing investment projects emerged and became increasing apparent through 1995. While the Bank undertook intensive efforts during 1995 and 1996 to improve project implementation, and the performance of the Bank's Russia portfolio improved, it also began to reexamine its strategy for lending to Russia. Largely to seek greater leverage for reform, the Bank moved, beginning in 1996, to a strategy that emphasized adjustment lending rather than investment lending. According to Bank officials, the Bank also believed at that time that, with the 1996 presidential elections past, political conditions for comprehensive structural reform were favorable. The Bank committed to a series of large, quick-disbursing adjustment loans, in some cases to be disbursed in multiple tranches, including (1) $1.3 billion for restructuring the coal sector between 1996 and 1998, (2) $800 million for adjustment of social protection programs in 1997, and (3) $2.9 billion to promote national-level reform on structural issues between 1997 and 1999. In some cases, these loans were structured to be disbursed in several tranches. As a result, as seen in figure 7, the World Bank's Russia portfolio significantly shifted toward adjustment lending. The Bank's overall portfolio performance ratings in Russia continued to improve until the August 1998 financial crisis, when many of the World Bank projects, particularly those involving regional loans, were rendered at risk. Potential World Bank financing through 1999 of $6 billion was part of a bailout package of more than $22-billion announced in July 1998. However, World Bank disbursements were far less than this amount, with $1.5 billion committed for a third structural adjustment loan, of which $400 million was eventually disbursed. The financial crisis resulted in intensive efforts to address problem loans, including substantial restructuring and canceling of projects, and portfolio performance improved significantly by late 1999. According to World Bank officials, as they revisit the World Bank's assistance strategy for Russia, they anticipate a long-term focus and modest levels of funding in the next few years.

The EBRD Has Focused on Russia's Private Sector Development

The EBRD's overall objectives in Russia have been to foster economic transition and promote private sector initiatives. It has used a variety of instruments including direct project lending, financing through intermediaries, equity investments, and use of technical cooperation funds. Direct project lending is done at market interest rates. Financing through intermediaries, generally called "on-lending," is used to promote the development of Russian financial institutions. The EBRD's equity investments are done through buying noncontrolling minority stakes in local firms. Technical cooperation funds generally are provided by bilateral donors to the EBRD to support project proposal review and preparation. Table 3 shows the evolution of the EBRD's strategy for Russia (see app. III for more information on the EBRD's programs).

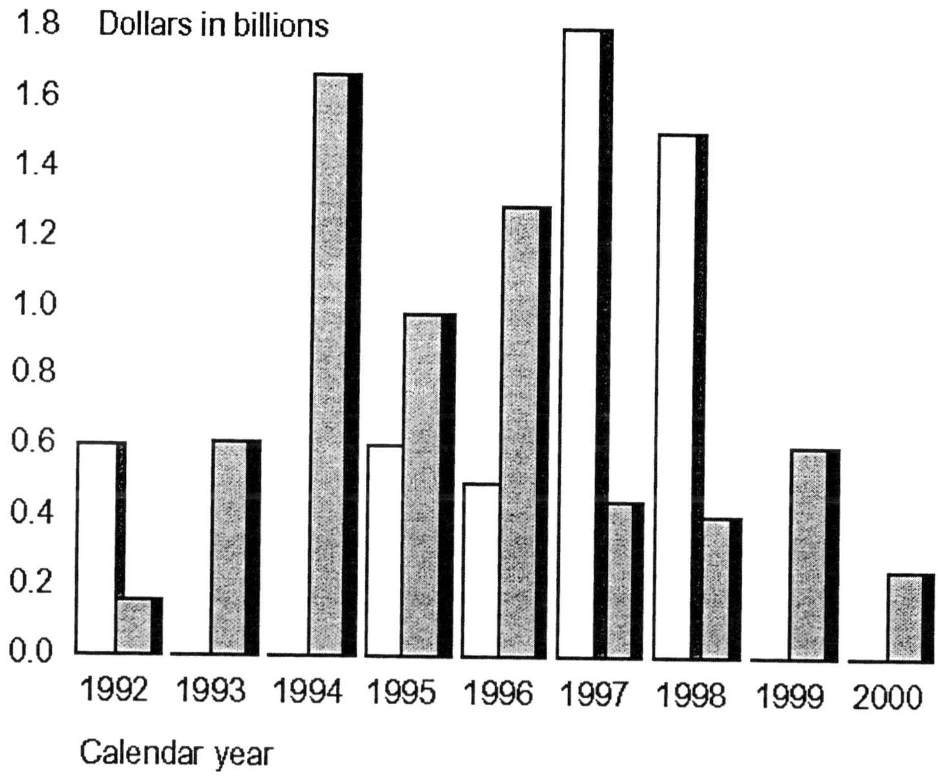

Figure 7: World Bank Approved Adjustment vs. Investment Lending, 1993-September 2000
Source: World Bank.

When the EBRD began its operations in April 1991 in the Soviet Union, there were very few viable business opportunities. As a result, the EBRD mainly provided technical assistance for training business people, supporting local privatization efforts in selected cities, and advising the government on drafting reform legislation. After Russia became a member in March 1992, much of the EBRD's early attention focused on providing technical assistance, most significantly in the area of privatization; trying to find financing partners; and identifying potential projects. Early EBRD plans lacked focus. For example, in 1992, the EBRD initially planned to spread its operations in Russia across 11 economic sectors, including privatization and enterprise promotion, financial sector development, military conversion and agriculture in an effort to support development of entrepreneurs and the legal, market, financial, and public infrastructures. However, the EBRD's resources proved to be relatively small compared to these objectives. By the end of 1993, the EBRD had approved 10 deals worth $362 million, with about two-thirds of these funds going to the oil and gas sector.

Table 3: Evolution of the EBRD's Strategy for Russia, 1991-2000

Time period	Highlights of the strategy
Early EBRD efforts for Russia focused on technical assistance: 1991-93	• Technical assistance targeted for privatization, training, and advice on reform legislation. • Initial plans for financing projects lacked focus; spread across 11 sectors. • Poor business climate in Russia limited sound financing opportunities.
Program development and growth: July 1993-early 1998	• Rapid growth in program; nearly $1 billion in new projects during 1996 alone. • Dropped emphasis on technical assistance, focused on fewer sectors, and tried to develop more realistic goals. • Focused on (1) financial sector, in part to promote development of small- and medium- sized enterprises; and (2) energy sector. • Conscious effort to cluster projects in reform-minded regions. • Relied on financial intermediaries for project implementation to encourage institution building.
Financial collapse and recovery: mid-1998 to the present	• EBRD suffered heavy losses, primarily in the banking sector, due to the crisis. • Very few projects approved in immediate aftermath; entire country portfolio closely scrutinized. • Cautious reengagement in Russia by mid-1999, with EBRD positioning self by mid-2000 for possible major return to Russian market. • Focus of operations continue to be small- and medium-sized enterprise development, financial sector enhancement, targeted support for larger firms, infrastructure and work with a small number of priority regions. • More direct promotion of lender and shareholder rights, business standards and creditor, shareholder and contractual rights.

Source: GAO analysis of EBRD documents and discussions with EBRD officials.

By late 1993, as it began to identify and invest in a growing number of projects, the EBRD's changed its overall approach to assistance to Russia. The EBRD dropped its emphasis on technical assistance;, developed more realistic goals to avoid making promises to the Russians that could not be fulfilled; and narrowed its primary focus to emphasize (1) strengthening the financial sector, especially in its support of small- and medium-sized enterprise development and (2) providing targeted support for the restructuring efforts of large firms, especially in the oil and gas sector. As seen in figure 8, more than half of EBRD financing to date has gone to the finance and energy sectors.

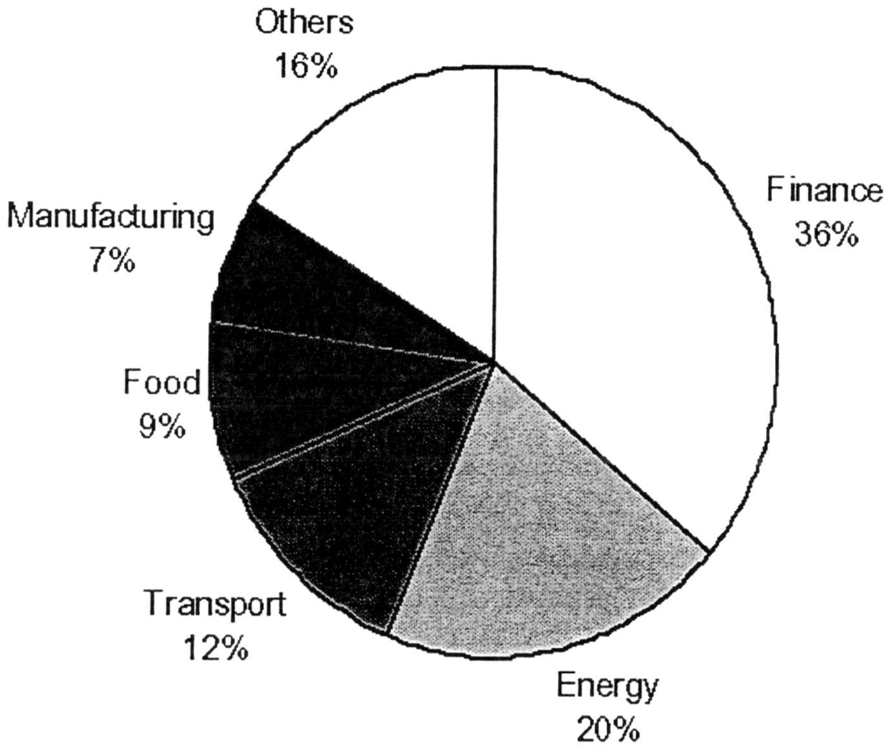

Figure 8: EBRD Funding for Russia by Sector, 1991-2000
Note: "Others" include mining, property, and public administration. Source: GAO analysis of EBRD data.

EBRD operations in the mid-1990s were characterized by rapid growth. From signing two projects in Russia worth $7.5 million in 1992, the EBRD signed 25 projects worth nearly $1 billion in 1996. The EBRD also made a conscious effort to cluster its projects in regions that were more reform minded. The use of financial intermediaries also increased over this period. Many of the EBRD's biggest programs in Russia, such as the Russia Small Business Fund, were actually implemented by Russian institutions. The EBRD believed that the use of intermediaries created opportunities for Russian institutions to learn how to operate in a market economy. This institution building aspect was an explicit part of the EBRD's strategy. However, the growing reliance on financial intermediaries, especially in the banking sector, meant depending on Russian institutions to implement the programs that were supposed to achieve the EBRD's overall objectives in Russia.

The August 1998 financial crisis was much worse than the EBRD and other institutions had anticipated and essentially destroyed the value of most of the assets on the balance sheets of most Russian banks. Because of the EBRD's emphasis on projects in the financial sector, the collapse damaged the EBRD's portfolio. Many of the EBRD's equity investments in Russian financial institutions became worthless, and the viability of several other projects was damaged. By the end of 1998, the EBRD had taken provisions of over $600 million, largely due to projects in the banking sector.

In the aftermath of the crisis, new EBRD operations in Russia almost came to a halt.[13] In the 6 months after the crash, the EBRD tried to salvage the projects it could and close out those that could not be saved. It signed only three new projects, worth $15 million. By mid-1999, as the Russian economy began to stabilize, the EBRD started to cautiously reengage in Russia. The EBRD exercised greater scrutiny of potential Russian business partners, with efforts supporting the development of Russia's small- and medium-sized enterprise sector taking highest priority. In early 2000, the EBRD was positioning itself for the possibility of a major return to the Russian market. The goals of the EBRD's core business in Russia reflected a continuation of earlier trends, with a growing focus on small- and medium-sized enterprise development, financial sector enhancement, infrastructure, targeted support for large firms, greater reliance on equity as an instrument, and active promotion of lender and shareholder rights in an effort to combat corruption and promote sound business practices. The EBRD's October 2000 country strategy for Russia called for targeting its investment priorities in these areas.

The U.S. Program Has Focused on Market Reform and Democracy

The primary objectives under the U.S. program, authorized by the 1992 Freedom Support Act, in Russia have been to promote market reform and democracy and to address urgent human needs related to Russia's transition to a market-based economy. From 1991 to the present, the relative emphasis on these objectives has shifted. While the Coordinator's Office at the Department of State oversees and coordinates U.S. assistance efforts, USAID has been the primary U.S. government agency involved in implementing Freedom Support Act programs. Table 4 shows the development of U.S. assistance programs for Russia (see app. IV for more information about Freedom Support Act programs).

Although some of the assistance that went to Russia in the early 1990s financed projects to support economic and democratic reforms, the main focus was on humanitarian assistance. The Departments of State and Defense collaborated on an airlift of medical, food, and other supplies to needy populations throughout Russia, called Operation PROVIDE HOPE, that has continued to the present. The economic and democratic assistance between 1992 and 1994 was generally spread across several sectors

[13] According to EBRD officials, the lack of new projects in Russia during this period was due to (1) a decrease in demand for EBRD financing stemming from the depressed economic conditions in Russia and (2) a decision by the EBRD to halt new operations in the banking sector.

in a deliberate effort to try different approaches and find out which ones were most successful.[14] During the pre-1993 period, the emphasis across the entire program was on speedy delivery and minimal effect on the U.S. budget.

With the change of U.S. administrations in early 1993, the approach to providing assistance to Russia evolved. Although humanitarian assistance has continued, the primary emphasis beginning in 1993 has been on working with the Russian government to develop and implement national reforms. In 1993, the Clinton administration sought to greatly increase the size of the U.S. program, expecting that U.S. help in key areas would jumpstart the reform process and assist in bringing about needed structural changes. In response to the assistance programs announced at the Vancouver and Tokyo summits in 1993, Congress appropriated the money necessary to implement these programs in September 1993, approving over $2.5 billion in the Foreign Operations, Export Financing, and Related Programs Appropriation Act, 1994, for assistance to Russia and the other former Soviet Union states.[15]

Although the general thrust of the program had shifted to emphasize economic reform, the U.S. program maintained the broad and disparate nature of the early 1990s. Projects were developed to support reforms in several sectors, including privatization, housing, agriculture, and energy. A wide variety of U.S. departments and agencies were implementing programs in Russia. In the past, we reported that 23 departments and independent agencies were carrying out programs in the former Soviet Union states. The sheer magnitude of this program made coordination difficult and complicated efforts to focus U.S. activities in a few key areas.[16]

During this period, the U.S. program focused on the need for quick implementation of assistance projects. Also, the United States moved away from having a single program for the entire former Soviet Union and started to develop formal country strategies. In mid-1993, the Coordinator of the U.S. program began writing the country strategy for Russia that was published in 1994. Country budgets for assistance were also developed.

Congressional support for assistance to Russia began to wane in 1994. Dramatic funding reductions were driven by two main factors. First, the relatively large appropriation for Russia in 1993 was presented to Congress as a onetime event to support what was likely to be a relatively short transition period. Indeed, the 1995 U.S. strategy for Russia supported this idea by stating that there would be no need for new funding for assistance after 1998. Second, Congress began to raise bipartisan concerns about the effectiveness of assistance to Russia and started earmarking significant portions of the Freedom Support Act appropriations for other former Soviet Union states, most notably Ukraine.

---

[14] USAID's grant assistance to help with the implementation of mass privatization is an exception. In that instance, the United States devoted relatively significant resources in a deliberate effort to influence a major aspect of the reform process. See chapter 3 for more information.

[15] P.L. 103-87. Approximately $1.6 billion of the funds provided by this measure was included as a fiscal year 1993 supplemental appropriation that was attached to the fiscal year 1994 foreign operations appropriation.

[16] Former Soviet Union: Information on U.S. Bilateral Program Funding (GAO-NSIAD 96- 37, Dec. 15, 1995)

Table 4: Development of the U.S. Assistance Program for Russia, 1991-Present

Time period	Strategy	Highlights of the program
1991-92	Humanitarian assistance predominates	• December 1991 United States outlined program to help Russia's transition. U.S. objectives paralleled those later articulated in the Freedom Support Act. • First Coordinator of FSU assistance designated. • February 1992 U.S. launched Operation PROVIDE HOPE to airlift emergency food and medical shipments to FSU. • October 1992, President signed Freedom Support Act. • During 1992 and 1993, State Department prohibited USAID's development of country strategies or country budgets because it wanted to develop regional approach for assistance to former Soviet Union states. • Economic and democratic assistance was generally spread across several sectors in deliberate effort to try different approaches and find out which ones were most successful.
1993-95	Focus on market reform	• January 1993 New administration brought evolutionary change in approach to providing assistance to Russia. • April 1993 U.S. pledged to provide $1.6 billion in assistance for Russia. • July 1993 U.S. portion of assistance package announced at Tokyo Summit totaled a new $1.5 billion for Russia. • Humanitarian assistance continued, but primary emphasis now on working with Russian Federation to develop and implement national reforms. • September 1993 — $1.6 billion fiscal year 1993 supplemental appropriation signed for FSU assistance. • January 1994 Coordinator published first assistance strategy for entire former Soviet Union. • May 1994 Coordinator published first assistance strategy for Russia. • Budgets for Russia dropped from $1.0 billion in fiscal year 1994 to $359 million in 1995 to $219 million in 1996, reflecting waning congressional support.
1996 to Present	Democratic reform becomes a priority	• Fiscal year 1996 assistance review and budget reduction forced near elimination of new budget authority to three USAID sectors. • 1996 development of Partnership for Freedom to increase impact of U.S. assistance at grassroots of Russian society, launched at the beginning of fiscal year 1997. • Assistance to Russian federal government would diminish as projects at national level ended, and new funding focused mainly on grassroots efforts at regional, local, or individual level. • U.S. assistance is now focused on efforts to promote (1) investment-led economic growth, (2) people-to-people linkages, and (3) development of civil society. • The Regional Initiative was also launched in 1997 to demonstrate what concentrated assistance in reform-oriented regions could do to improve lives of individual Russians. • 1998 Assistance dollars budgeted to democratic reform exceed dollars for market reform.

Legend: FSU = former Soviet Union; Source: GAO analysis of State Department and USAID documents and discussions with State Department and USAID officials.

In early 1996, the Coordinator reevaluated the U.S. program for Russia, because of significant decreases in funding, heightened concerns about program effectiveness, and a growing sense of unease about the state of transition in Russia. This review led to a significant shift in U.S. strategy. In mid-1996, the Coordinator announced a new U.S. approach, called the "Partnership for Freedom." Assistance to the Russian federal government diminished, and new funding focused mainly on grassroots efforts at the regional, local, or individual level. The new approach began in fiscal year 1997 and has continued to the present, focusing on efforts to promote (1) investment-led economic growth, (2) people-to-people linkages, and (3) the development of civil society. In addition, the recipients of U.S. assistance changed from organizations working largely at the federal level to those in regions that demonstrated more reform-minded policies. Under this aspect of the program, known as the "Regional Initiative," the United States targeted its assistance toward three Russian regions, whose local governments were deemed to be among the most reform minded and hospitable to investment. Moving to the regions was part of an approach to increase the bottom-up pressure for reform in Russia.

Figure 9 shows Freedom Support Act funds budgeted to Russia from 1992 through 2000. Although the total amount budgeted for promoting democracy from 1996 to the present does not exceed the total for promoting market reform, the amount for promoting democracy has increased relatively and in fiscal year 1999 exceeded the budget for promoting market reform. Figure 10 shows the proportion of Freedom Support Act funds budgeted to each objective from 1992 through 2000.

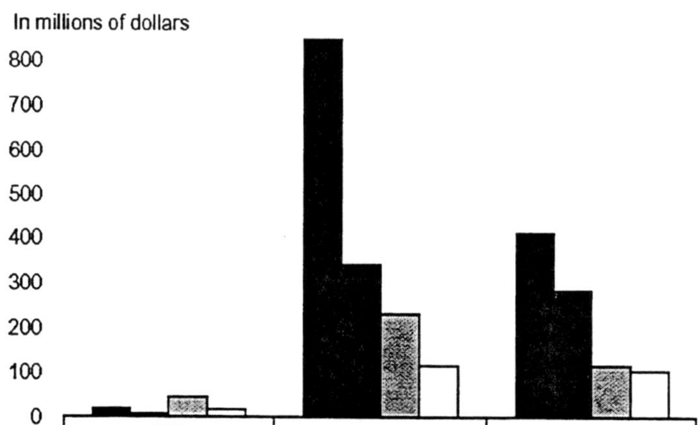

	1992	1993-1995	1996-Present
■ Promote market reform	$17.58	$988.22	$413.93
■ Promote democracy and rule of law	$8.05	$340.19	$282.94
▣ Address urgent human needs related to transition	$44.86	$231.31	$113.82
□ Nonproliferation/ security-related items	$16.14	$114.03	$104.35

Figure 9: Freedom Support Act-funded Activities Grouped by U.S. Objectives, 1992-Present
Source: U.S. Department of State and GAO analysis.

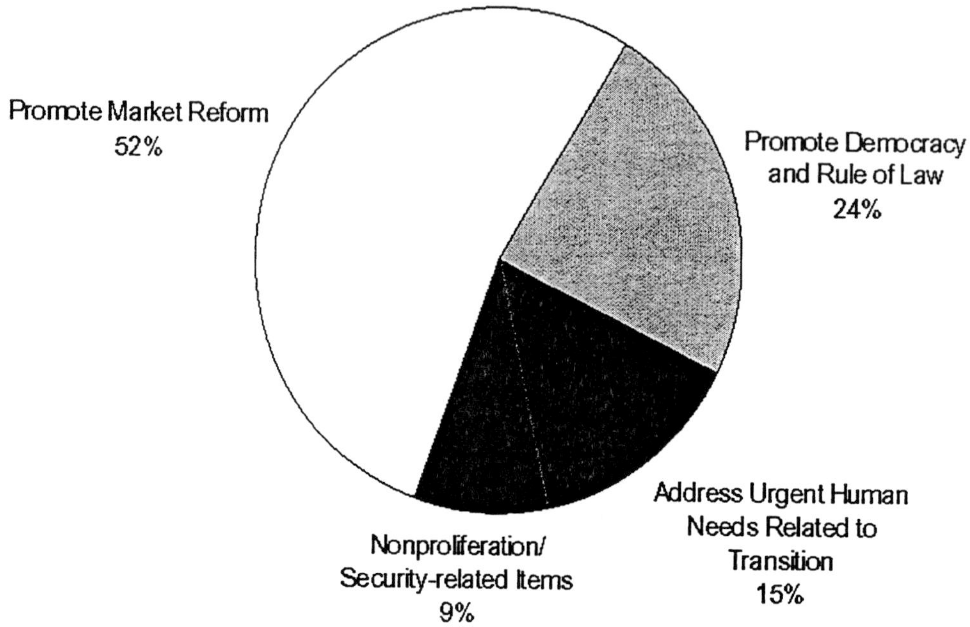

Figure 10: Portions of All Freedom Support Act Funds Budgeted for Each U.S. Objective, Fiscal Years 1992-2000

Source: U.S. Department of State and GAO analysis.

The European Union Has Provided Technical Assistance Aimed at Russia's Socio-economic and Democratic Reform Process

The principal objective of the TACIS program in Russia has been to accelerate the socio-economic and democratic reform process. The program relies primarily on technical assistance provided though policy advisers; training and advice to Russia's private sector; funding studies including preinvestment plans, market research, and feasibility studies; and linking Russian and EU institutions.

Drawing generalizations about strategy with such a broad and diverse program is difficult. Since 1991, TACIS has implemented more than 500 projects in Russia and as of August 2000 had about 100 projects underway. Although the TACIS strategy for Russia has evolved over time, some central tenants have remained. TACIS is still largely a technical assistance program that has delivered help to roughly the same sectors since 1991. Table 5 shows the evolution of the TACIS strategy for Russia (see app. V for more information about TACIS programs).

Table 5: Evolution of TACIS' Strategy for Russia, 1991-2000

Time period	Highlights of the strategy
Early efforts focused on quick impact: 1991-94	• Main focus on economic reform, little in democratic assistance. • Projects tended to be small and focus on quick impact. • Special attention to training Russians in market economics. • Many projects implemented at local level.
Greater emphasis on attaining systemic change: 1995-98	• Challenges of reform prove greater than expected. • Shift to larger projects and more frequent use of federal level partners. • Sectors largely unchanged; primary focus continues to be on economic reform. • TACIS efforts more closely linked to broader EU political goals in Russia.
Post-crisis reflection leads to modified approach: 1991-present	• Crisis reinforces assumption that transition would be a decades long process. • Greater focus on supporting development of (1) institutions for market reform, (2) rule of law, and (3) civil society. • More attention to supporting change at the grass-roots level. • Project selection begins to reflect greater emphasis on mutual benefits for EU and Russia.

Source: GAO analysis of TACIS documents and discussions with EU officials.

TACIS projects during the early years of the transition focused on having a quick impact, with special attention devoted to training Russians in market economics. Many of the early projects were small, emphasizing speed and meeting specific Russian needs, often involving study tours, conferences, or writing reports. There was also an emphasis on training as many people as possible in a variety of areas including banking, finance, and economics. From the beginning of the program, TACIS frequently implemented projects at the regional and local levels.

During the mid-1990s, support for economic reform and for democracy were the dual goals of the TACIS program in Russia. However, TACIS implementation continued to focus mainly on economic reform, with a greater emphasis on attaining systemic change at the federal level. TACIS shifted its focus from the regional to the federal level in an attempt to have greater influence on systemic reforms. TACIS implemented larger projects, but projects with federal institutions generally had activities in pilot regions. TACIS continued to operate in essentially the same sectors as it always had, adding environment to the initial areas of enterprise restructuring, human resource development, agriculture, energy, transportation, and telecommunications (see fig. 11).

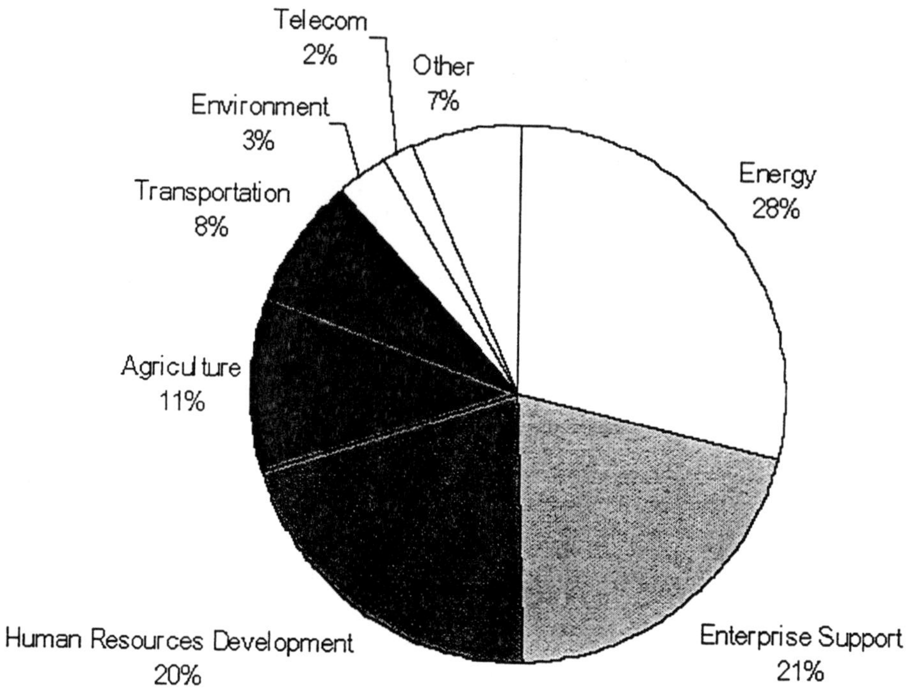

Figure 11: TACIS Funding for Russia by Sector, 1991-98
Source: European Commission.

The Russian financial crisis in late 1998 reinforced TACIS' earlier assumption that Russia's transition to a market economy would be a decades-long process. TACIS officials told us that it was clear the transition had not gone as well as initially expected, in part because (1) the institutional underpinnings for a market economy and democratic society were lacking and (2) the necessary political consensus within Russia on how to proceed was not developed. As a result, project selection began to include more grassroots efforts related to improving civil society and developing small- and medium-sized enterprises. The increased focus on the institutions necessary for a market economy and democratic society also led the European Union to add a third objective to the program: support for the development of the rule of law. By 2000, the TACIS annual program made democracy building the central focus for the first time. TACIS also placed greater emphasis on institution building, working at the grassroots level, and developing of more linkages—known as "twinning"— between Russian and EU institutions. TACIS projects were also increasingly being linked to the broader EU-Russian political goal of increasing Russia's integration within Europe. In practice, this meant development of projects like improving transportation links, upgrading border controls, and addressing environmental concerns in northwest Russia.

Coordination of Assistance Has Proved Difficult, With Some Improvements Over Time

In the years leading up to and the early years after the breakup of the Soviet Union, formal efforts to coordinate donor assistance programs had limited success. Over time, informal coordination mechanisms developed within the donor community. The donors believe these mechanisms are working relatively well, in terms of sharing information and reducing redundancies at the project level. The coordination between the Russian government and the international community is still problematic but has improved over time, especially in the aftermath of the 1998 financial crisis.

Early Coordination Efforts Had Limited Success

The initial attempts at coordinating the efforts of those interested in providing Russia with advice and assistance were impeded by lack of a clear western strategy during the breakup of the Soviet Union and difficulties in working with the Russian government. The Russian government appeared uninterested in coordinating donor assistance, according to officials we interviewed. Also, according to Russian and some donor officials, donors had difficulties in coordinating their own activities, particularly their technical assistance. Russian officials told us that problems occurred in the early 1990s with duplication and lack of communication among donors. U.S.-sponsored donor conferences in 1992 raised this issue but accomplished little.

In June 1993, the World Bank led an attempt to set up a consultative group to discuss priorities for structural reform and technical assistance needs. This effort was not successful. The reason given by many donor and institution officials who were involved at that time was that the Russian government did not want Russia to be treated like a third world country. Also, in 1993, the G-7 mandated the implementation of a formal coordination mechanism called the Support Implementation Group. The main efforts of the group were to work with the Russians to remove impediments to supplying assistance in the field, such as the Russian government's continued attempts to tax international assistance, and to accumulate a database of assistance projects in Russia. The group also tried to formalize the donor coordination process by creating a series of sector-based working groups. However, the group's efforts to formalize coordination proved to be cumbersome. Officials from all five institutions and donors in our review told us the group actually impeded the informal coordination process that evolved among the donors over time. Several told us that the data the group collected were not useful and meetings were not productive. As a result, the Support Implementation Group was disbanded in 1997. The Russian government has taken over the group's database, but it is unclear whether the data have been used.

Early coordination challenges were not limited to relations among donors. In some instances, donors like the United States experienced early difficulties in coordinating their programs internally. In February 1995, reports appeared on the ineffective coordination of the U.S. bilateral program for the former Soviet Union.[17] It was found that there were frequent, sometimes bitter, disputes among U.S. agencies over how the program should be structured and implemented and that other agencies and departments resisted, hindered, or overruled the State Department Coordinator's efforts.[18] After the report was published, the Coordinator's role was expanded. In December 1995, we reported that interagency coordination, while still marked by periodic disputes, had improved, as had the Coordinator's ability to oversee and coordinate the program.[19]

Informal Donor Coordination Mechanisms Have Evolved

Donor officials in Moscow said they prefer the informal coordination process that has evolved over time. According to donor officials in Russia, they interact frequently on an as-needed basis. They did not believe formal coordination mechanisms like the Support Implementation Group were necessary. Donor officials in cities outside Moscow echoed similar themes. In the GAO meetings in Russia, there arose little evidence of serious overlap in current programs and a general agreement on overarching goals and relative roles.

In some sectors, donors have established informal working groups to coordinate efforts in a specific sector. For example, in the health sector, several donors provide assistance for tuberculosis/acquired immune deficiency syndrome (TB/AIDS) control, including the World Health Organization; the European Union; the Open Society Institute; USAID, and other bilateral donors such as Canada, Germany, Japan, the United Kingdom, and Sweden. According to World Bank staff, in designing a World Bank-funded TB/AIDS project, they took into account the experience of other donors working in various locations in Russia, and other donor representatives have participated in Bank project preparation missions. World Bank staff said that the degree of coordination on the TB/AIDS project has reduced the possibility of duplication of efforts across donors. According to World Bank staff, better coordination among the 5 ministries and about 40 regions participating in the project has also been achieved. Donor working groups have also been established in some cases to address specific needs or concerns. For example, in 1996, in order to facilitate information sharing and promote cooperation among donors that provide grants in Russia, a group of western donors initiated a Moscow donors' forum. The forum is an informal coalition of representatives of about 25 private and

[17] Former Soviet Union: U.S. Bilateral Program Lacks Effective Coordination (GAO/NSIAD-95-10, Feb. 7, 1995).

[18] The Gore-Chernomyrdin Commission is one example of the complications the Coordinator faced. Originally established as a high-level mechanism for resolving U.S.- Russian problems in energy, space, and science, the Commission evolved into a multiagency effort to advance common U.S. and Russian interests in a number of other areas including commerce, environment, and defense diversification. Although the Commission had no direct coordination role, it did develop policies that had an impact on U.S. bilateral assistance.

[19] Former Soviet Union: An Update on Coordination of U.S. Assistance and Economic Cooperation Programs (GAO/NSIAD-96-16, Dec. 15, 1995).

public international organizations including, among others, the Eurasia Foundation, which is funded, in large part, by USAID. Participating donors are active in supporting the development of non-governmental organizations in Russia.

Donors also sometimes work together on the same project. USAID and TACIS officials often help lay the groundwork, through grants and technical assistance, for World Bank and EBRD loans in specific areas. For example, in the housing sector, USAID funded $10 million in technical assistance in preparation for a $400 million loan by the World Bank in 1995. The World Bank has also teamed with USAID and the U.S. Treasury in the tax administration area. In addition, the World Bank manages grants from the Japanese government to finance startups for numerous World Bank operations including, for example, a $2 million grant to support the preparation of a legal reform project. There have been areas, too, where the World Bank has put programs in place when other donors, such as USAID, have phased down their activities. For example, in 1996, the Bank committed $58 million for the legal reform project when USAID expected most of its larger law programs to end or taper off.

Coordination Is Still Challenging for Donors and the Russian Government

Some Russian government officials claimed, however, that there is room for improvement in donor coordination efforts. Some government officials stated that, in some cases, donors have had competing models in mind when working with them to set up new programs or institutions. For example, questions have arisen over whether Russia's capital markets would be structured more closely to that of the United States or of Germany. Some Russian officials said donors did not necessarily consider what was best for Russia in providing their advice. Russian government officials also commented that because assistance efforts affect more than one ministry in the Russian government, one ministry is not always aware of what assistance donors may be providing to another ministry. The tax area was mentioned as one in which this problem has occurred.

Donor officials said that coordination with the Russian government continues to be a challenge, although they noted some improvement has been made. One problem many donor officials mentioned was that their counterparts in ministries changed frequently. In many instances, donors would set up a program with a counterpart but, in a short time, that counterpart would depart, and it was possible that his or her replacement would not be interested in the program. Another problem is that no central location exists in the Russian government that has oversight over the entire breadth of assistance efforts. Over the years, the Russian government has tried to establish some procedures for dealing with lenders and donors, but constant changes in the format and personalities involved have limited the effectiveness of these efforts. For example, in 1995, the Russian government established the Federal Center for Project Finance to assist the government with the overall coordination of projects funded by the international financial institutions or other external sources. The government also created the Interministerial Commission for Cooperation with the International Financial and Economic Institutions and the G-7 to coordinate donors' technical assistance and the international financial institutions' lending programs. With the Federal Center for Project Finance serving as the secretariat, the Interministerial Commission is chaired by the deputy Prime Minister and comprised completely of high-level Russian government ministry officials.

Chapter 3

INSTITUTIONS AND DONORS HAVE HAD LIMITED SUCCESS IN MEETING THEIR OBJECTIVES

According to a number of indicators, Russian economic performance over the past decade has been poor. While there have been successes across individual program objectives of the institutions and donors we reviewed, officials have acknowledged that in many respects, there has been limited progress toward reaching their broad program goals. This is due to obstacles encountered in Russia, problems with design and implementation of the programs, and difficulties involving the scale of the challenge. Assistance efforts in four key areas—macroeconomic stabilization, social safety net protection, privatization, and banking sector reform—illustrate barriers to success and how limited reforms in some areas have undermined progress in other areas. Institutions and donors have modified their strategies and programs in Russia in different ways over the decade, but remaining engaged in Russia has been a common goal.

RUSSIA'S ECONOMIC PERFORMANCE OVER THE DECADE HAS BEEN POOR

According to a number of broad indicators, the Russian economy fared badly during the 1990s. Although declines in output during the initial transition period were expected and were in fact experienced across most transition countries in Eastern Europe and the former Soviet Union, Russia's economic decline was among the most severe and its recovery among the most limited. By 1995, the measured output of the Russian economy had fallen to about 65 percent of its 1991 level and then remained stagnant through 1998, with some improvement in 1999 and 2000. (Fig. 12 illustrates Russian gross domestic product (GDP) trends relative to those of several other transition countries.)

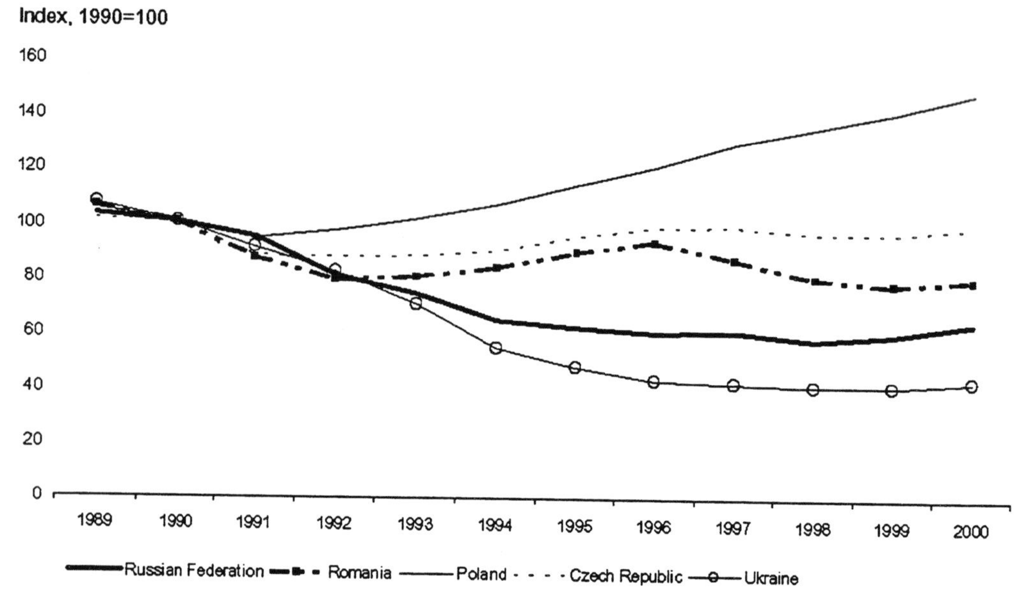

Figure 12: Trends in Real Output for Russia, the Czech Republic, Poland, Romania, and Ukraine, 1989-2000
Source: GAO analysis of data from the World Bank and PlanEcon, Inc.

Average labor productivity in Russia fell from about 30 percent of the U.S. average in 1991 to about 19 percent in 1998. Trends in social indicators show the personal impact of the decline, with average life expectancy declining from 69 years in 1991 to 64 years in 1994, and then rising somewhat but remaining below pretransition levels.

The problems in overall economic performance, and the hardships of many Russian citizens, have been linked to a number of conditions in the economy and society. These include, in part,

- • chronic macroeconomic instability,
- • the absence of effective competition in many economic sectors,
- • problems with the structure of the tax system and tax collection,
- • the lack of an efficient financial system,
- • the existence of widespread organized crime and corruption, and
- • the presence of a system of social services that fails to protect the poor and discourages economic restructuring.

Many of these weaknesses represent areas in which the international community has been actively engaged. While there have been a number of successes across individual program objectives (see the following sections), individual institutions and donors have acknowledged that in many respects there has been limited progress toward achieving broad program goals. For example, a 1999 USAID assessment stated, "Economic reform has not yet succeeded and no one should anticipate rapid progress."[1] Also, a recent TACIS report concluded, "Beyond the successful implementation of projects, the impact on the regulatory and policy framework has on the whole been limited."[2]

At the broadest, strategic level, assessing the impact of western involvement in Russia's economic transition over the past decade is extraordinarily complex. Clearly, the worst fears of the initial transition period have not been realized: anarchy has not prevailed; the nuclear arsenals of the Soviet Union are under control; there has not been a return to Communist rule; and in April 2000, Russia experienced a peaceful and democratic presidential transition.

The degree to which overall transition objectives have been achieved in Russia must be viewed in the context of the enormity of the challenge. Russia entered its transition burdened with economic and political legacies from decades of central planning geared disproportionately toward military output. Specialization of production and trade patterns had only a limited economic basis, many state-owned enterprises were burdened with obsolete capital, and, perhaps most important, many basic institutions ranging from banks to courts either did not exist or were poorly suited to supporting a market economy. Recent comparisons of the transition experiences of a number of European countries have concluded that the severity and length of economic decline may be linked to external incentives such as the potential for membership in the European Union, which has not been a realistic goal for Russia. By many indicators, Russia's challenge was huge.

SUCCESS OF INDIVIDUAL PROJECTS HAS BEEN MIXED

The success of individual projects in Russia implemented by the five institutions and donors in our review has been mixed, according to their own evaluations and the views of officials and analysts we interviewed. While some Russian officials were highly critical of international assistance efforts, others said that assistance programs have had a reasonable level of success, given the obstacles they have faced.

IMF Programs

Assessing the success of IMF programs is especially hard, given the IMF's broad objective of stabilizing the macroeconomy and the difficulty of isolating the impact of its program from other factors. The IMF has not comprehensively evaluated its own Russia program. There is a wide variety of views on the relative success of IMF programs in Russia. While Russia was finally able to bring inflation under control by late 1995, substantial imbalances remained in terms of the government's overall fiscal policies, which were highlighted by the 1998 financial crisis. A number of analysts and officials

[1] USAID Russia Country Strategy 1999-2003, April 5, 1999.
[2] TACIS Russian Federation Indicative Strategy Paper 2000-2003 (draft) (Brussels: Dec. 1999).

have taken issue with aspects of IMF policies and programs in Russia over the period and believe that the value of the IMF's assistance could have been greater. However, a number of analysts and U.S. and Russian officials stated that the policy advice and high-level dialogue provided by the IMF has been of value to Russia's transition in several respects. The IMF's technical assistance to several government ministries and the Central Bank of Russia is believed to have improved, for example, Russia's economic statistics, its ability to conduct fiscal and monetary policy, and its supervision of Russian banks.

World Bank Programs

World Bank officials, in their December 1999 country assistance strategy, characterized the success of the World Bank's efforts in Russia as mixed but overall disappointing relative to their expectations. According to the World Bank's periodic rating of loans in its Russia portfolio, the percentage of ongoing loans meeting both development and implementation objectives has ranged from 33 percent to 82 percent, showing improvement in 1996 and 1997 and then falling sharply after the 1998 financial crisis. Russia lending has at times had the poorest performance in the World Bank's portfolio, for countries with significant borrowing. The rating reported in June 2000—73 percent satisfactory projects—reflects a strong improvement following several post-crisis loan restructurings, and Bank staff said that the portfolio has shown further signs of improvement since then. According to World Bank documents and officials, the World Bank achieved limited success with a number of investment loans it made across several areas during 1993-95, ranging from agriculture to tax administration. World Bank officials point to greater success in the Bank's targeted structural adjustment lending, such as the productivity gains under the 1996 and 1997 coal sector adjustment loans and improved dialogue on social issues under the 1997 social protection adjustment loan. World Bank officials stated that the jury remains out on the successes of the Bank's adjustment lending in Russia. While citing gains in the quality of the World Bank's dialogue with the Russian government on structural policies, the December 1999 country assistance strategy concluded with respect to adjustment lending that "the Bank's efforts have not borne fruit to date on a scale commensurate with the increase in Bank exposure." According to World Bank officials, the value of the World Bank's adjustment lending program has become more apparent during the 9 months since the assistance strategy was written, based on the World Bank's ability to engage in high-level policy discussions with successive Russian governments.

EBRD Programs

The EBRD also rates the success of its efforts in Russia as mixed. By the end of 1999, the EBRD's project evaluation department had conducted evaluations of 31 completed EBRD projects in Russia. They rated 29 percent as highly successful or successful, 36 percent as partially successful, and 35 percent as unsuccessful based on the project's success in meeting a variety of goals, including transition impact, environmental impact and the project's financial performance. Compared to the EBRD's average across its entire portfolio, projects completed to date in Russia were significantly more likely to fail and less likely to succeed.[3] In February 2000, the EBRD reported that overall, its operations had had a positive influence on Russia's transition to a market economy. EBRD officials told us they believe they have been particularly successful in areas of small business development and other projects entailing work with smaller firms. They also acknowledged that the financial turmoil in 1998 damaged many EBRD efforts, particularly in the financial sector, and that the EBRD has had limited success in promoting economic restructuring in large Russian firms.

Russian officials had differing perspectives on the EBRD. Some believed it had generally done good work in Russia and had made important contributions to the transition efforts. Others thought the EBRD was not efficient and had had little impact in Russia. They criticized the EBRD for not being careful enough when selecting its partners, losing a lot of money in 1998, and acting overly cautious with new projects since then. Many private analysts were generally positive about the success of EBRD projects, with some noting significant improvement over time. However, several stated that the EBRD's role duplicates lending and investment functions that can be provided by the private sector and is therefore of limited value.

U.S. Freedom Support Act Programs

According to U.S. officials, the broad nature of the U.S. program complicates efforts to generalize about its effectiveness. Although no comprehensive evaluation of the entire U.S. program exists, an analysis of available evaluations, discussions with officials, and the results of prior work found that the United States has had varied results with Freedom Support Act projects in Russia. For example, a past review of nine projects showed mixed results in meeting project objectives: two projects—coal industry restructuring and housing sector reform—met or exceeded their objectives; five projects—voucher privatization, military officer resettlement, small business development, district heating, and agribusiness partnerships—met some but not other objectives; and two projects—health care and commercial real estate—met few or none of their objectives.[4] A review of democracy projects in Russia found that these projects were seen as valuable by Russian recipients but had mixed impacts.[5] USAID evaluations and State Department reports likewise noted mixed results in meeting objectives. One USAID Mission Director said that several projects that had funding stopped in 1996 had done no harm but little good. Several U.S. officials stated that, however effective and successful an individual project,

[3] As of the end of 1999, 54 percent of EBRD projects have been rated successful or higher, and only 18 percent have been rated unsuccessful.

[4] Foreign Assistance: Assessment of Selected USAID Projects in Russia (GAO/NSIAD-95- 156, Aug. 3, 1995).

[5] Promoting Democracy: Progress Report on U.S. Democratic Development Assistance to Russia (GAO/NSIAD-96-40, Feb. 29, 1996).

U.S. assistance as a whole helps Russia only at the margin. The most valuable part of U.S. assistance, according to some Russian and U.S. officials, has been an ongoing transfer of knowledge and exposure to western approaches.

TACIS Programs

The general assessment of TACIS projects in Russia is mixed, based on the EU's own evaluations and GAO discussions with EU officials. Russian and private officials we spoke with expressed sometimes serious concerns about the effectiveness of TACIS projects. Over the years, the European Commission's evaluations of the program have varied in their assessment of the program's success and impact. In 1994, the Commission reported that the program was generally meeting its objectives but was implementing effort to speed the disbursement of funds, improve the quality of projects, and sharpen the focus of the program. In 1997, it reported that TACIS had achieved a moderate degree of success in effectiveness and achievement of its objectives. A February 2000 report on the entire TACIS program for Russia found a mixed record of impact: high marks for education and training efforts and lower marks for enterprise restructuring and building the framework for a market economy.[6]

EU officials said that TACIS projects were generally effective in meeting their objectives, although they acknowledged substantial constraints. They believed the program was especially effective at supporting the development of higher education. Russian officials, as well as several analysts, focused on several problems with the TACIS program. Although some noted success in particular areas of assistance, such as education and a TACIS project that introduced foster parenting to Samara, these officials generally expressed concerns about the program's efficiency, impact, and timeliness.

SUCCESS OF ASSISTANCE PROGRAMS HAS BEEN HINDERED BY CONDITIONS IN RUSSIA AND LIMITATIONS OF PROGRAMS

Based on the documents from the reviewed programs as well as discussions with institution and donor officials, representatives of the Russian government, and private analysts, there are three main interrelated obstacles to attaining project and program objectives: (1) difficult conditions in Russia, including the lack of domestic political consensus behind reform, changing government officials, and widespread corruption; (2) limitations in the design and implementation of donor programs; and (3) the vastness of the scale of the efforts and the interdependent nature of the needs.

[6] European Commission Evaluation Unit, "Evaluation of TACIS Country Programme in Russian Federation" (Brussels: European Commission, Feb. 2000).

Institutions and Donors Faced Substantial Barriers in Implementing Programs in Russia

Russia proved to be a challenging environment for assistance efforts in several related respects, including a lack of political and economic stability, a lack of commitment in critical areas of the government to reforms institutions sought, limited institutional capacity, the rise of powerful economic interest groups with political influence, and corruption at some levels of government.

Political and Economic Instability

During the 1990s, Russia experienced a series of political and economic crises and distractions that diverted the energies and attention of the Russian government away from the transition, often leading to stagnation. These crises began with the struggles between the government and the Russian legislature, culminating in bloodshed in September 1993; the wars in Chechnya during 1994-95 and 1999-2000; and the efforts to attain President Yeltsin's reelection in 1996. (See app. VI for a timeline of major political events.) Although Yeltsin retained the presidency through 1999, that stability was undermined by serious health crises, periodic rumors of impeachment, and several changes in Prime Minister and other key ministers toward the end of Yeltsin's tenure.

Lack of Commitment to Reforms

In documents reviewed and discussions with officials, a frequently cited obstacle to success was the lack of Russian interest in or commitment to program objectives. Often, this lack of commitment was from high-level officials. In other cases, it was from institutions and donors' working-level counterparts. Lack of high-level interest was a serious problem during the early years of the World Bank's activity in Russia, when World Bank access to senior Russian officials was limited. Achieving dialogue on social sector programs was particularly difficult, according to World Bank officials. It was not until 1995, according to senior World Bank officials, that they began serious discussions with high-level Russians on the direction of the World Bank's program. According to World Bank staff and documents, commitments to World Bank lending projects were made in a number of areas, with little follow-through on reforms. Although dialogue with senior officials improved, commitment to carrying out program objectives continued to be problematic, as evidenced by the limited achievements in 1997 and 1998 of the World Bank's large structural adjustment loans.

Lack of commitment to agreed reforms was also a problem in the technical assistance programs of USAID and TACIS. For example, USAID concluded that its efforts to support reforms in the agricultural sector generally failed, in large part because the Russians were not interested in implementing key provisions to provide for the private ownership of land or the elimination of government-owned or monopolized distribution chains. EU officials cited their frustration in efforts to combat the spread of drug-resistant tuberculosis, when Russian officials, after agreeing to the program, refused to try new approaches to fight the disease. In extreme cases, according to officials, Russian counterparts would agree to programs simply to direct the training, equipment, or support to political supporters and not follow through on reforms. Officials from several institutions said that knowing when they have had adequate Russian commitment to program goals and conditions has been difficult, due both to changing views of officials they were dealing with and changes in which individuals were in positions of authority.

Closely related to limited commitment has been the lack of effective consensus within and between the executive and legislative branches and also regional governments. For most of the decade, the Duma was controlled by parties or groups that often opposed the reform policies of the administration. For example, after the Duma elections of 1993 and 1995, a combination of nationalists, Communists, and their supporters controlled about half of the legislative body. This coalition has been able to block a number of government efforts to pass legislation in the areas of tax reform, land code requirements, and bankruptcy provisions. In response to this opposition, the administration often sought to enact change through issuing decrees. Although these decrees allowed certain measures related to banking, bankruptcy, and tax reform to become law, they did not ensure the measures would be implemented or enforced.[7]

Limited Institutional Capacity

The lack of institutions to regulate market economic activities and provide the basis for a functioning democracy proved to be a significant challenge to reforms. Officials of the reviewed programs said, in general, the lack of these institutions created a barrier to project success across the board. At the same time, it proved very difficult to help Russia to create new, viable institutions. In some cases, reform efforts were passed into law by the Duma, but little changed because the federal agencies responsible for implementation and enforcement lacked the capabilities to follow through. For example, the United States and other donors provided assistance to support the creation of a Russian Federal Securities Commission. In 1996, the GAO reported that it was unclear whether the Commission had the necessary resources to fulfill its responsibilities.[8] Later that year, the political status of the Commission was downgraded by presidential decree, then partially restored, and in 1999, the head of the Commission resigned to protest the government's lack of support for the Commission.

In addition, limited technical capability to implement projects has plagued assistance efforts across the board in Russia. For example, the World Bank attempted to establish familiarity with World Bank lending operations and develop the government's capacity to implement projects with its 1992 rehabilitation loan. According to World Bank officials, although the Bank rated the project as satisfactory in terms of meeting its specific objectives, the Russian government's capacity remained far short of what was needed to implement Bank lending programs. Moreover, inadequate capability on the

[7] This approach proved controversial, even within donor organizations. For example, a USAID contractor provided extensive assistance to the Russian government's efforts to draft decrees. However, in 1996 we reported that the U.S. Ambassador to Russia and the USAID Office of Democracy opposed the use of decrees to achieve legal reform objectives because, in their view, decrees did not support the democratization process. See Foreign Assistance: Harvard Institute for International Development's Work in Russia and Ukraine (GAO/NSIAD-97-27, Nov. 27, 1996).

[8] See Foreign Assistance: Harvard Institute for International Development's Work in Russia and Ukraine.

part of the recipient to monitor either the financial or conditional aspects of the World Bank lending activity became apparent by 1994.

Rise of Powerful Interest Groups

The increasing concentration of economic power in Russia and the rise of politically powerful vested interests are widely viewed as impeding progress in meeting economic reform objectives. According to a number of analysts, incomplete liberalization of price and trade policies early in the transition created opportunities for individuals to acquire substantial wealth, and later measures, such as the privatization of the largest firms, led to further concentration of economic resources. Individuals were able to translate their wealth into political power—which they used to block reforms contrary to their financial interests. A primary example is the area of tax reform. A recent article by two IMF staff says that reforming the tax system and strengthening tax administration have often been opposed by vested interests in transition countries. Vested interests have found that many governments in former Soviet Union countries are willing to grant tax exemptions and even tolerate tax evasion, especially if given financial inducements.[9]

According to analysts, program officials, and documents, corruption within the government, particularly at the local level, has seriously undermined reforms, along with efforts to spur private sector activity. Uneven enforcement of requirements for licensing businesses and uneven tax collection are prime examples of the problems. Corruption has been of particular concern to the EBRD, because of its private-sector focus. EBRD officials stated that in some cases projects could not go forward because donors believed they could not trust their Russian partners. Corruption and crime also forced many Russian firms to focus on survival. Several small business owners in the Russian city of Samara said that running a growing, profitable business only attracts attention from corrupt government officials and organized crime. According to a Russian report cited in a State Department publication, small businesses spend 10 percent of their income paying off corrupt officials.[10]

Some donor officials claimed that in many respects their influence on the domestic political decisions of the Russian government was limited after the initial years of the transition period, as anti-reform elements were in control of the Duma; the oligarchs wielded significant power; crime and corruption were on the rise; and the population—after nearly a decade of economic and democratic reform dating back to the Gorbachev era—was weary, cynical, and skeptical. To many Russians, reform had become associated with declining living standards and loss of global power and influence.

---

[9] See "Political Economy of Stalled Reforms," Finance and Development, IMF, Vol.37, No. 3 (Sept. 2000).
[10] State Department Report to Congress on U.S. Efforts to Combat Crime and Corruption in Russia, Feb. 1999.

Limitations in Design and Implementation of Assistance Programs

Although conditions in Russia were major impediments to project success, limitations in the design and implementation of international assistance programs also created obstacles to achieving reform objectives. Some of these limitations were directly related to the mandates and traditional roles of the institutions and donors, and also to political guidance. Others stemmed from limited institutional and program capabilities and decisions about what strategies to pursue and how to implement them.

By the middle of 1992, the international lending institutions reviewed in this report faced pressures to lend to Russia quickly, given early evidence its economy was in serious decline. The World Bank, for example, was under considerable political pressure from its members, led by the United States, to develop projects and disburse funds as rapidly as possible. The World Bank also faced concerns from some members about Russia's ability to undertake agreed-to reforms and to repay World Bank loans. Many members were thus reluctant to put the Bank's financial soundness at risk by devoting too large a share of its lending to Russia. In the case of the EBRD, pressure to provide substantial financing to Russia heightened conflicting pressures already built into its mandate. By design, the EBRD was supposed to take risks but also ensure that its financing decisions followed proper due diligence to protect against financial losses. The EBRD, moreover, aimed to have its overall portfolio turn a small profit every year. Both World Bank and EBRD officials said that balancing these competing demands was difficult and complicated efforts to develop coherent strategies.

The IMF's mandate to provide balance-of-payments support for member countries was not well suited to Russia's transition needs, according to a number of officials and analysts. The IMF's role generally is to provide balance-of-payments support to a member country in need and help it to achieve macroeconomic stability to eliminate balance-of-payments problems. The IMF could not easily adapt its lending instruments just for Russia, according to IMF and other officials, although it did develop a new lending program, the Systemic Transformation Facility, specifically for transition countries. Although it needed budgetary support during its transition, Russia did not have a traditional balance-of-payments problem because it had high levels of commodity exports. While it did have problems with inflation, much of the basis for its financing need was due to underlying structural problems, such as lack of an effective tax system and inefficiently structured enterprises. While the IMF tried to address Russia's structural needs over time through the use of conditionality, many of those needs were in areas outside of the IMF's traditional expertise.

Both the international institutions, which had the lead in providing assistance for Russia's economic and political transition, and bilateral donors lacked significant experience with transition economies and depth of staff familiar with Russia. The World Bank and the IMF had limited experience with the region, the language, or the special challenges associated with transition economies. The EBRD and TACIS were brand-new organizations with no track record, simply trying to get operations up and running. USAID had not operated in the Soviet Union prior to 1992. According to some former U.S. officials, the program initially failed to adequately take advantage of expertise within the U.S. government on the unique political context of Russia's economic transition, and relied too much on personnel whose experience was primarily in poor developing countries. This was an obstacle in some cases to achieving the respect of and effective communication with Russian officials, according to these officials. Others have emphasized that no one within the U.S. government had both development and transition expertise.

Some donors, especially USAID and TACIS, were required to use private contractors to implement projects whenever possible. Initially, the Russians welcomed the experts but did so less over time. Russian officials and several donor officials noted that although many consultants offered excellent advice, the overall quality was very mixed. Russians were particularly concerned about the high pay received by consultants, the "fly in, fly out" approach taken by some, or the inexperience of many experts in a particular sector and the treatment of Russia as though it were like any other developing country.

Institutions and donors acknowledge that in some cases early pressures to get funds out quickly limited the program design and effective implementation. In the case of the U.S. program, for example, to show that funds were being obligated quickly, the program used large umbrella contracts, which in some cases were poorly managed.[11] For example, $300 million of U.S. assistance to Russia was overseen and strategically guided by the Harvard Institute for International Development with task execution by several U.S. contractors. This approach resulted in the Harvard Institute's having substantial control over portions of the U.S. assistance program with relatively little USAID oversight. USAID ended its contractual relationship with the Harvard Institute in 1997.

The broad scope of World Bank, EBRD, U.S. Freedom Support Act, and TACIS programs in the early years undermined potential impact, according to assessments by institutions and donors. As our prior program and strategy descriptions illustrate, assistance funds were spread broadly for a number of reasons, ranging from a belief that wide-ranging involvement was called for to pressure from different constituencies (such as agencies within the U.S. government or different EU member countries). The consensus among Russian government and program officials was that this broad dispersion of effort reduced impact. Unrealistic program objectives compounded the problem of lack of focus, according to Russian and program officials, with the gap between expectations and reality damaging the Russian perceptions of assistance programs and harming the credibility of later assistance efforts.

Interdependencies and Scale of Programs

Success in meeting different assistance objectives has clearly been limited by the interdependencies across Russia's needs and also the relative scale of assistance programs. Project objectives in specific areas have often been difficult to attain absent progress in key supporting areas. The scale of transition challenges dwarfed the size of some assistance programs and available resources. The following section analyzes

[11] See Foreign Assistance: Harvard Institute for International Development's Work in Russia and Ukraine.

examples of the interdependencies across several broad policy areas. Also on a smaller scale, there are many instances in which even very successful donor programs have had only a limited impact. For example, several donor and Russian officials pointed to the EBRD's Russia Small Business Fund as a successful project to help promote the development of small- and medium-sized enterprises in Russia. Although EBRD officials believe the fund has made important contributions, they recognize the fund's disbursement of $381 million in small loans since 1993 only begins to address nationwide Russian needs in the small- and medium-sized enterprise sector.[12] Several U.S. officials cited the success of USAID efforts to create public access Internet sites—giving 12,000 Russians access to the Internet.

Agricultural reform provides one example of how the full range of obstacles to program success can combine to limit effectiveness. The World Bank, USAID, and TACIS have undertaken agriculture reform projects, all with limited success. The World Bank and USAID have now limited their work in the sector. Program assessments and discussions with officials and analysts identified the following interrelated impediments to program success: the scale of the problem relative to the size of assistance programs, the lack of adequate expertise in designing and implementing programs, and the lack of serious interest by Russian officials in providing for private ownership of land or the elimination of government-owned distribution chains.

Four Policy Areas Illustrate Challenges and Interdependencies across Assistance Objectives

The successes and limitations of assistance in four key policy areas—macroeconomic stabilization, social safety net protection, privatization (particularly voucher privatization and the loans-for-shares privatization program), and banking sector reform—illustrate both the range of challenges faced and the degree to which the amount of progress in one area has affected reform efforts in other areas. For example, the limited degree of social services to cushion the impact of economic restructuring in Russia is widely believed to have been an obstacle to economic restructuring and may have constrained overall economic performance. While privatization of state-owned enterprises was an essential element of Russia's transition, the way in which some of the largest enterprises were privalized increased the concentration of economic power and made achieving reforms in areas such as tax collection more difficult. This, in turn, increased the fragility of Russia's macroeconomic situation.

[12] For a very rough order of magnitude comparison, note that the Russia Small Business Fund has disbursed in seven years roughly what the U.S. Small Business Administration lends to U.S. firms in a week.

Macroeconomic Stabilization

A stable macroeconomic environment was identified early on by the international community and some Russian government officials as a necessary condition for economic growth. Establishing such an environment has remained a challenge throughout the transition and has been the key focus of IMF programs in Russia. After 3 years of limited success, Russia finally brought inflation under control in late 1995. However, substantial macroeconomic imbalances remained, and the fragility of Russia's economic policies culminated in the financial crisis and debt default in August 1998. The issue of how much influence and leverage the IMF actually had on Russia's macroeconomic policies continues to be debated.

A stable macroeconomic environment consists of three interrelated elements: low, sustainable inflation; a sustainable overall balance of payments along with a relatively stable foreign exchange rate; and a government budget that does not require overly high domestic interest rates to finance any deficit. Macroeconomic stabilization policies in Russia have primarily focused on controlling inflation, with some success by late 1995. During 1992-94, Russia's budget deficit was largely financed by an expansionary monetary policy, with resulting high inflation. Between 1995 and mid-1998, less inflationary government bonds were used to partially finance the deficit, and a monetary policy based on maintaining a stable exchange rate helped in controlling inflation.[13] The inability to increase tax revenue, however, left a high and unsustainable fiscal deficit that made the Russian economy vulnerable when the external environment turned negative. Figures 13 and 14 illustrate trends in Russia's federal budget expenditures, revenues, deficit, and inflation over the transition period.

As illustrated in figure 13, cash revenues[14] generally declined during the 1992-1998 period, preventing budget deficits from falling below 5 percent of GDP despite substantial reductions in government expenditures. This decline in tax collections was part of a complex web of nonmonetary transactions throughout the economy. For example, large energy monopolies that failed to pay taxes also were often not paid by other firms or government entities such as military bases for their energy use. The government's noncash receipts—which includes the overpriced value of goods and services the government receives in return for canceling delinquent taxes—have been substantial, accounting for about 21 percent of total revenue during 1996-98. A number of efforts by parts of the Russian government, in some cases with international assistance, were made during 1996-98 to improve tax collection and compliance, but in general, they met with little success prior to 1999.

---

[13] In July 1995, the government adopted a managed exchange rate system. It targeted the growth of the money supply to maintain the ruble-dollar exchange rate within preannounced upper and lower bounds. The central exchange rate and its associated bounds were periodically devalued.

[14] Cash revenues include payments made through financial transfers and checking accounts, as well as payments made in actual currency.

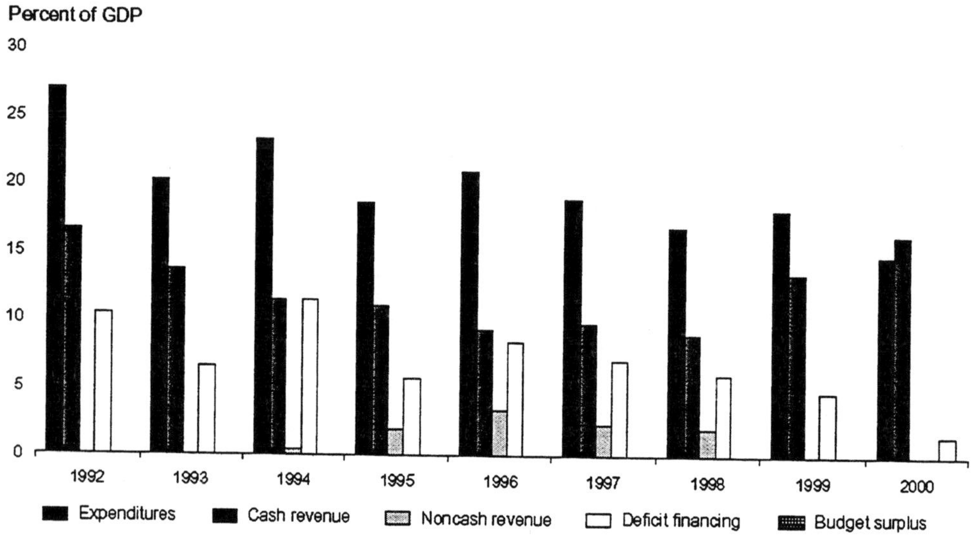

Figure 13: Russian Federal Government Budget Expenditures and Financing, 1992-2000
Note: The Russian Ministry of Finance counts noncash receipts as part of total revenue when calculating the budget deficit, as shown in the figure. The IMF computes the federal deficit on a cash basis resulting in a larger deficit. Source: Constructed from data from the IMF.

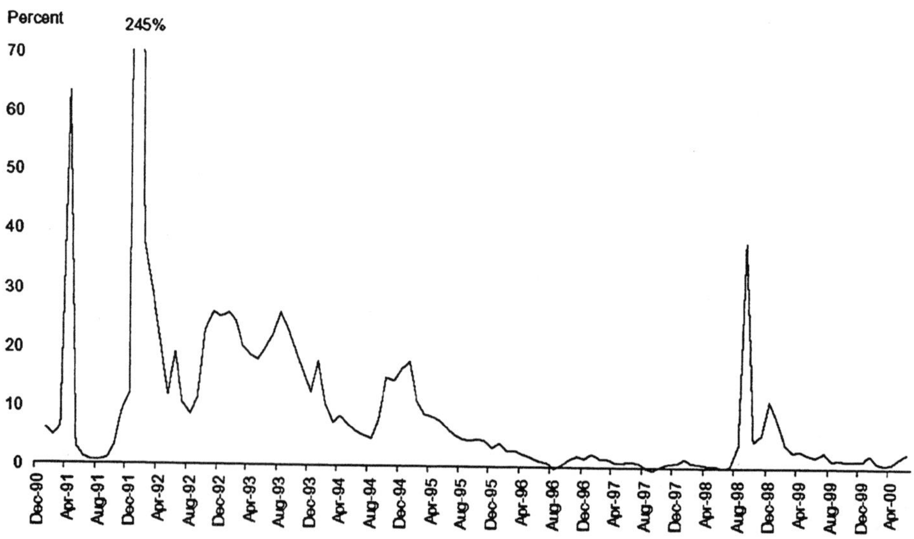

Figure 14: Russia's Monthly Inflation Rate, 1990-2000
Source: Russian Economic Trends

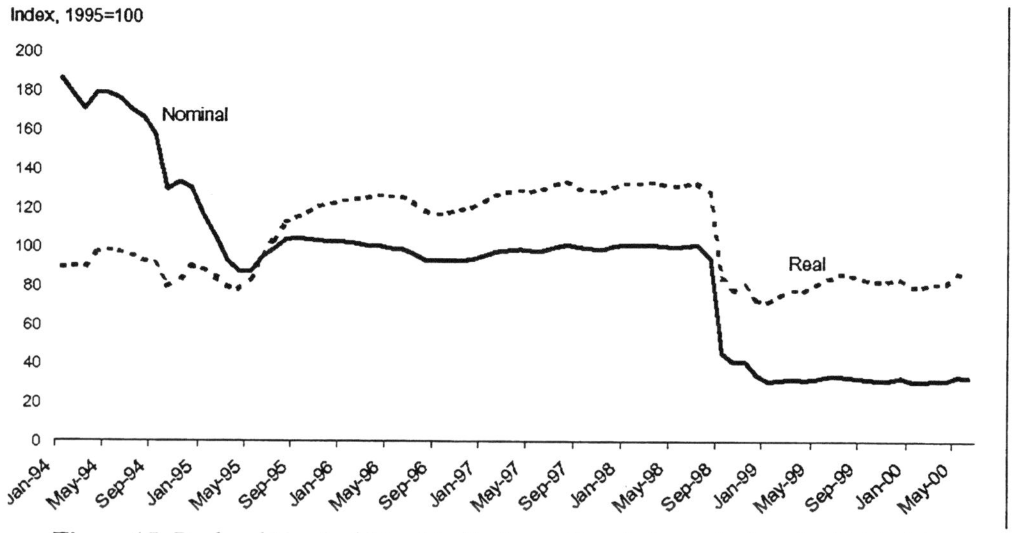

Figure 15: Real and Nominal Monthly Exchange Rate Indexes for Russia, 1994-2000
Note 1: The nominal effective exchange rate index is a weighted average of the ruble exchange rates of several of Russia's trade partners. The real effective exchange rate index adjusts for the relative inflation rates between Russia and these trade partners. The real index can be interpreted as the inflation-adjusted price of a traded unit of a Russian good or service, when the 1995 price was 100.
Note 2: An increase in the index reflects an appreciation of the ruble.
Source: Constructed from IMF, International Financial Statistics data.

Two issues of continuing debate regarding IMF policies in Russia over the period are the questions of how much leverage the IMF had in influencing Russia's macroeconomic policies, and whether the IMF supported an exchange rate that was too high. A number of officials and analysts, including IMF officials, have maintained that the IMF was "too soft" on Russia. For example, although the IMF delayed or reduced disbursements several times during 1996-98 when Russia missed some quantitative performance criteria requirements, it also granted waivers and made disbursements during this period when Russia had missed its targets.[15] Some officials and analysts argue that the Russian government would have implemented a stricter program if it knew it could not get disbursements otherwise. It is not possible to determine whether holding to stricter disbursement criteria would have resulted in better implementation of the economic program, given, for example, the key role of low tax collection in the government's failure to meet IMF performance criteria. Several international and Russian government officials interviewed stated that eligibility for bilateral debt relief may have been Russia's primary motivation in agreeing to IMF programs.[16]

The Russian government, with IMF advice and financial support, maintained a nominal exchange rate that was relatively stable from mid- 1995 to mid-1998 (see fig. 15). According to some analysts, this reduced inflationary expectations helping to reduce

[15] Missed criteria include, for example, international reserve, government revenue, and budget deficit targets.
[16] Russia or any debtor country is required to have an IMF program in place before it can receive debt relief from bilateral creditors through the Paris Club. The Paris Club is an informal group of creditor countries that meets, on an as-needed basis, to negotiate debt relief efforts on official debt.

inflation. However, analysts have also maintained that, with the benefit of hindsight, the exchange rate appears to have been overvalued, based on the strong performance of the Russian economy since the financial crisis. While that strong performance is partly explained by high oil prices, it is also largely attributable to a sharp rise in production by Russian firms, as the prices of Russian products became more attractive relative to imports after the government's move to a floating exchange rate in September of 1998 and the substantial depreciation of the currency. With high oil and export commodity prices and lower imports, Russia is running large trade surpluses in 1999 and 2000, adding to its international reserves.

Social Safety Net Protection

A social safety net to cushion the effects of transition on vulnerable populations, particularly dislocated workers, was identified early on by some in the international community as necessary to a smooth transition in Russia. It was recognized that enterprise restructuring, price liberalization, and other dislocations associated with Russia's transition to a market economy would inevitably affect living standards. Some analysts argued that a social safety net was essential to achieving objectives of privatization. They pointed out that the restructuring of enterprises, one goal of privatization, would necessarily entail periods of unemployment. In addition to loss of income, workers would be hurt by the loss of social services such as housing, kindergartens, and hospitals, which were traditionally provided to workers at little cost through their employers. The concern was that, absent an effective system of reducing the social consequences of unemployment, economic restructuring would not take place.

However, there was no real agreement within the international community about how support for an improved social safety net should be financed. One preliminary 1993 analysis by World Bank and IMF staff suggested additional international funding to help support a safety net with a very rough cost of $2-3 billion the first year. There was, however, little support among the G-7 members for directly financing social programs in Russia. According to several U.S. government officials, U.S. domestic political support for paying for pensions and other social needs in Russia did not exist. By the time of a summit between President Clinton and President Yeltsin in Vancouver in March 1993, bilateral funding for a social safety net was not included in plans for assistance to Russia.

The role of providing assistance to address the social impacts of transition thus fell to the World Bank. Within the World Bank, discussions about how best to provide that assistance were a part of the larger debate about the World Bank's assistance strategy for Russia. That debate included the issue of investment lending versus adjustment lending and what level of exposure to the possible nonrepayment of its loans the World Bank should assume.

The social sector did not consume a significant part of World Bank commitments or disbursement to Russia until 1997. A key reason, according to both World Bank and Russian officials, was the reluctance of Russian authorities to borrow funds for social needs. In November 1992, the World Bank approved a $70 million loan to strengthen the government's capacity to process unemployment benefits, in part through buying computers. However, the loan did not go into effect for 2 years and then had serious implementation difficulties.[17] A $200-million community social infrastructure loan approved in 1996 to improve the ability of local governments to provide essential social services in two regions, with the idea of possible expansion, was subsequently restructured with more modest objectives.

In June 1997, the World Bank approved an adjustment loan of $800 million tied to social sector reforms, and disbursed the first tranche of $300 million. The World Bank had, in 1995, indicated its willingness to consider such an adjustment loan and, according to World Bank officials, the prospect of an adjustment loan increased the interest of Russian government officials in discussing social reforms. However, a substantial period was required to work out loan conditions, since some Russian officials had initially viewed the loan as a source of general budgetary financing without expecting serious conditionality. The objectives of the loan were broad—reforms in social policy, pensions, unemployment assistance, social assistance, and social insurance. One goal was to improve targeting of needy groups within the government's existing social spending budget.

The World Bank disbursed a second tranche of $250 million under the social protection adjustment loan in December 1997, as scheduled, but the loan was restructured in July 1999; as of August 2000, all tranches had been fully disbursed and all loan conditions met. According to the World Bank, their most significant accomplishments under the loan have been in pension system reform, with little success in poverty reduction and the reform of social assistance. A World Bank official made several observations about the World Bank's work under this loan: It was important to have enough funding at stake to get the appropriate attention, but after that, the funding amounts have not been that important; working with regions was surprisingly positive; and while World Bank officials had anticipated the ability of special interests to block change, they had underestimated it.[18]

Russia's system of social protection remains poorly suited to protecting poor and vulnerable groups, according to U.S., Russian, and World Bank officials. Benefits are low—with unemployment benefits, for example, averaging 15 percent of the subsistence minimum—and badly targeted, with 20 percent of the poorest households receiving no benefits and the bulk of housing subsidies still going to those who are not poor. World Bank officials cited social protection components of Russia's 10-year economic development plan, which was adopted in July 2000, as indicative of more serious discussion within Russia concerning needed economic reforms in this area. Some officials also indicated that proposals within the plan draw heavily on work done with World Bank analysts over the past several years, particularly in the area of pension

---

17 A World Bank official cited that loan as an example of how success can take time. He stated that it had been a problem loan for a number of years and that the World Bank had wanted to cancel the loan; however, the loan had recently become an example of a very successful small project.

18 In addition to these programs, the World Bank's coal sector adjustment loans, with the primary purpose of overall restructuring of the coal sector, featured social safety net provisions for coal workers, their families, and communities adversely affected by mine closures and downsizing.

reform. However, there still are serious differences of opinion within the Russian government regarding the priority of government spending for social needs.

Voucher Privatization and the Loans-for-Shares Privatization Program

No aspect of Russia's economic transition has been more controversial than the privatization of enterprises. Privatization of over half of Russian state-owned industry was accomplished quickly during 1992-94, with the help of international funding. In Russia, specific motives for privatizing enterprises rapidly were to (1) decrease the chance of a communist resurgence, (2) impose some order on a process that had begun to occur spontaneously during the Gorbachev era, and (3) decrease the government's direct financial burden of subsidizing enterprises.

Beginning in early 1992 and ending in June 1994, the Russian government designed and implemented a mass voucher privatization program.[19] Through this program, over 16,500 medium and large state-owned enterprises,[20] representing more than half of Russian industry, were transferred to the ownership of more than 40 million Russian citizens. (Under the Russian privatization law, most shops and some smaller firms had been allocated to local governments to sell off.) This was accomplished through several steps: corporatizing the enterprises as joint stock companies; distributing vouchers to the entire Russian population; creating investment funds to channel purchases of larger firms; and organizing a system of auctions throughout Russia through which shares in the enterprises were distributed.

The international community strongly encouraged Russia's decision to privatize firms quickly and was significantly involved in the design and implementation of the voucher privatization program. In late 1991, the World Bank and the EBRD signed an agreement with the Russian government to act as lead advisers on a broad range of privatization issues. The World Bank began providing advice to the Russian Privatization Center in 1991 under its Technical Cooperation Agreement with Russia. In December 1992, the World Bank approved a privatization implementation assistance loan, for $90 million. The main objective of the project was to provide funding to design the voucher privatization program. However, that loan did not become effective until the end of 1993, due in part to legislative opposition, at which time the voucher program was nearing completion. Similarly, the EBRD did not carry out planned efforts to support the voucher privatization process. USAID became the primary source of international funding for implementing the program, providing about $58 million.

---

[19] The Russian privatization law was passed in July 1991 and included a basic emphasis on giving away shares of enterprises. The privatization program, headed by Anatoly Chubais, was adopted by the government and the parliament in June 1992, after intense negotiations. It contained the basic elements of corporatization and insider privatization, although not vouchers. Vouchers were chosen by Chubais as the mechanism for mass privatization in late spring 1992 and adopted by presidential decree in the summer.

[20] Small enterprises were defined as having less than 200 employees, medium enterprises as having 200-1,000 employees, and large enterprises as having more than 1,000 employees.

While the voucher privatization program was carried out with surprising speed and efficiency, assessments of its ultimate impact are mixed. The design of the program represented compromises to win the support of enterprise managers and of the Russian parliament. In particular, the program's most popular option allowed workers and owners to acquire a majority stake in their enterprises, resulting in "insider privatization," or what was effectively a management-employee buyout program. Although the program officially restricted privatization of the largest state-owned enterprises—more than 10,000 workers—a number of very large and strategic enterprises were ultimately privatized under the voucher program.[21]21

Although many believe that the insider nature of the voucher privatization process was crucial for its political feasibility, there is wide agreement that this factor undermined to some degree the potential economic and political benefits of the process. It limited the incentives of new owners—managers and their employees—to improve the efficiency of businesses by downsizing or restructuring their operations. A common although not consensus view among several officials and analysts is that, with the benefit of hindsight, the privatization of the largest Russian firms may have proceeded too quickly. The degree to which the disappointing economic and political benefits of privatization that have been realized to date are due to the timing and manner in which parts of the voucher privatization were carried out, and how much are due to other factors, including the loans-for-shares program, continues to be debated.

The loans-for-shares program, by far the most controversial aspect of the privatization of Russian enterprises, followed voucher privatization.[22] Through the loans-for-shares program, a handful of financial-industrial groups in Russia became controlling shareholders in some of the country's most valuable assets, including several large oil and metals companies. Under this program, carried out during the last quarter of 1995, the government auctioned off large stakes in these companies to banks, in return for loans, and in some cases, payments of firms' tax arrears.[23] This scheme was prompted by the government's need for a source of noninflationary financing of its budget deficit and also, according to some officials we interviewed, by President Yeltsin's desire to consolidate the support of Russia's business elite for his 1996 election campaign. Over the course of 1995, as revenues from other privatization efforts fell short of anticipated amounts, the government was failing to meet financing targets that had been agreed to with the IMF. Through loans for shares, the government was able to provide an additional $1 billion of budget financing and met the financing targets. According to IMF staff, alternative forms of financing were available to the Russian authorities.

---

[21] By June 1994, more than 300 of Russia's largest enterprises had in fact been privatized through special national voucher auctions, under pressures from managers who realized the benefits of gaining control of their enterprises.

[22] Following voucher privatization, Russia began a second round of privatization, with the objective of selling the remaining government holdings in order to raise cash. The cash auctions and investment tenders (bids) used were not transparent (open) and were poorly advertised, and the government fell far short of its revenue goals.

[23] The government maintained the right to repay its loans and thus buy back the shares until September 1996 although, according to some officials, there was little expectation among knowledgeable individuals that the government would repay the loans.

The loans-for-shares auctions are generally viewed as having been effectively rigged in favor of the large banks that were carrying them out. The Russian government had modified the original loans-for-shares proposal, made by a consortium of banks, from a closed process to auctions that would ostensibly be open, including to foreigners. However, in the actual auctions foreign investors were barred, the auctions were attended by a limited number of bidders, and the winning bids were lower than expected. The winners were generally the banks who were managing the auctions.[24]

The loans-for-shares program is widely considered a major setback in Russia's economic transition. It consolidated the fortunes of Russia's new "oligarchs." The program was criticized in the Russian press as evidence of corruption within the government and became an issue in the 1996 presidential election.

A number of western and Russian analysts have criticized the West for not being more outspoken in opposition to the scheme at the time. In contrast to its support for voucher privatization, the international community did not directly support the loans-for-shares program. It did not, however, strongly object, according to evidence we have reviewed.

The U.S. Executive Director of the IMF, in April 1995, in response to an early loans-for-shares proposal, went on record as asking for additional information regarding the proposal and potential negative impacts. The U.S. Executive Director said she was involved in other conversations regarding concerns about the loans-for- shares program, but U.S. officials did not provide us with any other documentation on objections. In an October 1995 staff report, IMF staff raised concerns about the way the loans-for-shares scheme was designed, but stated that Russian authorities assured the IMF that the government would exercise strong oversight to ensure that the program was operated fairly. In a December 1995 staff report, IMF staff raised concerns about the Russian authorities handling of the loans-for-shares program. In both instances, the staff recommended and the board approved further disbursements to Russia. A senior IMF official said that the IMF's focus was primarily on macroeconomic issues and less on the details of particular privatization schemes. USAID officials told us they had objected to loans for shares during 1995 but did not have information regarding the specific circumstances of the objection.

According to World Bank officials, a World Bank official in Moscow expressed serious concerns about loans for shares as the program was being implemented in 1995 and raised concerns to senior World Bank management, but high-level protests were not made by the World Bank. According to senior World Bank management, the World Bank's dialogue with Russian officials was generally not at a very high level during that time, and the World Bank was not in a good position to put major issues like the loans-for-shares transactions on the table. He stated that World Bank management concluded there was no way to reverse the program and that the World Bank needed to work to make sure that privatization was done more transparently in the future.

---

[24] Only 12 of the 29 companies that were initially identified by the government as candidates for the program were actually auctioned, due in part to efforts by company directors to avoid an auction.

Differing views were heard regarding how much difference clear western opposition to loans for shares would have made in 1995 and 1996. Several officials expressed the view that by the time the West realized the degree to which the outcome could further undermine reform objectives, it was too late. According to a former World Bank official, the only possible effective influence would have to have come from the U.S. President. Others stated that effective opposition would not have had to come from that level, with one former senior Russian official describing the overall western reaction to the program at the time as a conspiracy of silence.

Banking Sector Reform

During the Soviet period, the state bank had wide responsibilities for all banking-related activities in the Soviet Union. Five specialized banks carried out some of these tasks under the supervision of the state bank. Russia's banking sector began to evolve with the reform laws of 1988 and, with the dissolution of the Soviet Union in 1991, Russia introduced its own banking laws and created the Central Bank of Russia (which replaced the Soviet state bank) to issue currency and supervise banks. The new central bank followed a liberal policy of bank licensing, resulting in a rapid increase in the number of commercial banks. For example, in 1993, Russia had licensed 2,000 new commercial banks. Banks benefited from operating in an environment where there was limited prudential regulation, and inflation and currency depreciation created opportunities for quick profits. Although the vast majority of Russia's banks remained small and undercapitalized, the sector became dominated by a number of large banks that are at the center of industrial groups. Virtually all lending by Russian banks is short term. Banks concentrate their activities on trading in the treasury bill and foreign currency markets, lending to related entities, and on trade finance, and real estate activities.

Early on, several institutions and donors targeted Russia's banking sector as an area for providing transition assistance. However, for a variety of reasons, progress in strengthening Russia's banking sector has been limited. The 1998 financial crisis decimated Russia's banks and revealed the extent of their unsound financial condition. It also illustrated the need for better coordination between the government and donors on banking reform. Since the crisis, institutions and donors have provided substantial technical assistance on bank restructuring, but have been hesitant to commit significant financial resources for banking reforms, although some planning efforts were underway in summer 2000.

The financial institutions development project was approved in 1994 to support the institutional development of commercial banks, modernize the regulatory framework, and improve bank and enterprise accounting practices. The project was financed by a $200 million loan from the World Bank and $100 million loan from the EBRD, with some supporting grants from the EU and the Japanese government. In hindsight, the World Bank believes the accreditation process for financial institutions development project banks proceeded too rapidly. The project banks and outside investors saw the accreditation as the World Bank's "seal of approval" when, in reality, these banks were not necessarily following prudential banking practices. Implementation of these projects came to a halt following the 1998 financial crisis. The project was restructured in August 2000, with some small disbursements approved.

Under the Freedom Support Act program, USAID funded bank supervisor and commercial bank training programs in Russian cities. In its most recent country strategy document, USAID acknowledged that the success of such efforts has depended in part on the Russian government's commitment to specific reforms. USAID officials say they are working with other donors and government representatives on the Coordinating Committee to determine a useful role for its assistance. In addition, the U.S. Treasury provided resident advisers to work with the Central Bank of Russia; their activities included, among other things, helping to draft bank legislation.

From its earliest involvement with Russia, the IMF has targeted Russia's banking sector as an area that needed reform in order to support the country's economic growth. In the early years of its involvement with Russia, IMF staff provided technical assistance to the Central Bank of Russia on banking supervision, monetary and exchange operations, the payments system, public debt accounting, and bank accounting. In 1993, it also posted three resident advisers with the central bank. Although banking sector reform was mentioned in the government's March 1995 request for a Stand-by Arrangement, it was not until 1996, with the Extended Fund Facility program, that banking reform became a stronger focus of an IMF arrangement. In its February 1996 request for the Extended Fund Facility, the Russian government outlined its strategy for a comprehensive approach to strengthening the banking system. However, laws regarding bankruptcy and bank license revocation, identified as necessary for bank restructuring, were not passed or implemented. In addition, although all donors believed it was necessary to introduce the use of international accounting standards into Russia's banks, the Central Bank of Russia and the banks themselves resisted this change.[25] Only in 2000 did the authorities agree to introduce international accounting standards accounting for the Central Bank of Russia by year end-2000 and in commercial banks by year end-2001.

Experts have identified several factors specific to banking business that contributed to the breakdown of the market in 1998, including the use of Russian accounting norms rather than international accounting standards; inadequate credit risk analysis; and investment concentration in related borrowers, foreign exchange, and government securities.

The government's default on its securities, banks' failure to properly hedge their foreign exchange risks, and the sharp ruble devaluation are the factors that threw nearly all Russian banks into insolvency when the crisis hit. In addition, these measures resulted in a serious disruption in the payment system and a collapse of the domestic banking system. There were severe liquidity shortages as banks were unable to make payments or obtain liquidity through the usual channels, such as the sale on the open market of a portion of their portfolio of government securities.

[25] Russia's 1999 IMF program continued to acknowledge basic legislative needs related to the banking sector. It laid out a plan for bank restructuring that included developing a bank restructuring law and amending the central bank law, bank bankruptcy law, and civil code.

In the aftermath of the August 1998 financial crisis, the World Bank and the IMF convinced the Central Bank of Russia to conduct detailed reviews using western accounting standards of the financial condition of 18 large banks representing about 50 percent of the assets of the privately owned banking system. The audits found that 15 of the 18 banks were insolvent. According to World Bank officials, these results helped strengthen the credibility of the international financial institutions' advice in the eyes of the Central Bank of Russia.

In the wake of the financial crisis, two new bodies were formed to help deal with Russia's banking reform. One, the Interagency Coordinating Committee on the Restructuring of the Banking System, was established by the Central Bank of Russia with the multilateral donors as members. The Coordinating Committee, as well as the working groups formed under it, provide a forum for carrying out technical discussions between the Russian authorities and international experts on a wide range of issues and a means for coordinating technical assistance from the donor community.

The second, the Agency for Restructuring of Credit Institutions, was established in November 1998, with the task of restructuring large and insolvent banks. It has made progress in restructuring regional banks that voluntarily submitted to its oversight, but according to several officials from programs reviewed, progress in dealing with large, Moscow-based banks has been limited. Several officials in Russia stated that the restructuring agency has been relatively ineffective, due, in part, to a lack of political will on the part of the Russian authorities and, in part, to a lack of consensus on how these large banks should be treated as well as the limited financial resources for bank restructuring.

According to representatives from the World Bank/IMF technical assistance team, since the financial crisis, progress has been made in establishing the enabling environment for banking restructuring, but Russian authorities have failed to use this environment with full effectiveness. The team has identified areas in which the Russians must choose their strategy on fundamental issues, including the role of public versus private banking, the role of national versus regional banking, the role of domestic and foreign-owned banks, and the question of whether banks should be limited to traditional banking practices, such as taking deposits and making loans, or be permitted to conduct investment banking. Pending agreement on these fundamental issues, the World Bank/IMF team has proposed an action plan for 2000 that is divided into three strategic areas: (1) continued consolidation of the banking sector, (2) creation of a small number of viable core banks, and (3) establishment of a competitive and transparent environment for banking.

Views of certain Russian officials were mixed on the priority level of banking sector restructuring and reform. Although there is still little bank lending to small- and medium-sized enterprises, many experts felt the demand for such lending did not yet exist and that those needing finance were obtaining it from other sources, such as retained earnings. Many officials felt that the power of state banks impedes progress in creating a well-functioning commercial banking sector because it is hard for private commercial banks to compete with state banks. Also, restrictions on foreign banks limit citizens' choices. The Russian population in general is still suspicious of Russian commercial banks and is more likely to deposit its money with the state banks than with private commercial banks. (This suspicion is based on repeated cases of bank fraud, absconding with depositor frauds and freezing deposits which were never returned to their owners).

Changes in Assistance Programs Reflect Commitment to Staying in Russia

The evolution of international assistance efforts in Russia since 1992 reflects institutions and donors' continued commitment to remain engaged in Russia because of the country's strategic importance. While donors have faced a series of obstacles, they have never considered halting assistance programs altogether. Changes in the programs and assistance strategies have reflected responses to these obstacles, learning from experience, changing needs in Russia, and political guidance.

The rationale for continued engagement varies across institutions and donors depending on mandates and objectives. World Bank and IMF officials note Russia's strategic importance, and also their mandate to support member countries. Officials of these institutions have stated that they will continue to support Russia's process of reform, which they believe is likely to take a number of years. U.S. officials said that they will continue to implement projects in Russia as long as the Russians show continued commitment to supporting the process of economic reform and democracy building. The EBRD and TACIS were specifically created to help support reform in transition countries, of which Russia is the largest and most important. According to senior-level EBRD officials, the EBRD has remained engaged in Russia during times of crisis like 1998 and will continue to be engaged there. When the EU reauthorized its TACIS program in December 1999 for another 6 years, its Commissioner for External Relations noted that the program would help build closer and more constructive relations.

Changing Resources and Political Guidance Have Affected Assistance Strategies

Some shifts in donor strategy reflect differences in the nature, mandate, and political context of the institutions themselves. For example, the United States and the World Bank modified their assistance programs in sharply different ways over the decade. Their shifts are explained in part by differences in available resources, instruments, and mandates and may also reflect different perceptions of conditions and prospects in Russia.

- The World Bank's shift, beginning in 1996, away from subnational lending for investment projects to providing mostly large structural adjustment loans to the central government reflected an increasing emphasis on the importance of nationwide reforms and the obstacles to achieving reform objectives at the regional level. The shift also reflected institutional issues. For example, because the World Bank's charter requires it to lend only to, or obtain a sovereign guarantee from, national governments, implementing regional projects required complex negotiations regarding who would pay back loans and how funds would flow through the federal government before going to the regions.

- In contrast, in 1996-97, the United States changed its focus from working primarily with the federal government to working largely in specific regions on grassroots projects. U.S. officials explained that this change was driven by a number of factors, including (1) substantial reductions in U.S. funding which, in their opinion, greatly reduced the ability to obtain nationwide results; (2) the growing resistance within the Duma and federal government to enact meaningful reform, exacerbated by corruption within parts of the government; and (3) the importance of showing results of U.S. assistance to Congress and the White House. Several U.S. officials said that by 1994 or 1995, it was becoming clear that many U.S. efforts to promote change at the federal level were not achieving success. In addition, by the mid-1990s, Congress was placing a growing number of restrictions on Freedom Support Act assistance for the national government—restrictions that did not apply to assistance at the regional or local level. In addition, in contrast to requirements for World Bank loans, implementing Freedom Support Act projects at the regional level does not require detailed negotiations with the Russian federal government.

Political considerations have affected program implementation in a variety of ways for the institutions and donors we reviewed.

- IMF decisions regarding Russia have been affected by political concerns. For example, despite concerns regarding poor implementation of the first program, the IMF Board approved disbursement of $1.5 billion in March 1994 to show support for the Russian government. The December 1993 Duma elections had been widely viewed as a sharp repudiation of reform efforts and of the federal government by the Russian people. U.S. officials said that the political stakes in this decision outweighed concerns about lack of progress in meeting IMF requirements. In 1996, the IMF frequently reviewed the Russia program and modified target requirements for additional disbursements. According to the IMF, weak macroeconomic performance was felt to reflect instability related to the upcoming presidential elections and the board wanted to show continued support for the Russian government. Several Russian officials, however, were concerned that this action contributed to the belief that Russia did not have to comply with IMF requirements since Russia was too important to fail.
- In response to reports of massive civilian casualties and widespread human rights violations in connection with the war in Chechnya, the European Council adopted a resolution in December 1999 limiting new TACIS projects for 2000 to human rights, rule of law, and support for civil society.

Institutions and donors have recently reported the need to alter their approach for assistance to Russia because of changing Russian needs. According to a number of Russian and donor officials, Russia's assistance needs have changed to some extent away from basic transfer of know-how to assistance in implementing specific reforms. For example, in December 1998, a meeting of G-7 technical experts on assistance to Russia concluded that assistance projects showed the greatest success when they made use of both Russian expertise and western support. A February 2000 report on the TACIS program in Russia recommended that future assistance move away from the past focus on explaining the "right way" to the Russians and instead help them find "the best way in their conditions." IMF and World Bank officials expect the Russian government to have greater input into formulating its own program than in the past, and that they believed that their future programs with Russia would be more closely linked to supporting the government's implementation of reform packages than in the past.

Donors' Response to Crime and Corruption

Over time, resources allocated directly to developing judicial and law enforcement institutions in Russia have represented a relatively small share of international funding, reflecting the greater focus on economic policies and institutions. For example, $632 million, or 24 percent, of funds budgeted under the Freedom Support Act have been under the broad objective of promoting democracy and rule of law. In terms of a percentage of annual funding, however, funding for this objective has increased to 36 percent of funds budgeted for 2000. Specific programs include anticrime training and training Russian law enforcement officials. Some programs under the broad objective of promoting market reform have had direct anticorruption aspects, such as providing training to Russian businesses in western accounting standards. In the case of the World Bank, the structural adjustment loans it has extended to Russia have provisions that could reduce the potential for corruption, such as strengthening tax administration, and reforming key infrastructure monopolies and the banking sector by fostering competition.

The World Bank first explicitly addressed corruption in its 1999 country assistance strategy for Russia,[26] although according to Bank officials, several aspects of its Russia program over time have had an anticorruption aspect. A recent report of the World Bank's progress to help countries fight corruption indicates that, since the executive board endorsed an anticorruption strategy for the World Bank in 1997,[27] four of its active investment projects, involving $128.8 million in loans, relate to governance.[28]

---

[26] In January 1999, the World Bank issued new policy guidance that required every country assistance strategy to examine governance issues, including the extent of corruption. This was part of the anticorruption initiative that the Bank President launched in 1997.

[27] See World Bank: Management Controls Stronger, but Challenges in Fighting Corruption Remain (GAO/NSIAD-00-73, Apr. 6, 2000).

[28] The World Bank, Helping Countries Combat Corruption: Progress at the World Bank Since 1997 (Washington, D.C.: The World Bank, June 2000).

World Bank officials pointed to its coal sector lending as an example of a program where limiting opportunities for corruption has had an increasing focus over time. The World Bank's $500 million 1996 adjustment loan was designed to reduce the impact of the coal sector on the federal budget by decreasing subsidies to the sector. While progress was made toward this objective, including institutional changes to improve the targeting of subsidies, there was insufficient monitoring of funds from the Russian government that went to pay subsidies to coal companies and some evidence that such subsidies were not necessarily being allocated or used for their intended purposes. As a result, the World Bank's second coal sector loan approved in 1997, designed to further sector restructuring and promote privatization, more explicitly addressed controls over public funds. As a precondition for the loan, for example, the government made changes in sector governance and management of coal subsidies. This included changing its method of distributing coal subsidy payments.[29] According to World Bank officials, this change has substantially decreased the possibility of corruption within the government's system of coal subsidy payments.

The institutions and donors we reviewed have also implemented specific procedures to increase protection of their own funds from corruption and theft. These institutions and donors have reported either that they have not suffered serious theft or diversion of funds or that they have not suffered any theft or diversion of funds in Russia. We did not attempt to independently verify these claims during our review.

- Because technical assistance funds, which comprise the bulk of assistance under Freedom Support Act and TACIS assistance, have been paid to U.S. and European contractors, the potential for diversion has been limited. Since the early 1990s, State Department and USAID officials have testified and reported that the vast majority of the funds for the Freedom Support Act program in Russia were obligated to U.S. contractors, universities, and private organizations. Since 1995, USAID has implemented increasingly stringent financial controls for its operations in Russia. TACIS officials told us they believed their funds were adequately protected from misuse.
- In 1999, the IMF called for an investigation by an independent international accounting firm into allegations that its funds for Russia had been stolen or misused. The firms reported that they found no evidence that IMF funds were stolen, but they did find that Russia had misreported information to the IMF during 1995-98. This misreporting may have enabled Russia to obtain funds it may not have been entitled to. Based on these findings, the IMF determined that Russia had violated mandatory reporting requirements established in the IMF's Articles of Agreement. As a result, Russia agreed that new IMF funds would be

[29] They are now distributed through earmarked accounts in the regional offices of the federal Treasury and delivered directly to the intended beneficiaries.

held in an account at the IMF and go directly to repay Russian debt to the IMF. This procedure would apply to any new IMF program negotiated in 2000.[30]

- EBRD officials told us that an outside review of their Russia portfolio by an independent accounting firm in late 1999 found no egregious misuse of funds in any of its Russia programs and that the EBRD had instituted changes to tighten the EBRD's procedures for disbursing funds after the review.
- According to World Bank officials, none of their reviews have revealed any diversion of funds in Bank-supported projects in Russia. In June 1999, the World Bank, in response to concerns from its Executive Board, introduced new procedures to improve controls over the tracking of counterpart funds in adjustment lending disbursements. In addition, the World Bank has completed a draft country procurement assessment review, which is under discussion with the government. While World Bank policy now calls for country financial accountability assessments for its borrowers, such an assessment has not been completed for Russia. This was a matter of concern to some executive directors when the board discussed Russia's country assistance strategy in December 1999. In May 1998, the World Bank posted a procurement specialist to its Moscow office, and he was later joined by a financial management specialist in August 1999.

[30] See International Monetary Fund: Status of Efforts to Strengthen Safeguards Over Lending (GAO/NSIAD-00-211, Sept. 1, 2000).

Chapter 4

Conclusions and Lessons Learned

After nearly a decade of experience, a number of conclusions can be drawn about what has and has not worked in the international community's efforts to aid Russia's economic transition, some with implications for the design of future programs. The overarching lesson is that without some degree of consensus and political will within Russia, the impact of donor programs is generally limited. Expectations of quick results at the beginning of the transition process were unrealistic, and the international community now realizes that Russia's transition will be a lengthy one. In some areas, conclusions about what policies are appropriate remain difficult to draw. The surprisingly strong growth of Russia's economy during the past 2 years, for example, illustrates that, in some respects, the evolution and functioning of the Russian economy is still not well understood and Russia and the international community will need to work together to determine how policies should evolve.

Donors Assessing Status of Russia Programs

As of September 2000, the institutions and donors we reviewed are generally in the process of reevaluating, with the Russian government, the level and design of their assistance programs. Factors playing into these evaluations include: (1) the extent of Russia's current need for foreign funding; (2) Russia's desire for debt relief from bilateral creditors, which is conditional on having an IMF program; (3) the determination of what macroeconomic policies are appropriate at this point; (4) Russia's choice of direction for the government in terms of a number of reforms ranging from restructuring inefficient enterprises to overhauling social protection policies; and (5) the Russian' government's commitment and ability to address fundamental obstacles to change caused by corruption and vested interests.

Of great interest to the international community has been the 10-year economic strategy adopted by the Putin government in July 2000. The plan lays out ambitious reforms that address many donor concerns about structural impediments to reform. Developed by Russian officials, the plan was discussed with representatives of the international financial institutions and other analysts during its formulation. Although the Duma has adopted some reforms called for in the strategy, it is too early to conclude the degree to which needed changes will be approved, implemented, and enforced.

The international community is also closely watching political changes in Russia, with concerns about how proposals to alter the central-regional balance of power, for example, will play out. While some changes have been viewed positively, such as Duma approval of systemic tax reform, others are being viewed with serious concern, particularly moves against independent media, nongovernmental organizations, and political opposition. Given the complexities of Russian politics and economics, and an 8-year track record of periods of optimism followed by frustration, both donors and the Russian government have been approaching the design of future assistance cautiously.

Conclusions

Based on our work looking at the programs of five major institutions and donors over the period, the following conclusions appear to have strong support and particular importance. In some cases, they have clear implications for future assistance programs.

- The challenge of Russia's transition was enormous, greater than generally appreciated by the West, and far greater than those faced by Central European countries such as Poland and Hungary. Russia began the period with almost no exposure to the western market culture and principles it set out to adopt, and with a vacuum in terms of internal institutions to support a democratic society and market economy. In hindsight, expectations within Russia and among the donors of quick results were unrealistic. The transition process is likely to continue for many years.
- Some aspects of transition assistance that the international community identified early on as important proved difficult to provide, for several reasons, and have continued to be obstacles to needed reforms. In particular, the lack of a social safety net to cushion the impact of transition on workers and vulnerable groups has increased the social cost of transition, decreased Russian public support for reform, and contributed to the difficulties of economic restructuring.
- Russia's transition path has been made harder by the concentration of power and income in the hands of a few, which had begun prior to the transition process and was accelerated through the privatization of some of the most valuable enterprises in Russian industry. Donors agree that, in some respects, opportunities for reform and openness to international influence had diminished by the mid-1990s.
- Whether the international community, with different policies and levels of involvement, could have influenced a different path remains the subject of substantial debate. This question cannot be fully answered because what would have happened under alternative policies remains unknown. At different points,

complicated political choices were made by international players. However, many officials and scholars admit that, with hindsight, they would have made different choices in some cases. These include the push to privatize the largest firms quickly and the failure of the international community to object strongly to the loans-for-shares privatization program in 1995.

- The donors' initial expectation that Russians would accept and quickly implement advice proved unfounded. The transition to a market economy and democratic society in Russia required grassroots support and the development of effective institutions, laws, and enforcement. These changes have profound implications for Russian society and politics and required a degree of political consensus within Russia that did not exist for much of the decade.
- Little progress has been made in achieving reforms in areas where there has not been a commitment to reform and support from the Russian government, including the individuals and institutions with the authority to influence outcomes. It is ultimately up to those individuals to pass, implement, and enforce needed laws and develop and effectively operate the required institutions. Working to achieve and even identify adequate ownership has proved a challenge for all donors, however, because of change in Russian officials and government priorities.
- The unexpectedly strong performance of Russia's economy since the August 1998 financial collapse, due in part to high oil prices but also to increases in domestic production, underscores the limitations of how well the international community and Russians have understood the evolution and functioning of the Russian economy and demonstrates the lack of clarity regarding some policy choices.
- The Russian government's recent development of a long-term economic program demonstrates its capacity to seriously evaluate and debate the economic policy choices the country faces. Donors can take some credit for helping develop this capacity. The program and the debates surrounding its preparation also demonstrate that the policy choices facing the Russian government remain very hard ones.

LESSONS LEARNED

When taken together, these conclusions about past efforts to assist the transition in Russia have some important implications for future assistance efforts. Although there are no easy prescriptions for how best to support reform in Russia, the following lessons can be of value.

- In light of the realization that Russia's transition to a market economy will take longer than anyone initially thought, to have the ability to make a significant impact, donor programs need to be structured for long-term involvement in

Russia. For example, donors can help build grassroots support for the development of institutions in Russia to underlie a competitive market economy within a democratic society. This is likely to require involvement over many years. Donor-sponsored exchange programs have been frequently mentioned as an effective mechanism for transferring to the Russians knowledge about and support for how market economies and democracy function. The impact of exchange programs can be felt over time.

- The Russian government should be encouraged to develop and implement policies that will lessen the impact of restructuring on vulnerable groups, which should strengthen public support for needed reforms in the economy.
- Because progress on the path to democracy and a market economy may continue to remain uneven, donors need to maintain flexibility in their programs to the extent their mandates and instruments allow, so that they can respond to changing conditions and windows of opportunity.
- In light of the fact that Russian political will and consensus is so important to the success of reform efforts, donors may have a bigger impact if they concentrate their assistance efforts on the areas in which the Russians are open to making reforms. In many areas across the transition agenda, successful reforms may be geared toward policies and institutions that are in some respects different from western norms and reflect Russian priorities and experience. Working to develop commitment and buy-in as widely and deeply as possible within various levels of the Russian government and across society is likely to pay off in terms of assistance that will have the greatest benefit to the largest number of people.

Appendix I

INTERNATIONAL MONETARY FUND PROGRAMS IN RUSSIA

BACKGROUND

The International Monetary Fund, established in 1945, is a cooperative, intergovernmental, monetary and financial institution whose purpose is to promote international monetary cooperation. As of July 2000, it had 182 member countries. The IMF's Articles of Agreement (as amended), or charter, provides that it may make resources available, under "adequate safeguards," to members experiencing balance-of-payments problems.[1] The resources are intended to shorten the duration and lessen the degree of these problems.

Member countries govern the IMF through the Executive Board, which comprises 24 members, who are appointed or elected by one or more IMF member countries. The Executive Board is the IMF's permanent decisionmaking body and conducts the institution's day-to-day business. The United States is the largest contributing member[2] and therefore has the largest single share of voting rights on the IMF's Executive Board (17.67 percent).[3]

---

[1] A country's balance-of-payments accounts summarize its dealings with the outside world. A balance-of-payments problem occurs when its normal receipts from external transactions (e.g., export earnings, grants, loans, foreign direct investment and other financial inflows) are less than its payments (e.g., imports, interest and amortization). This external deficit may be financed by drawing down the country's international reserves and/or seeking exceptional financing, for example, IMF loans and debt relief.

[2] When a country joins the IMF and later when IMF members agree to an increase in the IMF's capital, the country pays a quota, or capital subscription, to the organization.

[3] Japan (6.33 percent), Germany (6.19 percent), France, and the United Kingdom (5.11 percent each) follow the United States in the number of voting shares allocated to them.

Overall Objectives and Initial Assumptions

The IMF's broad objective in Russia, to assist the country to (1) achieve macroeconomic stabilization, (2) increase sustainable output growth, and (3) facilitate the transition to a market-based economy has remained generally consistent from the beginning of Russia's transition period in 1991 to the present. The IMF intended to gain macroeconomic stabilization through controlling inflation and achieving sustainable fiscal budgets and balance of payments.

The main assumptions that guided the IMF's program for Russia were that

- the IMF would be Russia's main adviser in the international community's effort to promote macroeconomic stabilization and
- Russia did not require a fundamentally different approach than that for any other country transition country despite its unique history.

The IMF's Instruments

The IMF uses a variety of instruments designed to deal with the specific nature of the problems facing member countries. These instruments generally contain three elements: (1) conditionality, or required policy measures; (2) technical assistance and high-level dialogue; and (3) financing. IMF staff work with the member country's government to design a program that is mutually agreeable. Then the IMF's Executive Board approves programs before they go into effect and before any disbursements are made.

Conditionality

"Conditionality" is an important part of the IMF's agreement with a member country. Access to and disbursement of IMF resources are conditional on the recipient country's adoption and pursuit of economic and structural policy measures. Russia's IMF programs have generally contained quantitative conditions including, for example, requirements for the level of net international reserves held by the central bank and the level of the federal budget deficit. Structural conditions, or benchmarks, such as banking sector, tax, and legal reform, have been included as well.

Technical Assistance

The IMF provides technical assistance to members to assist them in building technical expertise and competency in a variety of government functions. Most of the IMF's technical assistance is given to the technical areas of the central bank, the Ministry of Finance, the Ministry of Trade, and the Ministry of Tax. The types of technical assistance provided include training in bank supervision, foreign exchange regulation, public debt management, and central bank. The assistance has been given in the form of seminars, workshops, training in the United States, and long- and short-term visiting experts.

IMF Financial Arrangements Used In Russia

For member countries using most types of IMF financing arrangements, the resources are provided in increments. The IMF periodically reviews the IMF programs, at which time the country's progress in meeting the agreed to conditions is examined, and the IMF Executive Board makes decisions on future disbursements. Although the IMF generally provides financing to countries' central banks, in Russia's case, on some occasions, the funds went instead to the Ministry of Finance and were used to finance the government budget's deficit.

The IMF's general instruments are as follows:

First Tranche Agreement: The First Tranche Agreement can be used provided that a member is making reasonable efforts to solve its balance-of-payments problems. A member can make use of IMF resources up to the limit of the first credit tranche, or 25 percent of its IMF quota, under fairly liberal conditions.

Systemic Transformation Facility: Established in 1993, the Systemic Transformation Facility is a temporary means of providing financial assistance to members facing balance-of-payments difficulties arising from shocks to their economy due to a shift from a centrally planned economy to a market-based economy. Use of the facility was limited to loans up to 50 percent of a member's quota. New loans were not possible under the Facility after December 1995 and the Facility no longer exists.

Stand-by Arrangement: A Stand-by Arrangement provides short-term assistance of generally one to two years for problems of a temporary nature, provided that the IMF member observes the terms set out in the supporting arrangement. This arrangement has conditionality requirements that a country is to meet in order to continue receiving disbursements.

Extended Fund Facility: The Extended Fund Facility provides longer-term, balance-of-payments assistance aimed at overcoming balance-of-payments difficulties resulting from macroeconomic and structural problems. Typically, an economic program, which includes conditionality requirements, for use of this facility states the general objectives for a 3-year period and the specified policies for the first year; policies for subsequent years are spelled out in program reviews, or annually.

Funding History for Russia

The IMF has approved loans of around $37 billion for Russia and has disbursed $22 billion as of August 2000. Currently, Russia has repaid around $8.3 billion[4] (See table 6 for the funding history of IMF programs with Russia.).

Strategy

The IMF first began its involvement with Russia prior to Russia's membership in the organization by participating in the 1991 "joint study" that reviewed the Soviet economy.[5] After the joint study was completed, the Soviet-IMF relationship was based on the Special Association of the Soviet Union to the IMF signed in October 1991, which led to the provision of technical assistance by the IMF. Russia joined the IMF in June 1992 and has negotiated seven agreements with the institution.

Table 6: Funding History of IMF Programs for Russia

Type of IMF program	IMF board approval date	Amount approved	Amount disbursed
First Tranche Agreement	August 5, 1992	$1 billion	$1 billion
Systemic Transformation Facility First Tranche	June 30, 1993	$1.5 billion	$1.5 billion
Systemic Transformation Facility Second Tranche	March 22, 1994	$1.5 billion	$1.5 billion
Stand-by Arrangement	April 11, 1995	$6.8 billion	$6.8 billion
Extended Fund Facility (3 years)	March 26, 1996	$10.1 billion	$6.2 billion
Interim financing package	July 20, 1998	$11.2 billion	$4.8 billion
Stand-by Arrangement	July 28, 1999	$4.5 billion	$640 million

Source: GAO analysis of IMF documents.

[4] The IMF's lending amounts to its members are fixed in Special Drawing Rights (SDR)—an international reserve asset created by the IMF in 1969 as a supplement to existing reserve assets, whose value is defined in terms of a basket of major international currencies that fluctuates with market conditions. As of August 31, 2000, Russia owed the IMF $12.4 billion, or Special Drawing Rights 9.5 billion, based on an exchange rate of $1.305 per SDR. Since the 1990s, the value of the dollar has generally increased against the Special Drawing Right. Thus, to the extent that the dollar-Special Drawing Right rate is stronger at the time of repayment than at the time of borrowing, it requires fewer dollars to pay off the Russia Special Drawing Right debt.

[5] The report, "A Study of the Soviet Economy," was done by the IMF, the World Bank, the European Bank for Reconstruction and Development, and the Organization for Economic Cooperation and Development and was issued in February 1991.

In Russia, the IMF has generally followed its traditional approach of requiring conditionality. Several aspects of IMF policies and conditionality in Russia, however, have been subject to recent debate, particularly given Russia's 1998 financial crisis and the country's subsequent relatively strong performance since the last quarter of 1998.

Some of these debates have to do with "technical issues" such as the exchange rate policies supported by the IMF. Others relate to whether the IMF paid adequate attention to the structural problems in the economy, such as indirect government subsidies and low tax collection rates. A controversial aspect of the IMF policy debate is whether the IMF was "too soft" on Russia, providing additional disbursements when Russia did not necessarily meet requirements. In addition to conditionality and financing, the IMF has also given technical assistance to Russian ministries and the Central Bank of Russia.

The IMF's task in Russia was complicated by several factors. Russia's economic transition was politicized both in Russia and abroad, and the Russian political consensus and will required to implement reforms were often nonexistent or difficult to attain. This situation dominated decisionmaking and reform implementation during the course of the IMF's involvement in Russia. While the IMF's initial broad strategy of controlling inflation and achieving sustainable budgets and balance of payments remained generally consistent over time, actually achieving these goals has proven elusive. Despite repeated difficulties in achieving macroeconomic stabilization, the IMF Executive Board has made the decision to remain engaged in Russia.

As discussed in chapter 2 and later in this appendix, the evolution of the IMF's strategy can be broken down into four stages: (1) efforts primarily to control inflation to bring about macroeconomic stabilization from 1992 to 1995; (2) continuing efforts to control inflation with increased stress on structural reforms from 1996 to mid-1998; (3) efforts to support the Russian government to help it deal with a growing financial crisis from July to September 1998; and (4) continued support of the Russian government with little funding in 1999 and 2000.

Efforts to Control Inflation: 1992-1995

During 1992-95, the IMF's primary goal in Russia was to reduce macroeconomic imbalances, particularly inflation, and to stabilize the macroeconomy. According to an IMF official, controlling inflation was paramount because inflation adds to uncertainty in the economy and discourages investment. Although the focus of the IMF's programs was to reduce inflation, the structure of the programs evolved according to agreements made between Russia and the IMF concerning Russia's perceived needs.

The first agreement, in August 1992, was a first tranche agreement of $1 billion—a 5-month package with a relatively limited number of conditionality requirements that sought to reduce inflation. To do so, Russia agreed to (1) cut its budget deficit by 11.5 percent of its gross domestic product (GDP), (2) limit money creation by the central bank, and (3) support a flexible exchange-rate policy within the framework of a ruble zone.[6] In addition, the program stipulated that the entire amount of the IMF loan was to be held as reserves by the Central Bank of Russia. The IMF funds could not be used to support the budget. The central bank financed the budget deficit by supplying credits, which was inflationary. According to IMF documents, Russia did not consistently implement the program. Moreover, Russia failed to achieve the goal of reducing inflationary pressures and progress on structural measures was mixed, particularly in the area of privatization.

1993

The IMF created a temporary Systemic Transformation Facility in 1993 because it recognized that some transition countries, including Russia, were not ready to meet the terms for full conditionality required under a Stand-by Arrangement. In June 1993, the IMF's Executive Board approved a $1.5 billion loan to Russia from the Systemic Transformation Facility. IMF documents stated that the main goal was to reduce the monthly percentage rate of inflation to a "low single digit level." Russia was to do so by limiting credit creation and reducing the government deficit to 10 percent of GDP. In addition, Russia agreed to meet some limited structural measures under the program, including further liberalizing the exchange rate and trade system and continuing with privatization and financial reforms.

According to IMF documents, the Systemic Transformation Facility program went seriously off track because the Russian government failed to abide by key commitments such as meeting the budget deficit target. According to a Russian government official, in September 1993, the Minister of Finance asked the IMF to discontinue the program because it was clear that the program had gone off track and that he would have more leverage within the government to improve the situation if there was no IMF financing. In late 1993, there was a marked shift in the political environment in Russia. Between October's attempted parliamentary rebellion and December's parliamentary elections, the government was briefly able to make some economic policy moves, bringing the Central Bank of Russia under executive control, reducing the budget deficit to 10 percent of GDP, breaking up the ruble currency zone, and abolishing most export quotas. However, the decline in the deficit was problematic: it was achieved by not paying wages and pension benefits to the Russian people. In the December 1993 parliamentary elections, the Russian public voted against the government "reformers" who, in turn, suffered heavy losses to the ultranationalists and Communists.

[6] Following the collapse of the Soviet Union, Russia and the other former Soviet republics (except the Baltics) agreed to maintain the ruble as their common currency, with the money supply controlled by the Central Bank of Russia. The newly created central banks from the republics were eager to expand their domestic credit, largely by obligating the Central Bank of Russia to provide financing and trade subsidies borrowing from the Central Bank of Russia. This indirect source of inflationary pressure led to Russia's withdrawal from the ruble zone in July 1993, contributing to its ultimate collapse. The Russians decided to discontinue making automatic extensions of credit to other central banks in July 1, 1992, which led to the creation of separate currencies.

1994

In March 1994, despite concerns regarding poor implementation of the first program, the IMF Board approved a new $1.5 billion Systemic Transformation Facility program to show support for the Russian government. According to an IMF official, the IMF Managing Director was under heavy pressure to approve the program. This agreement was reached with a Russian government that had changed significantly. The December 1993 Duma elections had been widely viewed as a sharp repudiation of reform efforts and of the federal government by the Russian people— Communists and ultranationalists who had gained seats in the December 1993 parliamentary elections were not supportive of the IMF's reform efforts. According to a Russian government official, a key reason for agreeing to go ahead with the Systemic Transformation Facility program, however, was the general concern at the time that without western support for Russia, there would be a heightened possibility of Communists taking over the government.

The main goals for the second Systemic Transformation Facility were to reduce the monthly rate of inflation to 7 percent by the end of 1994 and to increase gross international reserves to approximately $10 billion by that time. To achieve these objectives, the program conditions called for reduced expansion of the money supply by the Central Bank of Russia and a significant decrease in the budget deficit. However, by the end of the year, the IMF staff viewed Russia's overall performance as significantly worse than programmed. End-year inflation was more than twice as high as targeted, the net international reserve target was missed by a significant margin, and fiscal policy began to move considerably off track starting midyear due to continued weak revenue collection and an increase in government expenditures. In addition, the Russian currency devalued by 20 percent against the U.S. dollar in one day in the October 1994 exchange-rate crisis known as "Black Tuesday." This crisis, however, had the positive effect of leading to greater Russian government resolve to achieve macroeconomic stabilization in 1995.

1995

The IMF Board approved a new 1995 Stand-by Arrangement of $6.8 billion for Russia based on its assessment that the chances of implementing the agreed-upon program were better than they had been in the past. Russia had a more favorable political situation—the Russian President had replaced his economic policy team with more reform-minded players. At this point, the IMF changed from the limited conditionality and financing of the Systemic Transformation Facility to a stricter approach with considerably more financing under the Stand-by Arrangement. Not only were the conditions stricter, but also monitoring was also more frequent as Russia agreed to unprecedented monthly and quarterly IMF program reviews.

The key objectives of the 1995 program were to bring the monthly rate of inflation down very quickly to a rate of 1 percent. Russia was to achieve this by limiting the growth of the central bank credit to the government to 3 and restricting the government and Central Bank of Russia from extending credits or government loans to clear interenterprise arrears.[7] The government agreed to nearly halve the government deficit to 6 percent of GDP. The program also called for a continuation of the privatization program, including sales of public enterprises and large blocks of shares of those companies for cash. Privatization revenues were to be used to finance part of the budget deficit. During the 1995 Stand-by Arrangement, Russia's primary goal of reducing inflation was achieved, despite internal political pressures. The IMF reported that Russia was able for the first time to meet all of its macroeconomic targets, including its budget deficit target.[8] In addition, the Russian government passed the 1995 Budget Law that prevents the Central Bank of Russia from providing direct credit to the government. Also, in July 1995, in an attempt to stabilize market expectations, the IMF agreed to Russia's proposal to shift from a flexible to a banded exchange rate.[9]

Although there were significant positive changes in Russia in 1995, underlying problems in the economy began to emerge. Although Russia met its 1995 budget deficit targets, it was recognized at that time that the underlying budgetary situation was problematic and complicated by several factors. Russia met its budget deficit target by accumulating politically unpopular wage and pension arrears due to a shortfall in budget revenues. Although tax evasion was common, the shortfall in tax revenue collection in 1995 was also related to the lower inflation rate. In previous years, the nominal ruble revenue receipts were higher than expected because actual inflation was higher than projected. Expenditures were not indexed to inflation, and the budget deficit in ruble terms was reduced. With lower than projected inflation in 1995, the amount of nominal revenue receipts was less than projected, leading to a higher than anticipated ruble deficit. According to the IMF, Russia was able to meet its 1995 targets since the budget used outlays, not counting arrears, to measure the deficit. After the IMF recognized this trend, and as timely information on arrears became available, it changed the definition of budget expenditure so that arrears were also accounted for as part of the deficit, according to an IMF official. Inflation was reduced in part through the government's adoption of a banded exchange rate and in part by the government's pursuing supporting macroeconomic policies such as controlling the growth of the money supply and using government securities, called GKOs/OFZs, yielding high interest rates, for nonmonetary financing of the budget deficit. Although the exchange rate was relatively stable during this period, some argue that the Russian government maintained an overvalued exchange rate. While such a rate may have been suitable for the overall balance of payments, it made domestically produced goods less competitive with imported goods for the Russian consumer. In hindsight, the exchange rate issue became increasingly important because it led to a decline in domestic industrial output.

---

7 Interenterprise arrears occur when one enterprise does not pay another enterprise for goods or services.

8 A 1999 PriceWaterhouseCoopers audit shows that in 1995, Russia misreported required information pertaining to performance criteria to the IMF. The corrected figures show that Russia missed 2 targets during 1995.

9 A "banded exchange rate" is a mechanism in which the Central Bank of Russia undertook supporting measures and policies that attempted to maintain the exchange rate within a preannounced upper and lower range.

Toward the end of 1995, the Russian government faced serious pressures to raise revenue to pay increases in pensions and wage arrears and to finance reconstruction after the war in Chechnya in the runup to the 1995 parliamentary elections. In October 1995, the Russian government began its loan-for-shares program,[10] which resulted in privatizing some of Russia's most lucrative metal and energy enterprises for significantly less revenue than their market value—about $1 billion was raised. The loans-for-shares program dramatically altered the Russian economy, placing wealth in the hands of a few politically well-connected businessmen, called "oligarchs."

A Russian official we spoke with referred to the program as the "giving away of the family silver." According to IMF documents, the IMF raised concerns about potential abuses of the loans-for-shares program when it was initially presented by the Russian government, but were assured that the government would exercise strong oversight to ensure the program operated fairly. The final scheme differed in important respects from the one discussed with the IMF, and was implemented in a nontransparent and collusive manner. IMF staff noted these concerns in their staff reports in the fall of 1995 prepared for board reviews of the program, but recommended that the reviews be completed, and that disbursements continue to be made. The board approved these recommendations. In light of concerns over the loans-for-shares operation, the 1996 IMF program included Russian government commitments to transparency and an evenhanded privatization methodology.

Continued Emphasis on Controlling Inflation and Increased Stress on Structural Reforms: 1996 to Mid-1998

In March 1996, Russia and the IMF agreed to a 3-year Extended Fund Facility arrangement that signified a shift to focusing more on structural reforms than in previous programs. In the run up to the June presidential elections, a number of developments caused Russia difficulties in meeting fiscal targets, and the IMF modified the targets. The 1997 program emphasized tax collection targets to try to address Russia's budget deficit problem. As for the 1998 program, it was affected by a worsening economic situation in Russia.

---

[10] The 1995 loans-for-shares scheme auctioned ownership of some of Russia's most valuable companies (oil, metals, shipping) as collateral for hard currency loans and, in some cases, payment of some of the firms' tax arrears. Although the original plan called for open auctions, foreign investors were barred, while banks acting as the manager for a particular auction were allowed to submit bids –those managers won 2 of the 12 auctions. Suspicions of corruption were heightened by unexpectedly low bids: the loans yielded only 60-90 percent of the market value of the shares –and in eight cases, the winning bids were within 6 percent of the preestablished minimum bid. Although the scheme was presented as reversible, as of August 2000, the government had not repaid any of the loans nor had banks resold the shares they obtained. Donors, international financial institutions, Russian and U.S. officials, and academics we met with described the loans–for-shares scheme as highly corrupt.

1996

In 1996, Russia and the IMF embarked on a 3-year, Extended Fund Facility arrangement of $10.1 billion that marked a strategy shift from a focus on stressing macroeconomic stability to one that now included greater emphasis on implementing structural reform measures. The conditions for each year of the 3-year program were negotiated at the beginning of that year. According to an IMF official, the move from a Stand-by Arrangement to an Extended Fund Facility was predicated on the IMF Board's belief that Russia had made progress in stabilization and should focus on needed structural reforms. This agreement was the second largest loan the IMF had ever extended to one of its members.

At the time the 1996 program was being negotiated, serious budgetary imbalances existed. At the heart of the fiscal deficit problem was poor tax collection and government deficit spending. In addition, while many of the macroeconomic conditions negotiated in this program were similar to those of previous programs, meeting structural benchmarks played a much larger role in this arrangement.[11] Compared to earlier programs, the requirements for making structural reforms in the Extended Fund Facility were broader and more numerous than in previous programs, focusing on areas including strengthening the banking sector, privatization and restructuring of public enterprises, and energy sector taxation. At the same time, non-resident access to GKOs was officially permitted to provide an additional source of budgetary financing.

For the first half of 1996, Russian presidential election concerns dominated western decision-making toward Russia. According to a Russian official, President Yeltsin's reelection over Communist opposition was important to the west and the IMF and, despite Russia's poor performance, the IMF could not delay or suspend the program. According to the IMF, fiscal discipline eroded as the government increased spending to pay back wage and pension arrears. The IMF staff visited Russia on a monthly basis and frequently modified targets. According to the IMF, these target modifications were made because of unexpected events, especially the large capital outflow in advance of the presidential elections that made those targets unattainable.

Another factor that contributed to Russia's poor performance, according to an IMF official, was that in 1996, government leadership had changed and a less experienced team was attempting to implement the measures. As a result, while Russia had success in moderating inflation–the monthly average inflation rate for 1996 was 1.7 percent—it achieved less success in meeting its fiscal goals. After Russia's repeated failures to address its budget deficit, the IMF included a cash revenue receipt target as one of its quantitative performance criteria. For 1996, however, the federal budget deficit registered 6.3 percent of GDP instead of the planned 4 percent. In addition, federal revenues fell from 10.5 percent of GDP in 1995 to only 9.5 percent in 1996. Furthermore, although Russia had achieved limited structural reforms in instituting banking and tax-related fiscal measures and meeting many of the IMF macroeconomic conditions, progress in meeting IMF program goals generally fell short of its targets. IMF staff noted that, in

[11] "Benchmarks" are points of reference against which progress may be monitored, but disbursements are generally not dependent upon meeting them.

hindsight, the structural work plan might have been too ambitious for Russia to manage, given Russia's limited institutional capacity.

1997

Approval of the 1997 Extended Fund Facility program came after Russia implemented a series of "prior actions,"[12] all of which were structural measures. These included submission of the tax code and a new 1997 spending plan to the Duma,[13] a crackdown on large tax debtors, and the announcement of transparent privatization measures. Russian tax revenues were targeted to increase, on average, to 8.3 percent of GDP in 1997, compared to 7 percent in 1996.

Despite measures to improve tax collection, the lack of collection had become a perennial problem and, according to IMF officials, constant changes in government leadership and unclear federal government authority had contributed to the difficulties. In addition, an IMF official also stated that some government leaders fundamentally did not believe that tax collection was a priority and, at times, hindered efforts to collect taxes from large debtors.

According to an IMF official, over time, there was extreme concern that tax revenues in cash were not being recovered in Russia and that "tax offsets"— allowing firms to pay in-kind rather than in cash—promoted a culture of barter and nonpayments. The business community in Russia argued that it's total tax burden, should it fully comply with the tax laws, would leave an enterprise with almost no after-tax profit.[14] However, according to an IMF document, a firm's total tax obligation was widely viewed as a "negotiated settlement" between a firm and its tax inspector. The inspectors exploited the ambiguities in the tax code to adjust a firm's assessment and extract bribes. As a result, IMF documents state that tax evasion, by concealing income or nonpayment, had become increasingly sophisticated.

A stronger economic reform team; lower interest rates; and a large, transparent privatization venture increased Russian optimism despite fiscal imbalances and constant political conflicts between the President and the Duma. According to preliminary data, after 6 years of deep output declines the Russian economy had begun to turn around in 1997. This led to discussions in September 1997, in some circles, about the IMF's ending its assistance to Russia. In late 1997, however, the Asian financial crisis quickly spread to Russia, and Russia's economic recovery was halted.

In November 1997, a combination of domestic factors, such as a continuing large budget deficit, and external factors such as the aftermath of the Asian financial crisis and a sharp decline in world oil prices, led to pressures on the exchange rate. To support the ruble exchange rate, Russian authorities intervened in both the government securities

[12] "Prior actions" are policy measures that the IMF views as key to the effectiveness of a country's program. They may have to be implemented before the IMF board approves an IMF arrangement or disbursement. Such actions are particularly important if severe macroeconomic imbalances exist or in cases where the record of policy implementation has been weak.

[13] The Duma is the lower house of Russia's parliament.

[14] IMF documents state that for a firm to give an employee a take-home wage of $1,000 each month, the firm's total cost after taxes would be around $1,903.

(GKO) market by raising interest rates and the foreign exchange market. According to an IMF official, the IMF advised the authorities to support the exchange rate by continuing to raise interest rates in an effort to stem capital outflows, rather than expending reserves. The rise in interest rates was insufficient to stem the capital outflows and, in 3 weeks, the Central Bank of Russia expended approximately 25 percent of its international reserves before raising interest rates more decisively, which succeeded in stabilizing the situation. The rise in interest rates, however, also had the effect of weakening the commercial banks because it reduced the value of their current GKO securities holdings. Despite these efforts, there was significant capital outflow at the end of 1997.

According to IMF documents, at the end of 1997 the IMF and Russia created a fiscal action plan focused on tax collection and expenditure measures in order to bring the fiscal side of the program on track. On the revenue side, the plan included a measure to eliminate tax offsets, improve compliance by large tax debtors, and establish the right to seize and sell assets. Limits on energy consumption and administrative sanctions on officials who overspend their budgets were included on the expenditure side. By the end of 1997, however, IMF staff conceded that little had been accomplished on fiscal issues, particularly in the area of tax collection.

Early 1998

The 1998 Extended Fund Facility program was negotiated against the backdrop of pressures in Russia's financial markets, weaknesses in oil prices, and unexpected changes in government leadership. Due to Russia's poor performance in 1997, the 1998 IMF structural reform program required that Russia take a wide range of measures as prior actions before the IMF board would consider a disbursement. Structural reforms that would have important macroeconomic impact over the medium term were designated benchmarks. Some of the structural measures were taken from the November 1997 action plan and included (1) collecting taxes from large tax debtors, (2) identifying additional expenditure cuts needed to observe the program targets, and (3) establishing better monitoring and controls over expenditure.

Despite a developing crisis in Russia and reversal of market confidence, the 1998 Extended Fund Facility package was not agreed to until June 13, 1998. According to a Russian official, a change in government in March led to further discussions and renegotiations that delayed the process. On June 30, 1998 Russia received its first financial disbursement in 6 months. Only a few weeks later, a massive financial crisis hit Russia.

Support Government Efforts to Deal with a Growing Financial Crisis: July-September 1998

On July 20, 1998, in support of strengthened Russian government policies, the IMF agreed to lend Russia $11.2 billion in an interim package to ease the financial crisis that threatened to collapse the country's fragile economy; the IMF immediately disbursed $4.8 billion. In addition to IMF assistance, other sources announced additional financing bringing the entire package to over $22 billion. The announcement of the IMF's additional policy package had a positive, but very short-lived, effect on Russia's financial markets.

Prior to the first disbursement of the July 20 interim package, IMF and Russian government officials agreed to seek implementation of several prior actions including tax revenue, government budgeting, and pension measures. While President Yeltsin issued presidential decrees to ensure the implementation of many of the measures, the Duma delayed passing personal income tax and pension legislation. As a result, the IMF reduced the amount of the first disbursement from $5.6 billion to $4.8 billion. The government also offered to investors a voluntary debt exchange of government securities (GKOs) for longer-term Eurobonds in July 1998. Only about $6.5 billion of these government securities out of approximately $40 billion were exchanged.[15] The lack of significant response was interpreted as demonstrating that the markets had regained some confidence, according to a Russian government official. A Russian government official stated that overall, the package had temporarily increased investor confidence and the Russian government had believed that the crisis was temporarily halted.

In mid-August, however, market sentiment changed. As a result, domestic investors who had lost confidence in the government's ability to undertake reform led the massive capital outflow by converting their rubles into hard currency. Foreign investors—who may have believed that Russia was too big or too much of a nuclear power to fail—followed. IMF officials told us that, in hindsight, they recognize that no package may have been large enough to overcome investor concerns regarding Russia's fiscal and balance-of-payments situation. In addition, the IMF reduced the initial tranche based on the Duma's unwillingness to take action on key legislation. Investor confidence in the government's ability to deliver on the overall package fell. During this time, the Russian President announced that the government would maintain the value of the ruble.

On August 15, the Russian government and IMF officials met to negotiate strategies for handling the ensuing crisis. According to a former official of the Central Bank of Russia, the Russian government's major concerns at the time were related to the (1) government's inability to service its government securities (GKO) debt, (2) cost of maintaining the ruble band, and (3) foreign banking sector/external debt. The Russian government initially suggested a plan that provided for unequal treatment of domestic and foreign investors;[16] however, the IMF advised against it. Instead, the Russian government decided unilaterally to restructure the government's ruble denominated securities (GKOs). In addition, it decided to widen the exchange rate band in order to allow the ruble to depreciate within the band and to declare a 90-day moratorium on

[15] Of this amount, $4.5 billion was exchanged by Sberbank, a Russian government bank.

[16] The Central Bank of Russia viewed the key issue for residents as that government securities (GKOs) were the only liquid financial instrument available to banks and finance companies and the key issue for nonresidents as minimizing currency loss and maintaining the value of the investment. Thus, the central bank proposed that residents would receive 20-25 percent cash, exchanging the remaining value into 1-, 2-, or 3-year ruble securities with 50, 40, and 30 percent interest rates. For nonresidents, the central bank proposed to convert ruble securities into dollar-denominated securities with low interest coupons and maturities of 5-7 years.

external commercial debt for the banking sector. The Russian government informed the IMF of its plans.

Although the government placed a 90-day moratorium on commercial/banking external debt repayments, the remaining actions were more complicated. The government failed to clearly articulate a government securities (GKO) debt conversion scheme, adding to rising market uncertainty and upheaval after the Prime Minister was fired. Political factors at play within Russia during that period had a serious impact on the financial crisis. Although a new candidate for Prime Minister was nominated to replace the current Prime Minister, the Duma twice rejected his nomination. While the President and the Duma were engulfed in a political battle over the prime ministership, and despite heavy intervention by the Central Bank of Russia, the ruble continued to depreciate until the central bank finally allowed the ruble to float; the ruble then sharply devalued by over 40 percent in early September.

During this time, Russia missed interest payments due on August 20 on sovereign (government) debt dating from the Soviet era. In addition, the Central Bank of Russia offered a line of credit to the government because the 1995 central bank law prevented direct financing to the government. Meanwhile, the central bank continued to provide liquidity to the banking system while, at the same time, it was selling dollars for rubles to maintain the exchange rate band in the face of capital flight.

Immediately after the financial crash and before the July 1999 program, IMF officials stated that their primary post-crisis strategy was to remain involved in Russia to stabilize the situation. The IMF provided Russia with assistance and advice and conducted assessments of the post-crisis situation in the country. In addition, the IMF was attempting to negotiate a new program. According to an IMF official, the new government's announced monetary policy was geared toward creating money to pay off budgetary arrears. However, the government modified its intended policies because of concerns about hyperinflation and exchange rate pressures.

Continued Support of the Government, with Limited Funding Provided: 1999-Present

On July 28, 1999, almost 1 year after the financial crisis in Russia, the IMF approved a 17-month stand-by credit under a Stand-by Arrangement for Russia for approximately $4.5 billion to support the government's 1999- 2000 economic program. The first—and only—disbursement of $640 million for this program was retained in Russia's account at the IMF to be used for servicing Russia's debt to the IMF. According to IMF documents, the IMF executive directors were willing to approve the 1999 program because they wanted to focus the program on fiscal improvements and structural reforms in light of the difficult, post-crisis economic situation in Russia.

For the 1999 program, both structural and macroeconomic measures were included. The ruble exchange rate policy strategy shifted back to a flexible exchange rate policy allowing only limited intervention from the Russian authorities. New taxes, raising existing tax rates, as well as measures to improve tax compliance, were also stipulated.

The IMF also required the Central Bank of Russia to undergo an investigation of its financial transactions with its subsidiaries due to allegations of the inappropriate use of funds.[17] The program targeted an annual inflation rate of 50 percent in 1999, compared to 84.5 percent in 1998. Net international reserves were to increase by $2.2 billion in 1999, with gross reserves to be at least $1.7 billion during the last three-quarters of the year. Moreover, real GDP was assumed to decline by 2 percent in 1999.

The 1999 program was short lived. In December 1999, for the first time, the IMF, delayed a scheduled disbursement based on Russia's failure to meet structural benchmarks, while all macroeconomic requirements had been met. According to IMF staff, structural reform has become increasingly important in the task of achieving macroeconomic stabilization and, as a result, they held performance on these benchmarks to a higher standard. The IMF later stated that Russia had been required to meet several benchmarks related to financial audits of government agencies, tax collection, and legislation, which it had missed. Russia did not complete those structural benchmarks, and no further disbursements have been made.

Although the IMF has not made any disbursements to Russia since July 1999, it has continued to remain engaged in Russia through policy dialogue, program discussions, technical assistance, and its usual surveillance activities for members. IMF and World Bank staff have worked together on technical assistance missions, primarily to assist Russia with banking sector reform and restructuring.

Despite dire economic projections, however, in mid-1999, the Russian economy began to experience economic growth, largely due to a stronger than expected increase in domestic production. The increase in domestic production has been led by higher demand for less expensive domestically produced goods, as the devalued ruble made imported goods relatively more expensive. In addition, oil prices had begun to rise from their historically low 1997 prices. Although the IMF states that Russia's future balance-of-payments outlook is uncertain, Russia has emerged from these changes in 1999 with a substantial balance-of-payments surplus,[18] a budget deficit of only 1.7 percent of GDP, and a real GDP growth rate of 3.2 percent. For 2000, the IMF forecasts a balance-of-payments surplus exceeding 13 percent of GDP, a budget surplus of more than 4 percent of GDP, and real GDP growth of 7 percent.

As of August 2000, the IMF was in the process of negotiating a new program with Russia. While the specifics of the program are unclear, IMF officials cited that the IMF program would seek structural reforms in three main areas: tax reform, banking reform, and barter and arrears. In addition, the IMF program will continue to focus its attention on macroeconomic stabilization and fiscal and monetary policy.

---

[17] See International Monetary Fund: Status of Efforts to Strengthen Safeguards Over Lending.

[18] The 1999 current account surplus was $25 billion, more than 11 percent of Russia's GDP.

LESSONS LEARNED

Unlike donor agencies and some international institutions, the IMF has not formally identified institutional lessons learned from its years of involvement in Russia. However, through our review of IMF documents and discussions with IMF officials about their own experiences with Russia, some relevant lessons learned have surfaced.

- The IMF underestimated the complexity of Russia's transition process, in which the economic and political dimensions were intertwined.
- Russian political will is necessary for IMF programs to succeed.
- Russia's economic program is more likely to succeed if it is designed by the Russians themselves. The IMF's worldwide experience shows that economic programs are most likely to succeed when they are "owned" by the country implementing them.
- Achieving sustained, equitable growth in Russia will take a strengthening of macroeconomic stability and an intensification of sectoral structural reforms, including improving the social safety net.

Appendix II

WORLD BANK ASSISTANCE TO RUSSIA

BACKGROUND

Since its inception in 1945, the World Bank has grown into a family of five related institutions known together as the World Bank Group.[1] In addition to the International Bank for Reconstruction and Development, the International Finance Corporation—the arm of the World Bank established in 1956 to finance private sector investments in developing countries—has also been active in Russia.[2] We did not specifically examine the International Finance Corporation's lending program for Russia in this review.[3] Rather, our work focused on assistance provided by the International Bank for Reconstruction and Development.

Today, the World Bank is the largest source of market-based loans to developing countries and is a major catalyst for similar financing from other sources.[4] Its stated purpose is "to reduce poverty and improve living standards for people in the developing world." The World Bank has 182 members and a 24-member Executive Board—the Bank's primary oversight and decision-making body. The board decides overall World Bank policies, reviews country assistance strategies, and approves specific project proposals presented by the President of the Bank. As the largest contributing member of

---

[1] The World Bank Group comprises the International Bank for Reconstruction and Development, the International Development Association, the International Finance Corporation, the Multilateral Investment Guarantee Agency, and the International Center for Settlement of Investment Disputes.

[2] The focus of the International Finance Corporation's efforts in Russia has been privatization and capital markets. From the time Russia became a member in 1993 through August 31, 2000, the Corporation has approved $458 million in financing for 36 projects in Russia: $276 million in loans, $154 million in equity, $11 million in quasi-equity, and $17 million in a risk-held portfolio. As of August 31, 2000, the Corporation's disbursed and outstanding portfolio in Russia stood at $256 million; $54 million in disbursements were pending.

[3] We also did not review the Multilateral Investment Guarantee Agency, which has an outstanding portfolio in Russia consisting of 10 contracts of guarantee for a total gross exposure of $269 million (net exposure of $127 million). The Agency has facilitated a total of $1.17 billion in foreign direct investment in Russia. Its portfolio is composed of manufacturing (47 percent), financial (40 percent), and mining sectors (12 percent).

[4] The World Bank obtains most of its funds through the sale of bonds in international capital markets. Its lending terms are the average cost of borrowings plus a spread (typically less than 1 percent) for 12- to 20-year maturities, with a 3- to 5-year grace period for repayment on most loans.

the World Bank, the United States holds the greatest number of voting shares (16.5 percent) on the Bank's Executive Board.[5] Russia, which has 2.8 percent of the voting shares, is also represented by an executive director on the Board.

Overall Objectives and Initial Assumptions

The World Bank's stated broad strategy for Russia has focused on three key objectives:

- Support Russia's transition to a market economy based on private sector initiative.
- Protect the poor and vulnerable groups.
- Develop and strengthen institutions.

The main assumptions that guided the World Bank's program of assistance for Russia in the early years included the following:

- To shore up support for reform, the World Bank needed to move quickly.
- To have meaningful impact, the World Bank had to implement concurrent programs in several sectors because of Russia's size.
- To encourage change, Bank projects were to be implemented at the regional and local levels.

The World Bank's Instruments

To help Russia and other member countries with their development needs, the World Bank offers two basic types of lending instruments:

1. Investment or project loans that support investment activities with a long-term focus of 5 to 10 years. Most of the World Bank's lending has historically been for investment projects such as building roads and bridges, providing basic services in health and education, and increasing agricultural production.
2. Adjustment loans that provide quick-disbursing external financing to support policy and institutional reforms, generally with a short-term focus of 1-3 years. These loans are often used to finance balance-of-payments support while policy and institutional reforms are being implemented and to foster long-term economic growth.

The World Bank also offers guarantees to cover risks that the private sector is not normally in a position to absorb or manage. The first such project guarantee for Russia

[5] Japan (7.9 percent), Germany (4.5 percent), France and the United Kingdom (4.3 percent each) follow the United States in the number of voting shares allocated to them.

was approved in May 1997. The guarantee, for $100 million, protects commercial banks that lent funds to a joint international space launch vehicle venture. The guarantee provided protection against the possibility of nonpayment of the loan due to political risks in Russia.

In addition to making loans and guarantees, the World Bank also provides nonlending services, including economic and sector work and technical assistance. Through the World Bank Institute[6] the World Bank also provides training programs, which over the years have included such topics as macroeconomic management, intergovernmental fiscal relations, and governance.[7]

Finally, the World Bank administers trust funds that provide grants for specified purposes such as to cofinance some investment projects and provide technical assistance. For example, since 1994, more than $127 million in grant funds has been approved for Russia, including $83.3 million from the Global Environment Facility and about $34 million from the Policy and Human Resources Development Fund financed by the Japanese government.

Funding History for Russia

As of September 30, 2000, the World Bank had approved $12.1 billion for 46 projects in Russia (see table 7).

As shown in figure 16, a rapid buildup of the World Bank's portfolio occurred in the early years of the program. During fiscal years 1993 and 1994, the World Bank approved 10 loans worth nearly $3 billion for Russia—the fastest increase in World Bank operations for a new member country. Annual approved lending to Russia has been in the $1.3 billion-$1.9 billion range, except in fiscal year 2000,[8] when the World Bank approved only $90 million in new lending.

[6] Formerly the Economic Development Institute, the external training arm of the Bank, that was merged in March 1999 with the Learning and Leadership Center, the internal training unit for World Bank staff.

[7] The Institute has been involved in Russia since the beginning of the Bank's program, participating in the first World Bank mission to Russia. An office was established in Moscow as a separate operation in 1992 and staffed by locally hired employees, the only fully staffed unit of the Institute overseas.

[8] World Bank reporting generally goes on a fiscal year basis, starting from July 1 to June 30.

Table 7: Status of World Bank Loans for Russia, From Fiscal Year 1993 Through September 2000

Fiscal year and project title	Loan approved (in millions of dollars)	Date of Board approval [a]	Date of loan effectiveness[b]	Cancelled (in millions of dollars)	Disbursed (in millions of dollars)	Closing date[c]
1993						
Rehabilitation I[d]	$ 600.0	08/06/92	2/29/92	None	$600.0	Closed 9/30/94
Employment services and social protection	70.0	11/24/92	09/09/94	14.4	55.6	Closed 04/30/00
Privatization implementation assistance	90.0	12/17/92	12/07/93	3.95	86.1	Closed 6/30/99
Oil rehabilitation [e]	610.0	06/17/93	11/15/93	196.0	414.0	Closed 12/31/98
1994						
Highway rehabilitation and maintenance	300.0	02/17/94	10/21/94	19.2	280.8	Closed 12/31/99 9
Financial institutions development[e]	200.0	05/19/94	07/28/95	59.5	73.0	12/31/02
Land reform implementation[e]	80.0	06/16/94	04/26/95	None	28.7	10/31/00
Agriculture reform implementation[e]	240.0	06/16/94	11/21/94	115.2	110.4	12/31/00
Enterprise support	200.0	06/21/94	07/31/95	None	39.9	06/30/01
Oil rehabilitation II	500.0	06/29/94	05/25/95	53.5	346.5	Closed 12/31/00
1995						
Environmental management	110.0	11/08/94	08/30/95	None	49.5	12/31/02
Management and financial training	40.0	12/15/94	07/03/95	0.01	40.0	Closed 11/1/99
Portfolio development	40.0	02/16/95	01/02/96	None	21.2	12/31/00
Housing[e]	400.00	03/07/95	07/27/95	30.0	166.8	12/31/01
Tax administration modernization	16.8	03/09/95	07/03/95	None	12.0	12/31/00
Emergency oil spill recovery and mitigation[e]	99.0	04/25/95	06/29/95	None	82.6	09/30/01
Urban transport[e]	329.0	05/16/95	03/28/96	55.0	245.9	06/30/01
Rehabilitation II[d]	600.0	06/06/95	09/28/95	None	600.0	Closed 6/30/96
1996						
Standards development	24.0	11/30/95	06/05/96	None	17.7	12/31/00
Bridge rehabilitation[e]	350.0	03/28/96	08/19/96	158.0	106.6	12/31/01
Community social infrastructure[e]	200.0	04/30/96	01/31/97	43.5	40.2	12/31/02
Energy efficiency[e]	70.0	05/02/95	12/26/96	None	15.2	06/30/01
Enterprise housing divestiture[e]	300.0	05/07/96	11/18/96	23.2	30.1	12/31/03
Capital markets development	89.0	05/30/96	12/17/96	None	14.6	06/30/03
Medical equipment [e]	270.0	06/04/96	01/30/97	37.7	196.1	06/30/01
Legal reform	58.0	06/21/96	09/09/96	None	20.9	12/31/00
Coal sector adjustment loan[d]	500.0	06/27/96	07/02/96	None	500.0	Closed 12/31/97
Coal sector restructuring	25.0	06/27/96	07/25/96	None	13.7	12/31/01

implementation assistance						
1997						
St. Petersburg center city rehabilitation[e]	31.0	03/27/97	04/13/98	None	16.7	12/31/01
Structural adjustment loan[d]	600.0	06/05/97	06/17/97	None	600.0	Closed 3/31/98
Enterprise restructuring services[f]	85.0	06/05/97	N/A	85.0	None	Lapsed 8/3/98
Education innovation[e]	71.0	06/05/97	04/20/98	3.0	7.9	12/31/03
Bureau of Economic Analysis	22.6	06/05/97	12/18/97	None	13.3	09/30/03
Electricity sector reform support	40.0	06/05/97	08/12/98	None	None 12/31/01	
Health reform pilot[e]	66.0	06/05/97	04/17/98	None	13.6	04/30/04
Sea Launch guarantee operation	100.0	05/29/97	05/12/98	N/A	N/A	12/31/06
Social protection adjustment loan[d]	800.0	06/25/97	06/26/97	None	800.0	Closed 9/30/00
1998						
Social protection implementation	28.6	10/07/97	07/01/98	None	9.9	12/31/01
Second structural adjustment loan[d]	800.0	12/18/97	12/22/97	None	800.0	Closed 12/31/98
Second coal sector adjustment loan[d]	800.0	12/18/97	12/19/97	None	650.0	03/31/01
1999						
Third structural adjustment loan[d]	1,500.0	08/06/98	08/07/98	1,100.0	400.0	Canceled 8/5/00
Second highway rehabilitation and maintenance[f]	400.0	12/22/98	N/A	400.0	None	Lapsed 9/27/99
State statistical system	30.0	05/13/99	05/31/00	None	0.3	06/30/04
2000						
Regional fiscal technical assistance	30.0	12/22/99	08/30/00	None	0.8	12/31/04
Sustainable forestry pilot	60.0	05/23/00	Not yet effective	None	None	09/30/04
2001						
Coal and forestry guarantee facility	200.0	09/00	Not yet effective	N/A	N/A	
Total	$12,075.0		$2,497.2	$7,520.3		

Legend:
N/A=Not applicable
[a] The date that the Executive Board voted to approve the loan and the Bank is authorized to sign the loan agreement.
[b] The date when disbursements can be made under the loan.
[c] The date when all financial activities related to the project stopped.
[d] These are adjustment loans.
[e] Projects that had sublending to regional entities, including governments and private sector companies in the regions.
[f] These projects were allowed to lapse and were closed before they became effective.
Source: World Bank.

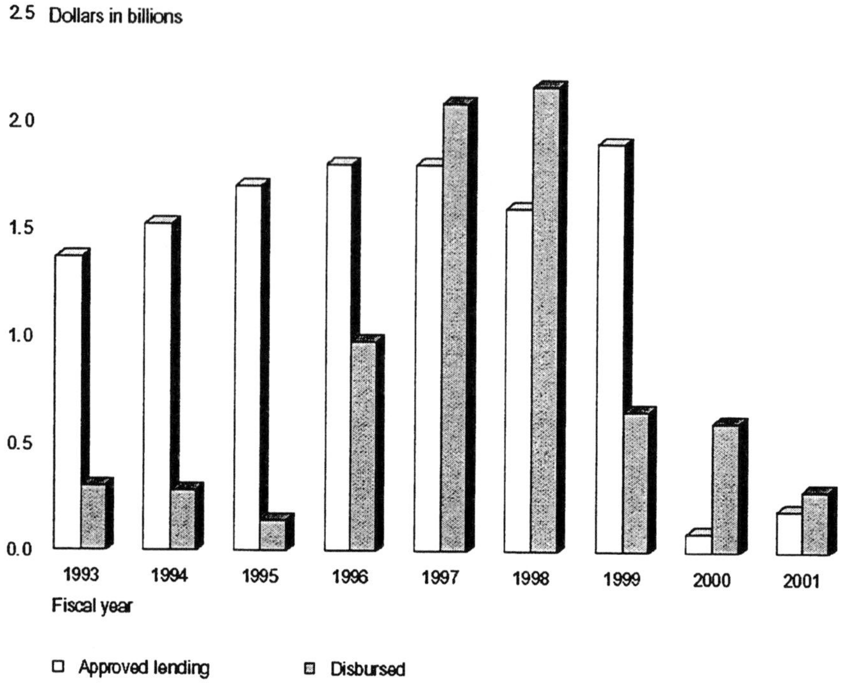

Figure 16: Trends in Approved World Bank Lending and Disbursements to Russia, Fiscal Year 1993 September 2000

Note: Fiscal Year 2001 reflects data for only one quarter, from July 1 to September 30, 2000. Source: World Bank.

Figure 17 illustrates the percentage of lending by type of instrument that the World Bank provided as of September 30, 2000.

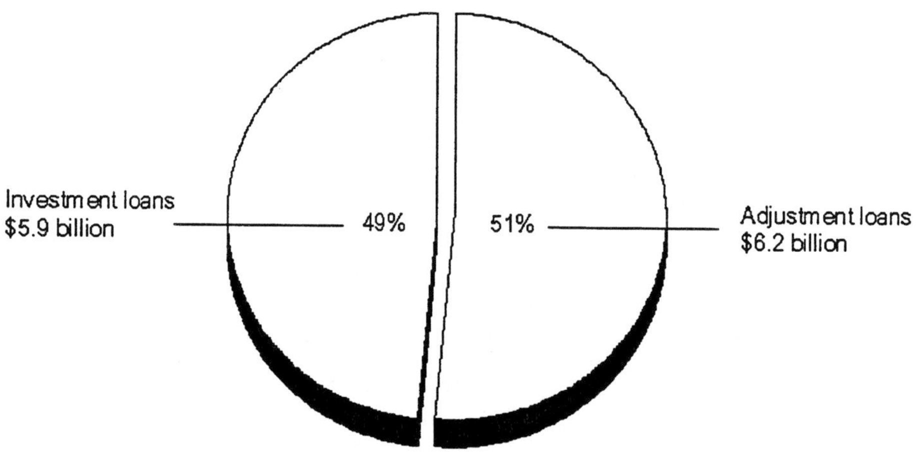

Figure 17: World Bank Lending to Russia, by Type of Instrument, Fiscal Year 1993 Through September 2000.

Source: World Bank.

Of the $12.1 billion in total lending that has been approved for Russia, $9.3 billion has been committed as of September 30, 2000[9]—$3.1 billion for investment projects and $6.2 billion for adjustment loans. About $2 billion has been cancelled, and $485 million for two loans was allowed to lapse before the loans became effective. The two most recently approved loans for $260 million had not yet become effective. Figure 18 shows the status of the World Bank's lending activity to Russia as of September 30, 2000.

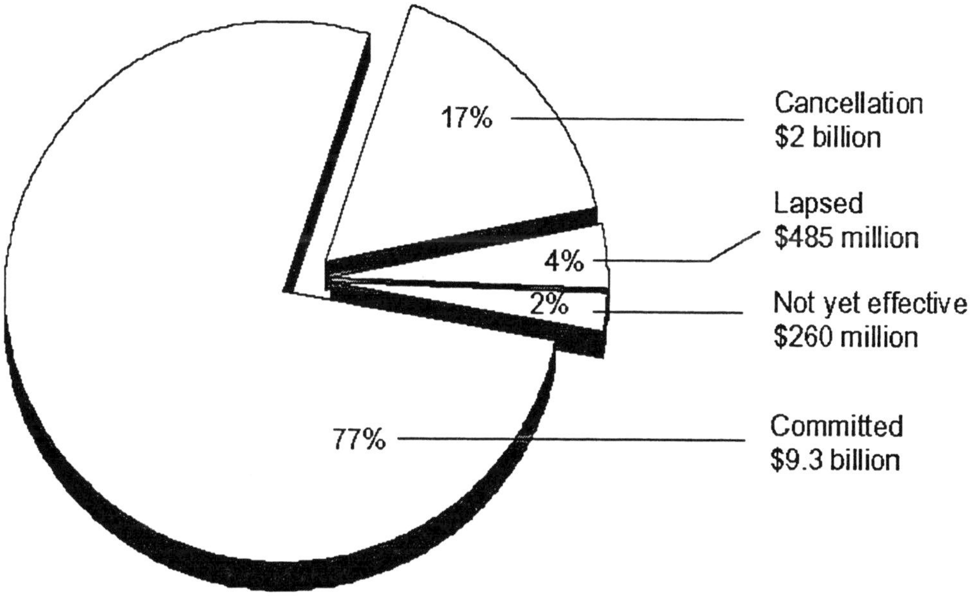

Figure 18: Status of World Bank Approved Loans to Russia as of September 2000
Note: Approved lending since 1992 totals $12.1 billion. Source: World Bank.

The World Bank had disbursed about 62 percent of approved loans—or $7.5 billion—as of September 2000. This makes Russia among the World Bank's largest borrowers in terms of commitments and disbursements to date. About $2.6 billion of the $7.5 billion in disbursements was for investment projects, and $4.9 billion for adjustment loans. The relatively slow disbursements, particularly during 1993-95, reflect the implementation delays that were commonly experienced in a number of projects in the Russia portfolio. These disbursements spiked in 1997 and 1998, following intensive efforts to improve the portfolio, and then declined with the deterioration of the portfolio after the Russian financial crisis in 1998 (see fig. 16).

[9] Commitments in this case include fully disbursed and closed loans, as well as effective loans after cancellations. Newly approved but not effective loans are not included.

STRATEGY

The evolution of the World Bank's program of assistance to Russia can be broken down into five stages: (1) the initial years between 1990 and 1992, which primarily involved activities to prepare the World Bank for a program of lending to Russia; (2) the early years of engagement between 1993 and 1994, which saw a rapid buildup of projects; (3) the transition years, between 1995 and 1996, when addressing poor project performance became a high priority, and the World Bank began to move toward adjustment lending; (4) the later years from 1997 to 1998, when the World Bank expanded its program of adjustment lending and the financial crisis hit; and (5) the post-financial crisis period, from 1999 to the present, when portfolio performance declined to its lowest levels as a result of the financial crisis and then rebounded following intensive efforts to improve it. Today, the World Bank is looking toward a long-term strategy to assist Russia address systemic weaknesses that remain.

The Initial Years (1990-92): Establishing the Russia Program

Russia became a member of the World Bank on June 16, 1992, although World Bank efforts to prepare for Russia's membership began prior to that time. In July 1990, in response to a request made by the Group of Seven (G- 7) industrialized countries at its Houston Summit, the World Bank—along with the International Monetary Fund, the Organization for Economic Cooperation and Development, and the European Bank for Reconstruction and Development—participated in a joint study of the Soviet economy.[10] In the fall of 1991, the Executive Board established a trust fund to provide technical assistance grants to the former Soviet Union republics. The $30- million technical cooperation program funded work on economic issues and culminated in a February 1992 report to the board. The report proposed undertaking the work and specific measures necessary to enable the World Bank to provide assistance for Russia and the former Soviet republics soon after they joined the Bank. These studies provided the basis for developing the Bank's initial assistance strategy for Russia. The trust fund also enabled the World Bank to set up a resident mission in Moscow in the fall of 1991, and on December 1, 1991, the Bank established a new vice presidency for the Europe and Central Asia region.

Shortly after Russia's independence at the end of 1991 and its membership in the World Bank in mid-1992, the Bank faced immediate pressure to organize itself and build its capacity to deliver a program of assistance as quickly as possible. On August 6, 1992, the first loan to Russia was approved—a $600-million rehabilitation loan that was essentially for balance-of-payments support. It was tied to the IMF's first credit tranche arrangement to support macroeconomic stabilization. However, the loan did not become effective for another 5 months. The rehabilitation loan was extended to finance imports needed to maintain production capacity and limit the decline in output while enterprises

[10] The report, entitled "A Study of the Soviet Economy," was issued in February 1991.

adjusted to the rapid devaluation of the ruble at the beginning of the transition. One objective of the loan was to initiate dialogue with the Russian government for longer-term reform and to build Russia's capacity to implement World Bank projects. Two other projects were approved later that year—an employment services and social protection loan for $70 million and a privatization implementation assistance loan for $90 million.

The Early Years (1993-94): Seeking Areas for Rapid Buildup of the Portfolio

As Russia's economic decline continued, pressure grew on the World Bank from western donors to quickly develop and implement projects. However, according to World Bank documents and officials, project implementation early on was fraught with difficulties. To some extent, this was due to the lack of institutional capacity on the part of both the World Bank and the government of Russia. Specifically, World Bank staff had limited expertise and experience regarding the Russian economy and institutions, while government officials did not know how to deal with international donors and how to implement World Bank-financed projects. Bank officials told us that they were frustrated with "bureaucratic inertia" and the lack of high-level engagement by their Russian counterparts. One World Bank official told us that their Russian counterparts changed roughly twice a year or about six times between 1992 and 1995, so it was often not clear who the World Bank was supposed to be working with. An additional impediment was the requirement early on that each individual project be approved by the Duma,[11] which was time-consuming. For this reason, the effective dates for first two investment loans approved for Russia were substantially delayed—it took about 1 year for the privatization loan to go into effect and nearly 2 years for the employment services loan to take effect.

Although it was clear to World Bank officials that they were expected to be engaged in Russia's transition to a market economy, the specific strategy for doing so was less obvious. According to these officials, it was difficult to strike the right balance between the World Bank's having a development impact and the financial risks that the World Bank could prudently assume, as well as what the proper mix, composition, and funding level of projects should be. The situation early on was chaotic, and a number of obstacles stood in the way of systematically implementing projects. In the end, the World Bank decided to implement concurrent projects, including operations at the regional and local level. This approach was driven, in part, by the belief that, given Russia's size, the World Bank needed broad involvement in order to have meaningful impact and a credible voice in the reform process. It was also borne out of the frustrations that World Bank officials faced as they tried to work with their Russian counterparts.

---

[11] The Law on External Borrowing was approved in 1995. It clarified the procedures for obtaining parliamentary authority for borrowing from the World Bank. While the Duma still authorizes an overall ceiling for borrowing, responsibility for approving the World Bank's lending program and reviewing the country assistance strategy has been placed with the Interministerial Commission for Cooperation with International Financial and Economic Institutions and the G-7.

According to World Bank officials, the Bank's initial approach was dictated, to a large extent, by areas where the doors for World Bank involvement were open. Between 1993 and 1994, the World Bank approved about $2.3 billion for nine projects in several sectors ranging from energy and infrastructure to privatization, agriculture, and institutional development. Although social protection[12] was an explicit focus of the World Bank's initial strategy for Russia, the social sector accounted for a small fraction of actual projects. However, by the end of 1994, only $655 million, or 23 percent, of the $2.9 billion approved for Russia had been disbursed due to start-up delays in project implementation. About 90 percent of these disbursements represented the $600-million rehabilitation loan; only $56 million were for investment projects. World Bank officials stated that a major factor that impeded their effectiveness during the early years was the Bank's limited presence and role in Moscow. Although the World Bank had a resident mission in Moscow since 1991, up until 1997, the Bank's operations in Russia, including project oversight functions, were primarily managed by staff at its Washington headquarters.

The Transition Years (1995-96): Addressing Project Effectiveness and Reassessing the Strategy

In June 1995, the World Bank approved the second adjustment loan of $600 million.[13] According to World Bank officials, the Bank was unwilling to make additional adjustment loans at the time because it did not think that there was sufficient consensus in Russia to carry out and sustain reforms, and it believed that large-scale lending would leave Russia with debt but little reform to show for it. Thus, between 1995 and 1996, the World Bank approved $2.3 billion for 14 investment projects in numerous sectors including transportation, energy, housing, public sector management, and the environment. Yet, even as new loans were being approved, delays in actual project implementation continued. By the end of 1995, less than 10 percent of lending approved for investment projects, had been disbursed. Improving the World Bank's Russia portfolio, especially the implementation of existing projects, became a priority of the World Bank beginning in late 1995. By the end of 1996, $875 million, approximately 19 percent of the $4.7 billion approved for investment projects, had been disbursed.

In 1996—following the presidential elections in July of that year—the World Bank began to shift the focus of the Bank's program and the lending instruments it employed. In response to encouraging political and economic developments, and the poor performance of many of the investment projects underway, the World Bank began to move in 1996 toward large, quick-disbursing adjustment loans. According to World Bank officials, it was becoming increasingly evident that investment loans— including those that funded regional projects such as urban transport, bridge rehabilitation, housing, and

---

[12] The World Bank defines "social protection" as a collection of measures to improve or protect human capital, including labor market interventions, unemployment or old-age insurance, and income support.
[13] The second rehabilitation loan was fully disbursed by October 1995.

medical equipment—were not addressing systemic structural issues. Furthermore, the lack of legal frameworks made it difficult to manage projects.

The Later Years (1997-98): Shifting the Strategic Focus to Federal Structural Reform

To support policy reform and institutional development, the World Bank extended adjustment lending to Russia in some key areas. Specifically, it approved (1) coal sector restructuring for $1.3 billion between 1996 and 1998, (2) social protection adjustment for $800 million in 1997, and (3) structural adjustment for $2.9 billion between 1997 and 1999. With these loans, the World Bank's emphasis shifted away from financing regional activities to providing support to the federal government with fewer but larger adjustment loans.

By the spring of 1998, there had been substantial improvement in the performance of the World Bank's Russia portfolio. According to World Bank officials, the improvement achieved in project implementation was due to the improved and higher-level dialogue with Russian officials. In addition, World Bank officials told us that the relocation of their work to the field in 1997[14]—including elevating the Bank's resident representative to the position of country director—increased their effectiveness. It has enhanced their ability to establish a high-level dialogue with Russian officials and work more closely with them to improve the implementation of projects. However, much of the progress they had made was wiped out when the financial crisis hit in August 1998. Potential World Bank financing of $6 billion was part of a bailout package of more than $22 billion announced by the World Bank, IMF, and the Russian government in July 1998, also including financing by the Japanese government. This included funds to be distributed through 1999, under a new third structural adjustment loan. However, World Bank disbursements over this period were far less than this amount with only $1.5 billion actually committed before the financial crisis and only $400 million eventually disbursed.

Post-Financial Crisis (1999-Present): Focusing on Long-term Efforts

The Russian financial crisis in August 1998 caused disruptions in project implementation and a deterioration in the Bank's Russia portfolio rating. In a review of the Bank's country portfolio performance in July 1999, only 33 percent of Russia's portfolio was rated "satisfactory"—down from 74 percent prior to the crisis. The remaining two-thirds of the portfolio (67 percent) were actual problem projects and were rated "unsatisfactory." Thus, the Russia portfolio performance became the Bank's weakest for any country with a significant portfolio. Three of the largest operations that

[14] As part of the World Bank's "Strategic Compact" initiative in 1997, the World Bank reorganized and decentralized many of its headquarters staff to the field. In addition, responsibility for the day-to-day supervision of project and management activities were largely delegated to the field.

were considered "at risk"[15] were adjustment loans for Russia, and half of the Bank's largest investment projects at risk were Russia projects. The World Bank has decided that, in order to qualify for any new investment lending, the Russian project portfolio must demonstrate satisfactory progress in meeting specified performance targets. Specifically, at a review of Russia's portfolio in July 1999, the World Bank and the government of Russia agreed to increase the share of satisfactory projects to 70 percent by January 2000, 80 percent by January 2001, and 85 percent by June 2001. According to World Bank officials, concerted efforts to address problem loans in the past year are showing encouraging results with 73 percent of the projects rated satisfactory in June 2000 and further improvement reported since then. See figure 19 for a review of Russia's portfolio performance from 1993 through June 2000.

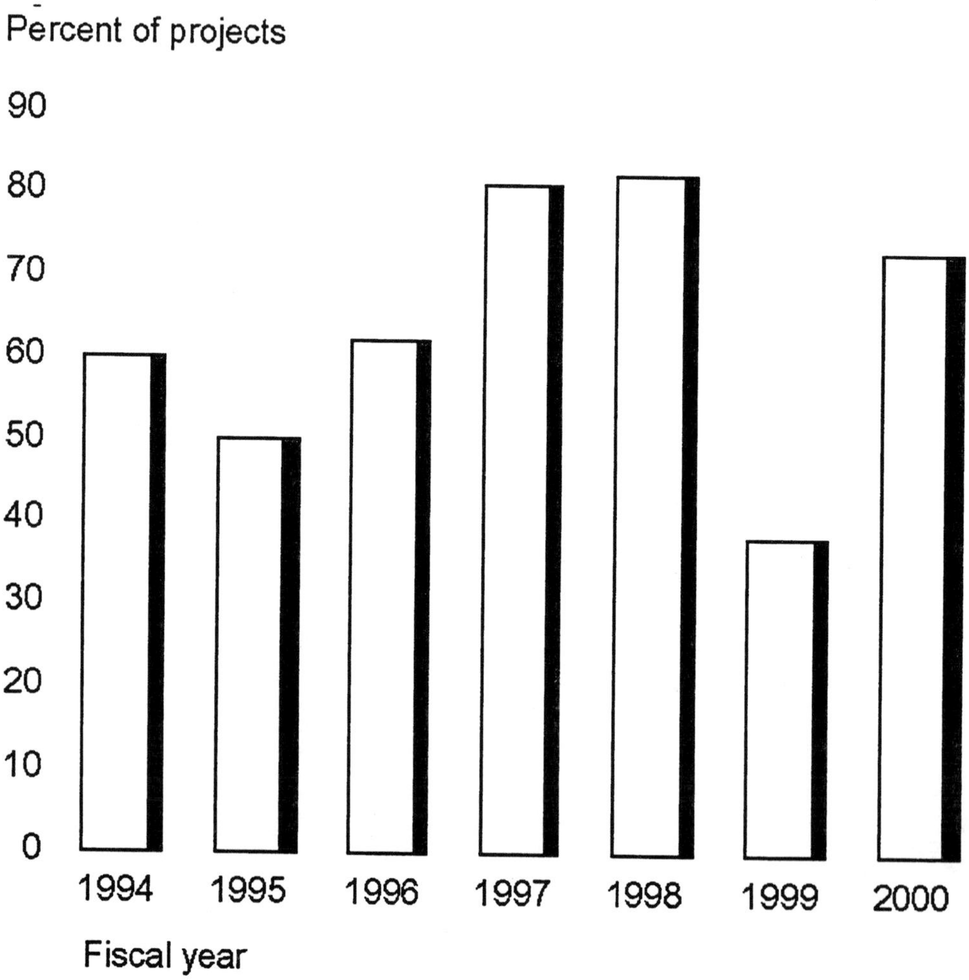

Figure 19: Russia's World Bank Portfolio Performance, 1994 to June 2000
Source: World Bank.

[15] "At risk" includes actual and potential problem projects.

As of June 30, 2000, Russia's projects and commitments at risk—despite marked improvement in overall project performance—were higher than the average for all World Bank projects worldwide and region-wide for Europe and Central Asia countries. See figure 20 for a comparison of Russia's World Bank projects and commitments considered to be at risk and those of the World Bank and the region overall.

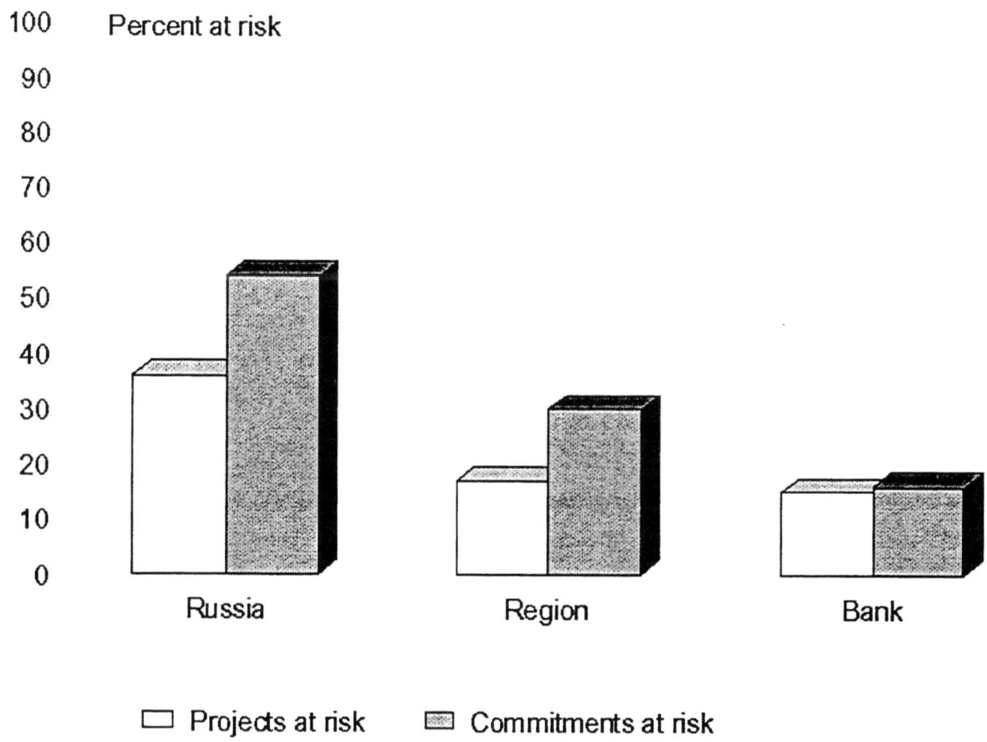

Figure 20: Russia's World Bank Projects and Commitments Considered to Be at Risk, June 2000. Source: World Bank.

On a project basis, few evaluations have been conducted because of the limited number of projects that have been completed.[16] World Bank staff prepare an implementation completion report after a project closes, and as of September 30, 2000, reports for 9 out of the 15 projects that have been completed, had been issued. In addition, the Bank's Operations Evaluation Department routinely conducts independent assessments of individual projects upon their completion and periodically conducts country assistance evaluations. According to World Bank officials, that department is expected to complete audits of several completed projects within several months, and is now undertaking a country assistance evaluation of the Russia program. In addition, in

[16] As of the end of September 2000, out of the 46 loans approved for Russia, 12 had been fully disbursed and closed; 2 projects had lapsed; and 1 has recently been canceled. There are presently 31 active projects in the portfolio.

the spring of 1999, Bank staff conducted an internal retrospective review of the Bank's Russia program at the Board's request,[17] and according to Bank officials, a number of conclusions from that review are reflected in the December 1999 country assistance strategy.

CURRENT STATUS OF THE WORLD BANK'S RUSSIA PROGRAM

Today, the World Bank's program of assistance to Russia is at a crossroads. The Bank's overarching objectives—promoting structural reform, protecting the poor, and developing institutions in Russia—are expected to remain largely the same. However, the strategy that the World Bank uses to implement its program of assistance for Russia—in terms of the type of lending instruments, the level of funding, and the mix and composition projects—will need to be revisited in light of changing conditions, according to World Bank officials.

World Bank officials have told us that the strategy for their involvement in Russia must be long term. Yet, at a time when some donors are looking to the World Bank to take the lead in the structural reforms that must take place in Russia, more modest levels of lending are anticipated. During the past fiscal year, which ended June 30, 2000, the World Bank approved a program of lending that was its lowest ever—$90 million for two projects, just a fraction of the Bank's lending program in years past.[18] While this decision appears to signal a dramatic shift in the Bank's strategy, World Bank officials pointed out that this level of funding is consistent with the reduced lending levels that the latest country assistance strategy calls for. Moreover, they believe that the Russians, in the years ahead, will look to the World Bank not so much for financial support but for the policy advice, analytical advice, and assistance that the Bank can provide as the country moves further with transition.

LESSONS LEARNED

The World Bank routinely documents and disseminates "lessons learned" from its past work, operations, and strategies. The following discussion highlights some of the themes from key lessons learned during the course of the Bank's experience with its Russia operations over the years.

- Ownership is key to success. Numerous World Bank officials emphasized that Russian government commitment to and ownership of reform is needed to achieve success. For instance, a World Bank evaluation of the structural adjustment loans it provided to Russia in 1997 and 1998 indicated that the

---

[17] This paper was not formally presented to the Board and therefore was not available to GAO.

[18] Since then, a coal and forestry guarantee facility for $200 million has also been approved. Because it was approved in September 2000, this loan is reflected in fiscal year 2001 data.

implementation of reforms was "complicated by extremely strained political relations—among and between the President, the Prime Minister, the Federation Council, the State Duma, and regional governments." As a result, implementation of the reforms in some areas proved more difficult than anticipated.

- Consensus-building efforts are needed. The lack of consensus building around World Bank-financed programs made early reform efforts difficult to implement. In addition, the government must reach out to the public and be more open and transparent in explaining its programs to the public. For example, the coal sector adjustment loans—cited by World Bank and government officials as relatively successful—enjoyed broad support from the central government. High subsidies, somewhere in the order of $2 billion to $3 billion per year, provided the incentive for the government's commitment to restructure the coal sector. While the road to reform was not easy, with numerous vested interests at stake, ownership improved as even initially reluctant parties began to see the benefits of coal restructuring.

In contrast, the World Bank's experience in the social sector is generally viewed as somewhat less successful due to little government ownership and cooperation. The motivation to borrow money to address this important area did not come about until 1996 with the promise of an adjustment loan. But even with a substantial amount on the table, according to World Bank officials, progress on social reform has been slow, albeit steady.

- Financial support provides limited leverage. World Bank officials we spoke with generally agree that money itself is not the most important factor in assisting a transition process. For instance, while financial support was an important incentive to move along on reforms in the coal sector and on social protection, it did not seem to make much of a difference on effecting reforms under the third structural adjustment loan, which was stalled last year after the first disbursement. Nonetheless, as was the case with the first rehabilitation loan, World Bank officials told us that financial assistance helps open doors. For example, in the second half of the 1990s, the World Bank put more money on the table directly to support core ministries such as the ministries of finance and economy. A senior World Bank official said this was one of the factors that facilitated a closer relationship with these ministries. Moreover, the financial investment lends credibility to the Bank's efforts and advice. For example, the intensive dialogue that took place to turn around the Russian portfolio in 1999 made it clear that the World Bank was serious about not making disbursements until project performance improved. Furthermore, in some cases, World Bank financing attracts additional financing from other donors and lending institutions, thereby increasing the Bank's leverage. For example, on the second coal sector restructuring adjustment loan, the Japan Bank for International Cooperation provided $800 million in cofinancing, thus having the effect of doubling the World Bank loan.

- Long-term World Bank involvement will be necessary. World Bank officials now acknowledge that expectations for rapid results were unrealistic and that its long-term involvement will be necessary. According to a World Bank assessment, the devastating impact the 1998 financial crisis had on Russia showed that not enough progress had been made in addressing major structural problems such as the issue of corruption, the lack of fiscal and financial discipline, and the deterioration of the social safety net. Further progress in building institutional capacities also needs to be made, and addressing these and other systemic weaknesses will take years. As a result, the World Bank will need to plan on more modest levels of financial support in the years ahead in order to ensure that Russia remains well within its lending ceiling.[19]
- Finally, a number of people we met with suggested that what needs to happen is a "generational change." A former senior World Bank official stated that transformation must go beyond the transfer of knowledge, technical know-how, and institutional development—it will require Russians believing and behaving entirely differently than they have in the past. Not only must old systems of control be abolished, but also new institutions must be built and the legal and regulatory frameworks established—all of which take time.
- World Bank lending needs to be more selective. The latest country assistance strategy for Russia emphasizes the need to be more selective in the programs that the World Bank supports in the near future, particularly in light of an anticipated reduction in new lending. This means focusing on projects that seek to achieve the Bank's overall objectives—structural reform, social protection, and institution building. For example, in an effort to develop a positive investment climate, the strategy calls for reforms in financial management and administration to improve the performance of public institutions such as the ministries of finance and taxation. The U.S. Executive Director has also advocated public sector reform as a way to fight corruption— viewed by many as a symptom of weak institutions and lack of transparency—and for an independent judiciary and the rule of law.

The World Bank has drawn a number of lessons learned from its experience in working with the regions. The 1999 country assistance strategy states that support for regional projects may have been premature for several reasons:

- Implementation capacity, especially fiscal management, is still weak.
- Results are localized and do not address systemic problems.
- Supervision of projects is resource intensive and costly.

---

[19] The lending ceiling is determined by the Executive Board annually. For the fiscal year that ended June 30, 2000, the limit was set at $13.5 billion for any single country. The limit for this fiscal year, which ends June 30, 2001, remains the same.

We note that a number of the local government officials in Novgorod and Samara—the two regions we visited—expressed interest in increased lending from the World Bank despite their complaints about the lengthy delays they experienced in implementing Bank-financed projects. Regarding adjustment loans, the World Bank has learned that

- those loans need to be disbursed in association with significant structural reform;
- loan conditions should be based not on interim steps but on outcomes, so that disbursements, for instance, would be based on legislation enacted by, rather than simply submitted to, the Duma; and
- multiple disbursements for loans seem to be effective in certain situations, such as in the second coal sector adjustment loan, where splitting the loan into "bite-size chunks" enabled the World Bank to be engaged in the sector longer and resulted in better compliance.

Several Russian officials we met with expressed a preference for sector-specific adjustment loans over structural adjustment loans. They felt that the sector adjustment loans are more focused and, as such, they are easier to manage and implement, and the results are more measurable.

Appendix III

European Bank for Reconstruction and Development Programs in Russia

Background

In May 1990, representatives from 40 countries, including the United States and most European nations, signed an agreement creating the European Bank for Reconstruction and Development.[1] When the EBRD began its operations in April 1991, it was specifically tasked with assisting formerly communist nations with their transition to market economies, with a particular focus on promoting the development of the private sector. In developing strategies, the EBRD must balance several competing aspects of its mandate. The charter requires the EBRD to devote at least 60 percent of its total portfolio to financing private sector projects and forbids concessional (below market interest rate) loans or grants. The EBRD must also follow sound banking principles in its investment decisions, and achieve profitability. At the same time, the EBRD must be willing to take risks and make sure its projects further the recipient country's transition efforts. The EBRD frequently works in concert with private sector investors and lenders to help share the costs of projects but ensure that its efforts do not crowd private sources of financing out of the market.

Overall Objectives and Initial Assumptions

At the broadest level, the EBRD is supposed to "foster the transition towards open market-oriented economies and to promote private and entrepreneurial initiative in...countries committed to and applying the principles of multiparty democracy, pluralism and market economics." The EBRD's focus on the private sector is supposed to complement the International Monetary Fund's work on macroeconomic stabilization and the World Bank's sectoral work.

---

[1] The United States has 10.3 percent of the voting share at the EBRD. Institutions and member countries of the European Union have a combined voting share of 58.0 percent

Throughout its operations in Russia, the EBRD's strategy has been guided by a relatively stable set of assumptions:

- The ability to achieve reform depends on the desire of the Russians to change. Since most of the EBRD's financing in Russia goes to the private sector, the EBRD relies heavily on the recipient's government to establish and enforce the proper legislation necessary for an enabling environment. It must also rely on the recipients of its financing to make promised changes.
- The EBRD recognized that it could not expect to have a major influence on national-level reform efforts. While its resources can play a significant role for an individual project or company, they are small relative to the size of Russia and its transition needs. Consequently, assistance needs to be focused on particular sectors or regions to ensure transition impact beyond the individual project.
- Since 1993, the EBRD has assumed that it will have greater impact working directly with the private sector in reform-minded regions. Like other donors, the EBRD has targeted its work in a number of regions.
- The EBRD has also assumed that it can influence the process of institution building in Russia by encouraging or requiring recipients to meet western financial standards. Indeed, institution building has been an explicit goal of its strategy since 1992. EBRD financing can directly support institution building or provide an inducement to convince existing institutions to change.

THE EBRD'S INSTRUMENTS

The EBRD has primarily relied on four instruments to achieve its goals in Russia: direct project lending, equity investments, financing through intermediaries, and technical cooperation funds.[2]

Project lending: The EBRD loans money to mainly private sector firms at market interest rates.[3] Although the terms can vary depending on the project, the EBRD typically requires repayment within 5-10 years. About three-quarters of the EBRD's total commitments for projects in Russia to date have been through loans. For example, in May 2000, the EBRD approved a $150 million loan to Lukoil, a large Russian oil company. Lukoil will use the funds for export-related payments, crude-oil production, and oil processing. As a condition for receiving EBRD financing, Lukoil agreed to increase its financial transparency, implement an initial public offering of its shares, and improve its environmental standards.

Equity investments: The EBRD also buys noncontrolling stakes in firms. Its charter generally prohibits the EBRD from taking a controlling interest, although in some cases the EBRD will work with other western investors to obtain a majority interest and thus have an important voice in how the firm is organized and run. The EBRD sees itself as a

---

[2] The EBRD has also provided a small number of guarantees for projects in Russia.
[3] Actual rates for private sector projects vary depending on the EBRD's assessment of project risk.

medium-term investor and generally plans to hold equity investments for 5-6 years before selling and hopefully turning a profit. For example, in July 1996, the EBRD approved a $30 million investment in the Russian Black Earth Regional Venture Fund. This fund invests in Russian companies in southwestern Russia to help them modernize and restructure their operations.

Financing through intermediaries: Many of the EBRD's lending and finance projects are implemented via Russian financial intermediaries. The EBRD believes this not only contributes to the primary goal of developing the private sector in Russia, but it also promotes the development of Russian financial institutions. Some of the EBRD's most well-known projects, such as the Russia Small Business Fund and Regional Venture Funds, are implemented on the ground by such intermediaries as contractors, private firms, and Russian financial institutions. For example, in July 1999, the EBRD invested $6 million in a bank in which it was the principal shareholder, reorganized it into a bank that finances micro- and small enterprises, then provided it a $30 million loan. Since then, the EBRD has used this bank to lend to small- and medium-sized enterprises through its Russia Small Business Fund.

Technical cooperation funds: The EBRD has provided a significant amount of technical assistance to Russia—nearly $300 million for 425 projects from 1991 to1999. Most of this assistance supports preparing projects and improving project implementation. About 95 percent of the EBRD's technical assistance efforts are financed through reimbursement by clients or grants from other donors, including the European Union's Technical Assistance for the Commonwealth of Independent States (TACIS) program. For example, in 1992, the EBRD approved a $7-million technical assistance program, financed entirely with funds from TACIS, to provide advice to the Russian government on the implementation of its mass privatization program.

The EBRD also pursues its objectives in Russia through methods not directly tied to specific projects. For example, recipients have to comply with EBRD requirements about transparency or corporate governance to receive funding, a tool the EBRD frequently uses to advance transition efforts. The EBRD also provides advice to government officials at the national and regional level. And since the financial crash of 1998, the EBRD has aggressively sought legal channels to obtain repayments from defaulting loan recipients. EBRD officials told us they believe this approach protects their interests, forces the Russian judicial system to operate, and sheds possibly unwelcome light on its activities if cases are not handled fairly.

FUNDING HISTORY FOR RUSSIA

Since 1991, the EBRD has approved $5.5 billion worth of projects for Russia, of which $4.4 billion were eventually signed.[4] Roughly half of the signed projects—$2.2

[4] After the EBRD's executive board approves financing for a project, EBRD staff negotiate the specific terms of the operation with the Russian recipient. When agreement is reached on these terms, the project is signed,

billion—has been disbursed, and about $600 million has been repaid as of May 2000. Most of the EBRD's projects with Russia were signed in the mid-1990s, with new activity falling off dramatically since the 1998 financial crisis (see fig. 21).

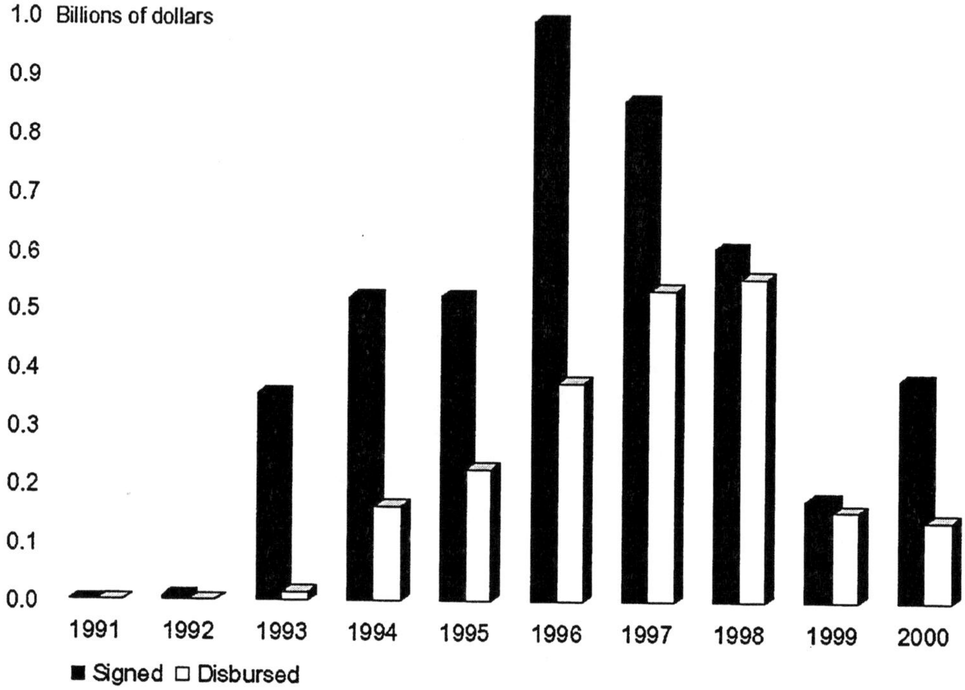

Figure 21: Annual EBRD Funding for Russia Projects, 1991-2000

Source: EBRD.

More than half of the EBRD's signed projects to date have been for the financial and energy sectors, with transportation and food production also getting significant amounts.[5] However, the EBRD has financed projects in over two dozen sectors across the Russian economy (see fig. 22).

---

and disbursements can begin. In some instances, the amount of financing changes between approval and signature. In other instances, approved projects are not signed.

[5] EBRD activities in the food sector primarily represent investments in and loans to firms that manufacture food or drink products.

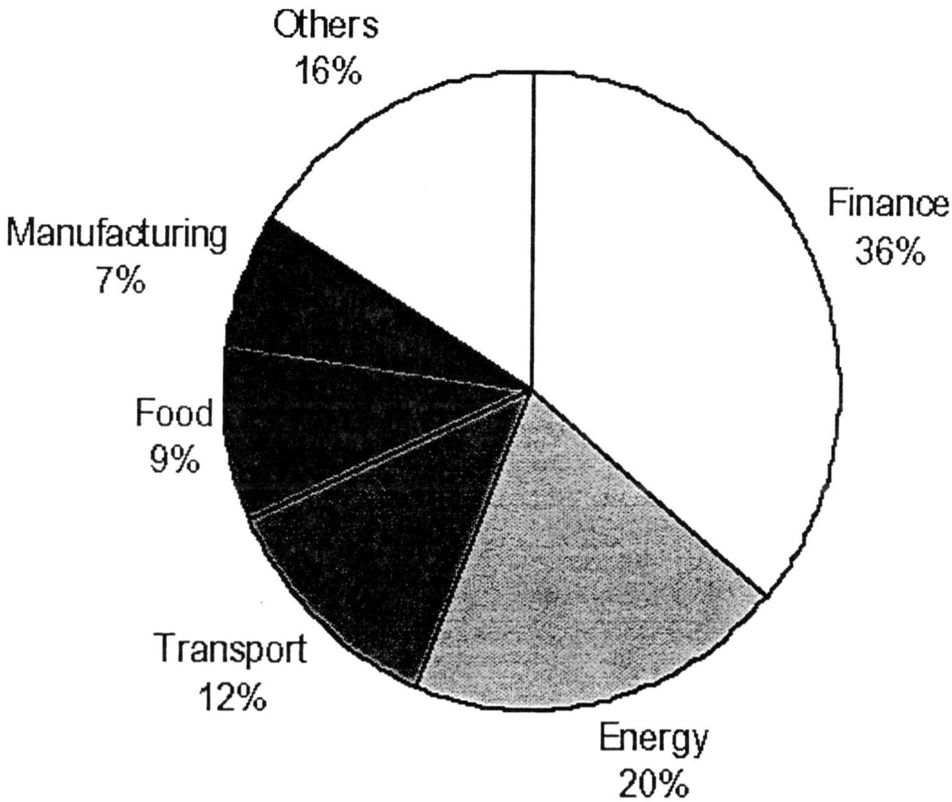

Figure 22: EBRD Lending and Equity Investment for Signed Projects by Sector in Russia, 1991-2000

Source: EBRD. Note: "Others" include mining, property, and public administration.

STRATEGY

The EBRD's strategy for providing assistance to Russia has changed over time. Its initial approach stressed engagement across several sectors, relying heavily on technical assistance due to the lack of viable projects. Later, the EBRD narrowed its primary focus to emphasize the financial sector, especially as it pertains to supporting small- and medium-sized enterprise development, and to provide targeted support for the restructuring efforts of large firms, especially in the oil and gas sectors.

Early EBRD Efforts for Russia Focused on Technical Assistance: 1991-93

When the EBRD began its operations in April 1991, the Soviet Union was one of its charter members. However, the charter allowed the EBRD to provide no more than $300 million worth of assistance to the Soviet Union over 4 years—an amount equal to the initial Soviet capital contribution.[6] As it turned out, there were very few viable business opportunities in Russia at that time, so the EBRD mainly provided technical assistance for training business people, supporting local privatization efforts in selected cities, and advising the government on drafting reform legislation. It also approved two small loans in late 1991. By the end of 1991, the EBRD had approved $17.5 million in financing and spent about $8.3 million on technical assistance for the Soviet Union.

After the formal dissolution of the Soviet Union in December 1991, Russia became a member of the EBRD in March 1992. The EBRD began operations in Russia facing significant challenges. The EBRD was a new organization starting programs in a new country in the midst of rapid and dramatic political and economic changes. With no road map, no historical precedents, and no institutional history or experience to fall back on, the EBRD found that its early plans lacked focus. For example, in 1992, the EBRD initially planned to spread its operations in Russia across 11 economic sectors, including privatization and enterprise promotion, financial sector development, military conversion, and agriculture, in an effort to support development of entrepreneurs and the legal, market, financial, and public infrastructures.

However, the EBRD's resources proved to be relatively small compared to these ambitious objectives. Much of the EBRD's early attention was focused on identifying potential projects, trying to find financing partners; and providing technical assistance, most significantly in the area of privatization. By the end of 1993, the EBRD had spent more than $68 million for 122 technical assistance projects, largely in the area of private sector development, and signed 7 loans and 3 equity investments worth $362 million, with about two-thirds of these funds going for the oil and gas sectors.

Program Development and Growth: July 1993-early 1998

The EBRD had not been set up to provide technical assistance, and its own reports questioned the wisdom of devoting so much energy to this area. By late 1993, as it began to identify and invest in a growing number of projects, its overall approach to assistance to Russia changed. The EBRD shifted its emphasis from technical assistance, tried to narrow its focus to fewer sectors, and developed more realistic goals to avoid making promises to the Russians that could not be fulfilled.

The foundation for much of the EBRD's new approach in Russia was laid at the G-7 Tokyo Summit in July 1993. Coming into the meeting, the EBRD hoped to play a central role in Russia's ongoing privatization efforts, small- and medium-sized enterprise development, nuclear energy safety, and oil and gas sector support. Several of the EBRD's major programs for Russia were launched at the Tokyo Summit. For example, the EBRD felt it had a comparative advantage in finance and banking and attempted to

[6] The United States had resisted allowing the Soviet Union to join the EBRD, on the grounds that the Soviet Union was not part of Europe. However, the European countries believed it was important to include the Soviet Union, and their position prevailed. As a compromise, the United States insisted on including limitations on the amount of assistance the Soviet Union could receive from the EBRD.

directly shore up the Russian financial sector by providing advice and equipment through the Financial Institutions Development Project.[7] The EBRD also pursued the dual objectives of small- and medium-sized enterprise development and institution building in the banking sector in several projects, most notably the Russia Small Business Fund. Through this program, the EBRD provided funds to Russian banks, which then lent them to small- and medium-sized enterprises. According to EBRD, Treasury, and State Department officials, Russian banks learned how to lend to small businesses, small businesses learned how to organize their operations and pay loans, and the small- and medium-sized enterprise sector began to grow. The EBRD also provided financing for some larger firms such as Kamaz and GAZ (major Russian truck manufacturers) and Chernogoreft (oil production) to improve production and the company's environmental programs.

In addition, the EBRD made a conscious effort to cluster its projects in regions such as St. Petersburg, Vladivostok, and Samara that were more reform minded or more open to investment. In general, the EBRD believed it could have a better impact by supporting three good projects in one region than by spreading three good projects across three different regions. This approach required the EBRD to learn more about the various regions and led to greater deployment of resources and authority in the field. The use of financial intermediaries also increased over this period. Many of the EBRD's biggest programs in Russia, such as the Russia Small Business Fund, were actually implemented by Russian institutions. The EBRD viewed this as an inexpensive way to have greater impact at the smaller end of the economic scale. Almost as important was the belief that use of intermediaries also created opportunities for Russian institutions to learn how to operate and flourish in a market economy. This institution-building aspect of the program was central to the EBRD's strategy for having an impact on the transition to a market economy.

EBRD operations during this period were characterized by rapid growth. For example, the EBRD added 25 projects to its portfolio in Russia worth nearly $1 billion in 1996. At the same time, the growing reliance on financial intermediaries meant placing a lot of trust in Russian counterparts and relying on Russian institutions to implement the programs that were supposed to achieve the EBRD's overall objectives in Russia. By late 1997, the EBRD was the largest single foreign investor in Russia; had seats on the boards of several Russian enterprises and banks; and, through its various operations, had staff on the ground throughout Russia. The country strategy for 1997 noted that Russia had made important progress in the transition but continued to be dogged by persistent economic problems and a mixed record on political commitment to reform.

Financial Collapse and Recovery: mid-1998 to the present

By mid-1998, the EBRD realized that its rapidly growing portfolio in Russia could be threatened by the escalating financial trouble in Russia. In April 1998, Tokobank, a major

[7] The EBRD and the World Bank jointly implemented this project.

Russian bank in which the EBRD had taken a $32 million equity position in 1994, collapsed. In June 1998, the EBRD updated its Russia strategy due to the increasing financial and economic uncertainty there, calling for continued engagement, retaining the emphasis on institutional development, setting standards for business practices, attracting foreign and domestic investment, and engaging in policy dialogue.

Although the June 1998 EBRD strategy update noted the potential for a crisis, what happened 2 months later was much worse than the EBRD and other institutions had anticipated. The collapse in the value of the ruble made it more expensive for Russian firms and banks to repay dollar-denominated debt. A moratorium on foreign exchange payments by domestic banks led to defaults on foreign debt, and the Russian government's defaulting on domestic debt essentially ruined the domestic government securities market. The combination of these factors essentially destroyed the value of most of the assets on the balance sheets of Russian banks. Many of the EBRD's equity investments in Russian financial institutions became worthless, and the viability of several other projects was damaged. By the end of the year, the EBRD took provisions of over $600 million for loans and investments for the year, primarily for banking sector projects in Russia.[8] Some of the EBRD's Russian partners defaulted on loan repayments or stripped assets from institutions partially financed by the EBRD. In a few months, the overall state of the EBRD's portfolio in Russia and the region suffered as the Russian economy went into a tailspin. The EBRD responded to the collapse by evaluating the quality of its investments in the region, increasing provisions, restructuring its Russia portfolio, and almost entirely halting new operations in Russia. In the 6 months after the crash, the EBRD only signed three new projects for Russia, worth $15 million. According to EBRD officials, the lack of new projects in Russia during this period was due to (1) a decrease in demand for EBRD financing stemming from the depressed economic conditions in Russia and (2) a decision by the EBRD to halt new operations in the banking sector in Russia. The EBRD also tried to salvage the projects it could, and close out those that could not be saved. The EBRD immediately took advantage of its rights as a preferred creditor to protect most of its investments outside the financial sector.[9] This action allowed the EBRD eventually to salvage much of its investment outside the banking sector. Without these rights, the EBRD could have been in an even worse position.

By mid-1999, as the Russian economy began to stabilize, the EBRD started to cautiously reengage in Russia. The EBRD exercised greater scrutiny of potential Russian business partners. Guided by a May 1999 country strategy update, the EBRD noted that its role in Russia was now even more important, since the transition would take longer than initially envisioned. Its operations focused on portfolio management and selection of only the highest-quality projects, with efforts supporting the development of Russia's small- and medium-sized enterprise sector taking highest priority. In early 2000, the EBRD was positioning itself for a major return to the Russian market, pending the

---

[8] The EBRD's operating loss for 1998 was $293 million.

[9] This step enabled the EBRD to obtain an exemption from the Russian government's halting of foreign exchange payments.

outcome of presidential elections and potential change in the overall reform environment. The goals of the EBRD's core business in Russia reflected a continuation of earlier trends, with a growing focus on small- and medium-sized enterprise development, financial sector enhancement, infrastructure, targeted support for large firms, greater reliance on equity as an instrument, and active promotion of its lender and shareholder rights in an effort to combat corruption and promote sound business practices.

In recent months, the EBRD has restated its commitment to remain engaged in Russia and has announced several new projects there. During January-June 2000, the EBRD had approved about $300 million in new projects for Russia, or more than in all of 1999. In addition, senior EBRD officials have publicly stated that the EBRD could commit about $1 billion per year for Russia, in an effort to provide an inducement for reform and change by the Russians. At its annual meeting in May 2000, the EBRD board approved a medium-term plan to devote 30 percent of the Bank's portfolio to Russia, provided the Russian government establishes the proper reform framework and Russian enterprises adopt more transparent and fair business practices. A shift to 30 percent would represent a substantial increase from the current level of 22 percent.

However, EBRD officials noted the difficulties in identifying and securing deals within Russia. Because the EBRD generally seeks co-financing, it has to find viable Russian business partners and private sector co-investors willing to share the financing and risks with the EBRD. This has been difficult to do ever since the crash of 1998 and raises questions about the EBRD's ability to meet its 30-percent medium-term financing goal.

In addition, the EBRD's strategy toward Russia is part of a larger debate within the EBRD on the relative level of resources to devote to Central Europe versus the former Soviet Union. Investments in Central Europe to support countries like Poland and Hungary can help their efforts to meet EU standards for eventual membership in the EU. Investments in these countries may also be more profitable, since they are further along in the transition process. However, most Central European countries are capable of raising finances on the private capital markets, and some argue that EBRD resources should be shifted out of these countries and into the former Soviet Union where the greater transition challenges lie. This approach emphasizes the EBRD's mandate to support transition but entails greater risks and possibly lower profit. How the EBRD decides to balance these conflicting objectives will have important implications for its future strategy for Russia.

In October 2000, the EBRD publicly released its new country strategy for Russia. The EBRD plans to commit from $300 million to $1 billion per year for projects in Russia, depending on government actions to improve the investment climate. Future investments will be targeted to improve corporate sector governance and transparency, promote financial sector competition, rapidly build-up small business financing, and increase support for infrastructure. The EBRD also intends to:

- increase the share of equity and public sector projects in its Russia portfolio,
- develop long-term strategic partnerships with selected companies, and
- continue to aggressively defend its legal rights in Russian courts.

The EBRD plans to remain realistic about its ability to affect change within Russia. Although it will continue efforts to promote national level change through high-level policy dialogue and technical assistance, the EBRD's main focus will be on achieving change at the corporate level.

LESSONS LEARNED

According to the EBRD's 1999 Transition Report, which assesses the EBRD's experience with transition since 1989, countries that pursued rapid liberalization and sustained macroeconomic stabilization were able to lay the basis for economic reform and gradual institutional change. However, countries such as Russia that did not follow this path suffered slow and uneven progress and faced threats to economic stability from continued soft budget constraints. The report also found that corruption was a major impediment to transition in several countries, including Russia.

Additionally, the EBRD also has a formal, institutional "lessons learned" process. EBRD staff identify and enter lessons learned into a large database.[10] A summary of these lessons is presented annually in evaluation overview reports, with additional lessons noted in country strategies and individual evaluation reports. Based on our analysis of these lessons and our discussions with EBRD officials, the following lessons regarding the EBRD's experience in Russia have broad application.

- The ability to create and sustain transition in Russia depends on a demonstrated commitment to reform, sound macroeconomic conditions, transparent and consistent rule of law, and progress in furthering institutional reform.
- Sustainable transition requires strong grassroots support.
- Russia and the problems it faces are so large that EBRD cannot expect to have major, nationwide impact. The EBRD can play an important role in supporting transition by developing projects that can have important demonstration effects or by clustering projects in reform-minded regions to enhance the impact at the local level.
- Good, consistent monitoring of the project enhances impact, maintains important lines of communication, and builds trust.
- Projects with clearly defined objectives tend to be more successful than projects with broad, vague objectives.

---

[10] The EBRD does not currently allow access to this database, but plans to put an amended version on its website in 2001. Some of the main themes each year are presented in the Annual Evaluation Overview Report, which is distributed to the board but not the public. However, the EBRD's lessons from the 1998 financial crisis in Russia were publicly presented in its 1999 annual report.

Appendix IV

U.S. FREEDOM SUPPORT ACT PROGRAM IN RUSSIA

The United States began providing limited assistance to the Soviet Union in December 1990 to support the reform effort and then increased its aid after the Soviet Union dissolved in December 1991. U.S. assistance has taken many forms: the Cooperative Threat Reduction program, which provides aid to safeguard and dismantle nuclear weapons and other weapons of mass destruction; support for programs provided through international financial institutions; food aid provided by the U.S. Department of Agriculture; and programs authorized by the Freedom Support Act, implemented mainly by the U.S. Agency for International Development (USAID). In addition to these funding sources, many federal agencies have used funds from their regular appropriations to provide technical assistance and other types of aid to Russia. Figure 23 shows the budget[1] and spending patterns for the major U.S. programs with Russia since 1992.

The Freedom Support Act, enacted in October 1992, signaled a change in the character of U.S. aid to the former Soviet Union, from a period of ad hoc assistance, including agricultural commodity credit guarantees and food and medical aid, to a long-term development effort characterized by provision of technical assistance in a variety of sectors and by U.S. private sector investment support. Nearly half of all expenditures related to the Freedom Support Act for the former Soviet Union from 1992 through 1999, or $2.26 billion, went to programs with Russia.

[1] The Coordinator allocates funds appropriated for the former Soviet Union to each of the countries, creating country budgets.

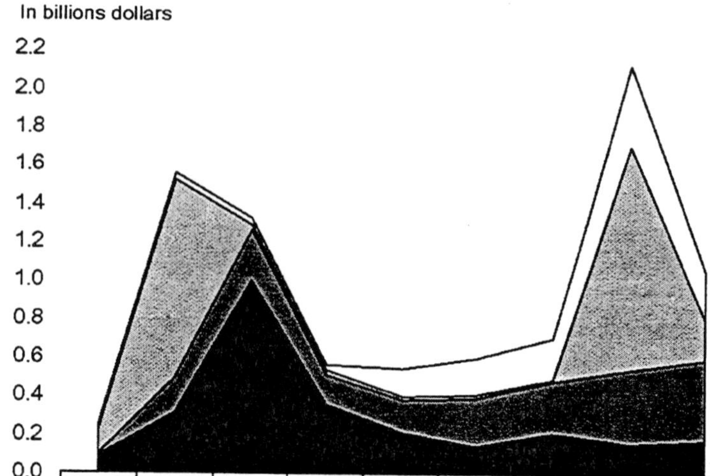

	1992	1993	1994	1995	1996	1997	1998	1999	2000
□ Other	0.02	0.04	0.03	0.02	0.14	0.19	0.22	0.42	0.25
▤ Agriculture	0.13	1.03	0.03	0.03	0.02	0.01	0.00	1.16	0.20
▦ CTR Nunn-Lugar DOD	0.01	0.17	0.26	0.15	0.17	0.25	0.28	0.39	0.43
■ Freedom Support Act	0.09	0.31	1.00	0.36	0.22	0.14	0.21	0.16	0.18

Fiscal year

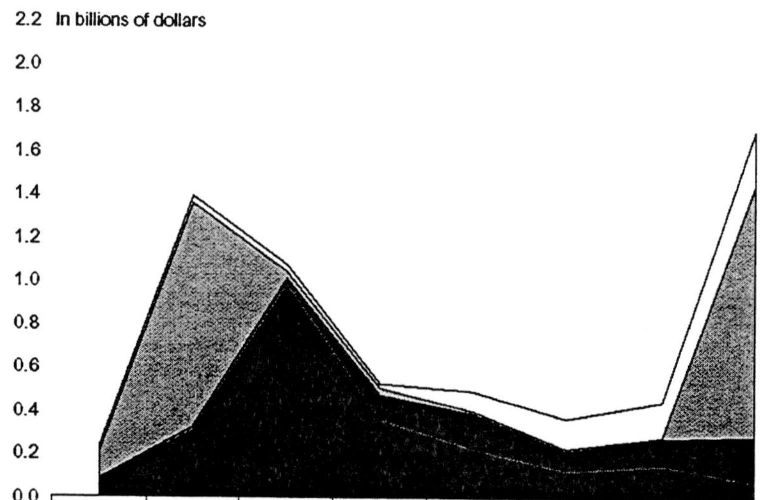

	1992	1993	1994	1995	1996	1997	1998	1999
□ Other	0.02	0.03	0.03	0.02	0.09	0.14	0.17	0.25
▤ Agriculture	0.13	1.03	0.03	0.03	0.02	0.01	0.00	1.16
■ CTR Nunn-Lugar DOD	0.00	0.02	0.04	0.12	0.17	0.09	0.13	0.21
■ Freedom Support Act	0.08	0.30	0.97	0.35	0.22	0.12	0.15	0.07

Fiscal year

Figure 23: Funding Levels for Major U.S. Programs With Russia Since 1992 (Budgeted and Expended, Respectively)

Legend:
CTR = Cooperative Threat Reduction;
DOD = U.S. Department of Defense
Source: U.S. Department of State and GAO analysis

The goal of the Freedom Support Act was to provide the expertise and support necessary to ensure Russia's continued progress on economic and political reforms. The Freedom Support Act authorized bilateral economic assistance activities in at least 13 sectors, including humanitarian needs, educational television, administration of justice, and civilian nuclear reactor safety. Congress stated that technical and managerial assistance should be provided on a long term, on-site basis, supplying practical management and other problem-solving advice, and encouraged assistance to be provided through nongovernmental organizations, enterprise funds to invest in the Russian economy, and cooperative development and research projects.

The Freedom Support Act also established in law the Coordinator of Assistance to the former Soviet Union. The Coordinator was a State Department official, answering ultimately to the Secretary of State. The State Department's involvement in all assistance to the former Soviet Union demonstrates the political sensitivity of the program. The Coordinator was to (1) design an overall assistance and economic strategy for the former Soviet Union; (2) ensure program and policy coordination among U.S. agencies and foreign governments and international organizations; (3) ensure proper management, implementation, and oversight by U.S. agencies; and (4) publish an annual report on U.S. assistance for the former Soviet Union. The effect of this broad assistance program was to allow the President and his Assistance Coordinator wide latitude to design the U.S. assistance strategy. USAID became the primary implementor of Freedom Support Act assistance.

OBJECTIVES AND INITIAL ASSUMPTIONS

Since 1992, the United States has pursued three objectives for assistance to Russia through the Freedom Support Act:

- The first objective was to foster the emergence of a competitive, efficient, market-oriented economy in which the majority of economic resources were privately owned and managed, so that economic decisions were based primarily on individual choice.
- The second objective was to foster transparent, open, and accountable governance; the empowerment of citizens, working through their civic and economic organizations; and democratic political processes that ensure broad-based participation in political and economic life and respect for human rights and fundamental freedoms.
- A third objective was to foster redefined public and private sector roles in the management of humanitarian, health, and related social services fundamental to a successful transition to stable democracy and a market-based economy.[2]

[2] A fourth objective, related to Cooperative Threat Reduction funding rather than Freedom Support Act funding, was to accelerate demilitarization and promote responsible security policies. This objective became

The relative priority[3] of the objectives has varied over the years. In the earliest years from 1991[4] through 1992, the third objective, providing "humanitarian assistance," was the priority. As the technical assistance program developed from 1993 through 1995, the market reform objective assumed the priority. With the development of the Coordinator's new "Partnership for Freedom" approach (for more information, see later paragraphs), the democratic reform objective has been emphasized since 1996. During fiscal year 1995, as a response to U.S. budget cuts, the humanitarian assistance objective was dropped outright, only to be reinstated as budgets increased in the late 1990s.

The U.S. program was built on a number of initial assumptions about how Russia might make the transition to a market economy and the role foreign assistance could play in that transition. Some assumptions identified by State and USAID included the following:

- Russia was wealthy in natural resources but misdeveloped. Russia had a generally healthy, educated, and productive populace, a significant industrial base, and a potentially strong agricultural base. Russia was misdeveloped, especially in respect to many institutions essential for a market economy and democratic politics. The challenge was not to develop basic human and physical infrastructure but to assist Russia in redirecting resources to support open and participatory political and economic systems.
- Assistance had to happen quickly. If assistance were not provided quickly, the Russian state might revert to Communism. This assumption drove the United States to expend assistance funds as quickly as possible, sometimes with minimal concern about the effectiveness of the activity.
- Russians had to want change. Just as no outside agency, institution, or country could substitute for or replace Russian reformers themselves, so no one country or agency by itself could shoulder the task of encouraging Russian reform at the margin. Only Russians would be able to create the political will to do what they must.
- Protracted support was not needed. Russia was a well-endowed country, fully capable of remaking itself into a full, democratic, prosperous partner in the international community, with the help of strategically targeted support during the critical period of economic and political transition. U.S. programs would be of limited duration.
- Aid should follow reform. Former Soviet Union states and regions within countries would receive aid based on their progress toward democratic and economic reform.

---

a regular part of the Coordinator's reports in April 1996, reporting on fiscal year 1995. The report consistently presents data about the Cooperative Threat Reduction program.

3 These objectives were routinely listed in early Coordinator's reports without ordinal numbers beside them.

4 Before the collapse of the Soviet Union, the United States had provided humanitarian assistance in the form of pharmaceuticals and medical supplies worth $39.1 million under the President's Medical Initiative. This assistance precedes the Freedom Support Act and the Coordinator's reports, which first express the objectives.

- Projects should be generally regional and managed from Washington. Organizing projects across the former Soviet Union would allow the United States to respond quickly to the changing circumstances in the former Soviet Union states and keep design and contracting actions to a manageable number. Achieving U.S. assistance objectives and developing assistance priorities was to be most effectively accomplished through a Washington-based Coordinator responsible for overseeing policy development and implementation of the assistance effort. The whole assistance program was to be managed from Washington, with a small number of USAID officials in the former Soviet Union.

THE FREEDOM SUPPORT ACT'S INSTRUMENTS

U.S. Freedom Support Act assistance program has used the following instruments from the beginning of the program to the present.

- Technical assistance has been provided by U.S. contractors and agencies, primarily USAID, to Russia to convey know-how.
- Exchanges run by the U.S. Information Agency, USAID, and other agencies bring Russians to the United States for training and exposure to the U.S. style of democracy and capitalism and the institutions that underlie them, thus supporting the transition to free market economies and democratic society. The exchanges, which could help create people-to- people linkages, run the gamut from secondary school students to Russian parliamentarians. Many U.S. citizens are also sent to Russia.
- Commodity import programs, such as the Russia Energy and Environmental Commodity Import Program, have introduced U.S.- designed equipment to Russia. The purpose of this particular program was to improve the efficiency of energy use and improve environmental quality, primarily in the energy sector.
- Enterprise funds, primarily The U.S. Russia Investment Fund or TUSRIF, also have been used to make equity investments in and provide loans and technical assistance to Russian businesses. Most of these investments have been in small- and medium-sized businesses.
- Trade and investment programs have been established through the Overseas Private Investment Corporation, the Department of Commerce, the Trade Development Agency, and the U.S. Export-Import Bank. The Freedom Support Act authorized supplementing these agencies' regular appropriations to pay for programs of technical assistance, feasibility studies, and orientation visits. The act also paid for programs fostering long-term commercial ties between Russia and the United States to help American companies defray the costs of hosting Russian managers and scientists for hands-on training. These programs are viewed as assistance. On the other hand, to the extent that these agencies'

programs have funded export credits or insurance, they are not usually considered assistance.

- Programs providing small grants have been used to promote democracy and market reform. The Eurasia Foundation is a prime example of a provider of small grants. The Eurasia Foundation is a privately managed grant-making organization, originally funded by USAID and dedicated to funding programs that build democratic and free market institutions in Russia.

FUNDING HISTORY FOR RUSSIA

From fiscal year 1992 through 2000, the United States budgeted $2.68 billion for Freedom Support Act programs in Russia.[5] From fiscal year 1992 through 1999, the United States expended $2.26 billion in programs authorized by the Freedom Support Act in Russia, which comprise about 36 percent of the U.S. assistance expenditures. USAID was responsible for spending almost 75 percent of the funds for programs authorized under the Freedom Support Act. Figure 24 shows how funds for programs authorized under the Freedom Support Act were budgeted among the primary U.S. objectives.

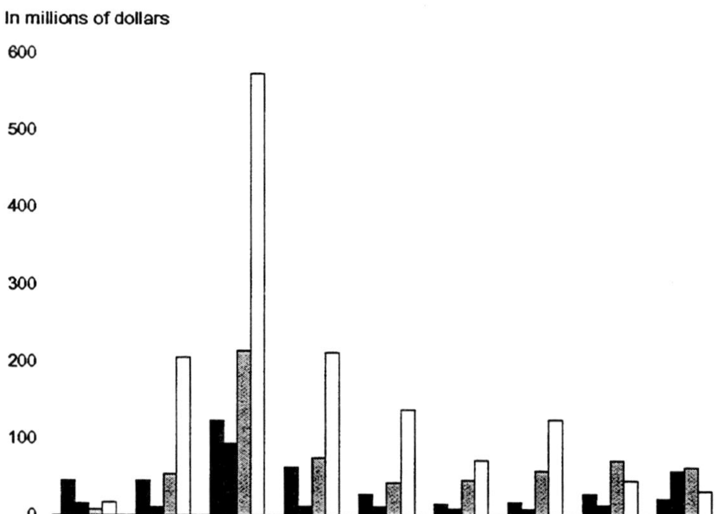

	1992	1993	1994	1995	1996	1997	1998	1999	2000
■ Address Urgent Human Needs Related to Transition	$44.86	$45.41	$123.32	$62.58	$27.84	$15.76	$18.10	$28.80	$23.32
■ Nonproliferation/ Security Related Items	$16.14	$10.25	$92.28	$11.50	$12.00	$9.50	$9.05	$15.45	$58.35
▨ Promote Democracy and Rule of Law	$8.05	$52.86	$213.33	$74.00	$42.40	$46.56	$57.48	$72.44	$64.06
□ Promote Market Reform	$17.58	$205.09	$572.30	$210.83	$136.66	$72.23	$125.69	$46.83	$32.53

Figure 24: Funds Budgeted for Freedom Support Act Assistance to Russia, Fiscal Years 1992-2000 (in $millions)

Source: U.S. Department of State and GAO analysis.

[5] The Coordinator allocates the appropriation for assistance to the former Soviet Union among the countries, creating country budgets.

STRATEGY

Humanitarian Assistance Priority: 1991-1992

Prior to the passage of the Freedom Support Act, there were several projects in process that paralleled the objectives in the Freedom Support Act. During the early years of U.S. assistance to Russia, there was no written U.S. strategy nor specific authorizing legislation to guide the program.[6] In fact, according to officials, the State Department prohibited USAID from developing country strategies or country budgets because it wanted to develop a general approach for assistance to the entire region of the former Soviet Union. Therefore, to determine the strategy for 1991 and 1992, we relied on the Coordinator's early annual reports and our previous work (see Related GAO Products section). The United States' general approach assumed that the needs of the former Soviet Union states were similar and that the same project could be implemented across several countries.

Although some of the assistance that went to Russia in the early 1990s financed projects to support economic and democratic reforms, the main focus was on humanitarian assistance (see fig. 24 for specific sums). The Departments of State and Defense collaborated on a large-scale airlift of medical, food, and other supplies[7] to needy populations throughout Russia, called Operation PROVIDE HOPE. The economic and democratic assistance from this period was generally spread across several sectors[8] in a deliberate effort to try different approaches and find out which ones were most successful.[9]

The emphasis across the entire program was on speedy delivery and limiting the cost visible in the U.S. budget. The State Department emphasized quick-impact projects in an effort to show that the United States was engaged in and making an effort to help with the reform process. At the same time, domestic budgetary and economic problems in the United States created pressure to find ways to deliver assistance without having to seek additional appropriations. Thus, Operation PROVIDE HOPE shipped surplus commodities from the Defense Department as well as commodities from private donors. The initial economic and democratic assistance programs were financed from the transfer of U.S. economic support funds initially designated for Pakistan and the Philippines.

---

[6] The Freedom Support Act was signed into law in October 1992.

[7] These supplies were a combination of Department of Defense surplus items and donations from private organizations. From fiscal year 1992 through 1999, the estimated value of the items was $602 million. The Freedom Support Act paid for the transportation costs, which were $59 million.

[8] In a December 1992 report, Former Soviet Union: Assistance by the United States and Other Donors (GAO/NSIAD-93-101), we reported that the experience gained in Central and Eastern Europe would help shape the aid program in the former Soviet Union, according to U.S. officials. U.S. officials cited lessons they learned and intended to apply, including that aid should be concentrated in a few priority areas to prevent a proliferation of projects.

[9] USAID's grant assistance to help with the implementation of mass privatization is an exception. In that instance, the United States devoted relatively significant resources in a deliberate effort to influence a major aspect of the reform process.

The nature and approach for the assistance were greatly influenced by initial assumptions and the domestic political environment in Washington. For example, part of the rationale for running the program from Washington and not developing country strategies stemmed from efforts to limit the numbers of State Department new embassies and USAID new missions in the former Soviet Union and the accompanying costs. This pressure, in turn, arose from the administration's desire to reduce the deficit and combat the recession underway in the United States during the early 1990s. In the earliest years of the program, this may have made sense because assistance officials generally knew little about how the Soviet economy and the economies of the former Soviet Union states worked. However, according to U.S. officials, the policy of not having country-specific budgets actually undermined Washington management and control of the assistance program. Project managers, implementing work in one sector across several countries could leave a given country out of the project by committing all funds to projects in other countries. This limited the ability of officials at the Coordinator's office to control the program.

Market Reform Priority: 1993-95

The approach to providing assistance to Russia and the other former Soviet Union states evolved with the change of administrations in early 1993. Although humanitarian assistance continued, the primary emphasis was now on working with the Russian Federation government to develop and implement national reforms. Using the authority provided by the Freedom Support Act, the new U.S. administration sought to increase dramatically the size of the U.S. program in an effort to increase its impact on the reform process in Russia. The hope was that U.S. help in key areas would jumpstart the reform process and assist in bringing about the numerous structural changes needed in Russia for a democratic, market-based economy. For example, large contracts were created to assist Russians with privatization, and capital markets development. By September 1993, 8 U.S. firms were working in these areas under contracts worth up to $60 million.

The United States developed the overall approach for these programs in preparing for two major international summits in mid-1993. At the April Vancouver summit meeting with Russian President Yeltsin, President Clinton announced a $1.6-billion bilateral package of humanitarian and technical assistance for Russia. Components of the package had been announced before and required no new appropriations. These programs were designed to be implemented very quickly to ensure that the U.S. bilateral program was having tangible effects for the Russian population to see.

At the annual summit of the world's seven largest industrial economies (the G-7) in Tokyo in July 1993, the leaders of the G-7 countries approved a plan to extend an additional $3 billion in financial assistance to Russia. The U.S. portion totaled $1.5 billion for Russia in addition to the amounts pledged previously at Vancouver and consisted of private sector development funds, including grants; trade and investment money, including commodity import programs; democracy initiatives; funds to support troop withdrawal from the Baltics; an energy and environment program; and humanitarian assistance.

In September 1993, Congress appropriated the money necessary to implement these programs, approving over $2.5 billion in the fiscal year 1993 supplemental fiscal year 1994 appropriation for assistance to Russia and the remaining former Soviet Union states.

We have reported about the complex iterative interagency process involved in developing these packages.[10] Several groups, whose membership included many different U.S. agencies convened by the National Security Council, met to develop programs for Russia and the remaining former Soviet Union states. These programs focused on specific sectors such as Agricultural Technical Assistance, Anti-crime, Democracy, Energy, Environment, Enterprise Fund, Financial Sector, Food Aid, Law Enforcement, Rule of Law, Trade and Investment, and Russian Officer Housing and Retraining. Several officials described the challenges of making a coherent program with so many agencies. Although the general thrust of the program had shifted to emphasize economic reform, it maintained the broad and disparate nature of the early 1990s. By 1994, a wide variety of U.S. departments and agencies were implementing programs in Russia, including the Departments of Commerce and Energy, as well as the U.S. Information Agency and the Environmental Protection Agency. In December 1995, we reported that 23 departments and independent agencies were implementing over 200 programs in the former Soviet Union —including 180 in Russia. The sheer magnitude of the U.S. bilateral program made coordination difficult and complicated efforts to focus U.S. efforts in a few key areas.

In 1993 and 1994, the U.S. program still stressed the need for quick implementation due to pressure from Congress and the White House. However, the rationale for speed changed. In the early 1990s, U.S. officials believed that rapid humanitarian assistance could stave off social unrest and show the Russia public the benefits of the new economic system. In the mid-1990s, the desire for rapid assistance in market reforms was driven by the belief that rapid reform would improve reform results and decrease hardship for the population in the long run.

By mid-1993 the United States moved away from having a single program for all the former Soviet Union. In late-1993, the Coordinator began writing the country strategies that were published in 1994, with the first country strategy being completed for Russia. Country budgets for assistance were also developed, and program design and management moved more to the local USAID mission and U.S. embassy. The Coordinator told us that, because of the Russia program's sensitivity, it would always receive more scrutiny than other country programs.

As State and the other agencies implemented the emphasis on market reform throughout 1994 and 1995, congressional support began to wane. After budgeting $1.0 billion for Russia for programs authorized under the Freedom Support Act in 1994, Congress cut funding to $359 million for 1995 and $219 million for 1996. These dramatic funding reductions were driven by two main factors. First, the large

[10] See Former Soviet Union: U.S. Bilateral Program Lacks Effective Coordination (GAO/NSIAD-95-10, February 7, 1995).

appropriation for Russia in 1993 was presented by the administration to be an exceptional, onetime event to support what was likely to be a relatively short transition period. Indeed, the 1995 U.S. strategy for Russia supported this idea by stating that there would be no need for new funding for assistance to Russia after 1998. Second, Congress began to raise bipartisan concerns about the effectiveness of assistance to Russia and started earmarking significant portions of the Freedom Support Act program's appropriations for other former Soviet Union states, most notably Ukraine. Officials told us that the decrease in funding to Russia stemmed from a desire to do more in other parts of the former Soviet Union and not necessarily to do less for Russia.

Democratic Reform Priority: 1996 to Present

The significant decreases in U.S. funding, heightened concerns about the program's effectiveness, and a growing sense of unease about the state of transition in Russia combined to bring about the next shift in U.S. strategy. Faced with these challenges, in early 1996 the Coordinator began to reevaluate the U.S. program for Russia. He found many problems affecting project effectiveness, which were published in the annual report.

- Since a large amount of funding was appropriated early in the process, the rate at which a project was able to expend its funds became an important criterion in the initial rush to move money out the door, in some cases sacrificing cost-effectiveness. Under political pressure to expend as much money as possible, the Coordinator's office and the implementing agencies could not take time to figure out what projects worked. Contracts were let with objectives so large and vague that the money would always be spent.
- During the first several years of providing assistance to Russia, the desire to start up programs as quickly as possible, in combination with the need to ensure strict control over program implementation, resulted in a heavy reliance on large contracts for program implementation. For example, as we reported, under USAID's cooperative agreement with the Harvard Institute for International Development, the Institute oversaw the work of contractors involved with Russian privatization with minimal oversight from USAID.[11] According to the

[11] In Foreign Assistance: Harvard Institute for International Development's Work in Russia and Ukraine (GAO/NSIAD-97-27), we reported:

The Harvard Institute for International Development conducted this project with minimal oversight from USAID. USAID did not always enforce the reporting requirements contained in the cooperative agreement, did not set measurable goals, and was not aware of decisions HIID was making that could have resulted in added cost to the government or significantly affected U.S. strategy. In addition to assistance provided to Russia directly by HIID, HIID also helped USAID to manage and oversee contractors and consulting firms. The U.S. contractors were paid by USAID, not HIID. The total value of USAID'S obligations for 1992- 96 for the Russian privatization program as of May 10, 1996, amounted to about $325 million, including approximately $40 million for HIID.

Coordinator, the United States had to move away from primary reliance on the large-contract mechanism.

- The difficult and rapidly changing environment in Russia, as well as the need for outside expertise, led to the predominant use of U.S., rather than Russian contractors in the early years of the program. The Coordinator concluded that the United States also had to make greater use of alternatives to U.S. contractors, such as local Russian nongovernmental organizations and experts.

As a result of the Coordinator's review, State, USAID, and other agencies began to close down projects considered to be less effective or less important to the overall effort, including efforts in (1) agriculture, (2) energy reform, and (3) housing. Several USAID and State officials told us that the dramatic cuts in funding for Russia forced them to prioritize stringently their assistance efforts and limit strictly the scope of assistance.

As Figure 24 shows, the United States began shifting funds away from the market reform objective and toward promoting democracy in fiscal year 1996. Since 1995, budgets for promoting market reform have generally dropped from a high of $572.3 million in fiscal year 1994 to $46.83 million in fiscal year 1999. For promoting democracy, the trendline since 1996 rose steadily, with the exception of a $12 million decrease in 2000. The funding for Promoting Democracy surpassed the funding for Promoting Market Reform in 1999 by $24 million.

The Coordinator's review also led to a significant shift in U.S. strategy. In mid-1996, the Coordinator formulated a new U.S. approach, called the "Partnership for Freedom." Assistance to the Russian federal government would diminish as projects at the national level ended, and new funding would focus mainly on grassroots efforts at the regional, local, or individual level. Implementation of the new approach began in fiscal year 1997 and has continued to the present. The restructuring focused U.S. assistance efforts on promoting (1) investment-led economic growth; (2) people-to-people linkages, bringing citizens of Russia and the U.S. together;[12] and (3) the development of civil society. In Russia, according to the Coordinator, technical assistance provided by the United States and other donors had played an important role in helping to begin building the basic institutional building blocks for developing a market economy and a democratic government. Nonetheless, implementation of many institutional reforms was blocked in the Russian federal government. Under the new approach, the United States would remain involved to support the development of small- and medium-sized enterprises and civil society. The United States also place a greater emphasis on partnerships between U.S. and Russian universities, hospitals, nongovernmental organizations, cities, and business and professional associations as well as exchanges between U.S. and Russian students, professionals, and entrepreneurs. The purpose of this grassroots effort was to demonstrate to Russians the value of reform and the values of a democratic society.

[12] In fiscal year 1997, people-to-people linkages included low-cost, high-impact activities such as community-based exchanges and training, and U.S.-NIS institutional partnerships which were designed to be increasingly self-sufficient and ultimately self-sustaining.

Connecting Russians with the world beyond their borders is supposed to encourage pressure for reform from below.

In addition, the recipients of U.S. assistance shifted from organizations working largely at the federal level to organizations in regions that demonstrated more reform-minded policies. Under this aspect of the program, known as the Regional Initiative, the United States targeted its assistance towards three Russian regions— Novgorod, Samara, and the Russian Far East[13]— whose local governments were deemed to be among the most reform minded and hospitable to investment. Moving to the regions was part of the approach to increase the bottom-up pressure from Russian citizens for reform in Russia. Supporting the development of nongovernmental organizations, financing public access Internet locations, and helping independent media were intended to bolster the development of a pluralistic democracy. Similarly, the United States hoped that providing advice to businesses, training in international accounting standards, and microlending opportunities would bolster the development of a vibrant small- and medium-sized enterprise sector that, in the long term, would grow large enough to counteract the influence of large enterprises controlled by the "oligarchs."

These shifts involved rejecting a number of old assumptions. First, the Coordinator recognized that the transition process in Russia would extend over generations and that U.S. assistance in these efforts would last beyond fiscal year 1998, which was the initial end date in the original 1994 Russia strategy. As a result of the changed assumption, many U.S. programs, such as Junior Achievement programs or exchanges for young Russian leaders, became rooted in "investing in the future." Second, the U.S. embassy and USAID mission in Russia played an increasing role as more U.S. assistance was targeted for specific regions within Russia. Finally, U.S. assumptions about what its assistance could accomplish were scaled back. The earlier emphasis on impacting national-level reforms shifted to hope that creating "success stories" at the local or regional level would spread, over time, throughout Russia.

The election of President Vladimir Putin in 2000 and the renewed possibility of reform driven at the federation level presented the United States with a quandary. So much of the U.S. assistance funding was committed to the Partnership for Freedom and the Regional Initiative that little was available to move back to the federation level to encourage reforms there. The Coordinator told us that the United States will continue to emphasize work at the grassroots level away from Moscow. Such assistance corresponds with the U.S. long-term perspective in Russia and with U.S. political realities. According to the Coordinator, if the Russian government makes specific requests for assistance, the U.S. government will consider responding positively if (1) a significant opportunity exists to advance reform; (2) the U.S. government has a comparative advantage in providing assistance in the requested sector; and (3) the Russian government is judged not to have sufficient resources to purchase assistance from private sources or the assistance requested is not available from private sources. If a large number of requests is received, the Coordinator may have to consider reallocating current budgets, or, in an extraordinary case, asking Congress for additional funds. U.S. officials expect to

[13] The Tomsk region joined the Regional Initiative in 2000.

maintain some bilateral engagement in support of economic and democratic reforms in Russia over the long haul, believing that needed changes in Russia will require generations.

LESSONS LEARNED

U.S. agencies implementing assistance in Russia learned many lessons about assisting the transition to a market democracy. In general, the magnitude of change in Russia posed challenges greater than expected. The very difficult operating environment limited the progress of the program. The following are key lessons learned based on our review of U.S. documents and discussions with State Department and USAID officials.

- The Russian economy did not perform as predicted. According to U.S. officials, incomplete implementation of the reforms contributed to the failure to perform as predicted. Stabilization, liberalization, and privatization were supposed to transform centralized economic systems into competitive market economies. Economic reform was supposed to lead to growth, which would generate the money to pay for social programs. However, the hardships resulting from incomplete transition, economic stagnation, and collapsing social services, created greater resistance to reform.
- A lack of political will and consensus slowed the implementation of the transition. The governing elite in Russia, supporting the transition, was supposed to provide leadership for reform, and a growing middle class was to provide grassroots support for economic reforms, making them sustainable. However, the Russian transition has not spawned a growing middle class. Russian Federation officials were not committed to specific transition policies, despite professed official statements to the contrary. Because the United States believed that the "ideas" of reform were so powerful, the United States underestimated the political dynamics in Russian society, particularly the struggle between reformers and entrenched power center, including the oligarchs.
- Lack of consensus in Russia about what kind of society was ultimately desired resulted in fundamental disagreements about the institutional arrangements needed for transition. Where entrenched interests dominate the Russian national level, leadership for reform may need to come from the grassroots level (for example, business associations, nongovernmental organizations, community organizations, and local government). Because the next generation will provide tomorrow's leaders, it is in this generation that the United States must seek a reform orientation to deepen and consolidate the transition. Building the political will for reform after so many problems is a more difficult task now than it was in 1992 and must be viewed as a longer-term process.
- Russian commitment to assistance projects is vital. Russia must be ready for and open to the type of change that the assistance activities are designed to promote,

and there must be willing private and public sector officials who can be full partners in reform. By requiring Russian partners to share program costs, the United States can accomplish two objectives: (1) reduce the costs of U.S. programs and (2) ensure that the recipient actually wants the program. Involving Russian staff in projects as much as possible is also important, because it teaches them new skills.

- The United States underestimated the difficulty in reorienting existing Russian institutions toward the principles and practices of market democracies. New economic reform policies–even once passed into law–were difficult to carry out due to insufficiently developed institutions in either the bureaucracy or the newly created private sector. Formal and informal public and private sector institutions fundamental to the operations of a market economy and democracy were and still are lacking or severely underdeveloped in Russia. By itself, training in how western systems work has limited effect when the trainees must return to the Russian environment. Likewise, new institutions filled with people who have not adopted new approaches will not be institutions of change.
- Corruption is a pervasive major constraint to reform. Corruption is pervasive in Russia and is a major constraint to the development and growth of the private sector. Powerful private interests use their connections to the state to block reforms. Economic restructuring will not be successful without addressing corruption.
- Relations between the United States and the Russian Federation will fluctuate based on international politics or the pace of reform in Russia. However, there are useful, long-term programs mutually beneficial to the United States and the people of Russia that remain relatively immune to fluctuations in the pace of governmental reforms. These include (1) training and exchange programs that increase exposure to and knowledge of democracy and market economies among those involved; (2) direct assistance to independent media or democratic political institutions; (3) help for the emerging private sector; and (4) people-to-people, and institution-to-institution programs.
- Sustained contact with assistance recipients enhances projects: A regular complaint from Russian and other former Soviet Union officials was that technical aid consisted of too many assessments and too few actions. Effective aid projects, such as housing reform by the Urban Institute, relied on sustained contacts between American experts and Russian counterparts, not whirlwind site visits by consultants.

Appendix V

ADDITIONAL INFORMATION ON THE EUROPEAN UNION'S TACIS PROGRAMS IN RUSSIA

BACKGROUND

In December 1990, the European Council decided to offer technical assistance to the Soviet Union in an effort to bolster the reform agenda and help foster the development of a market economy and a democratic society.[1] The European Union (EU) was concerned that the growing economic and political instability in the Soviet Union could affect the EU's member countries. EU members believed that aiding the transition could stave off large refugee flows, help ensure that nuclear reactors operated safely, and maintain economically important trade ties. However, the EU was aware of the potentially large sums of money that could be spent on transition efforts. The German government was just beginning to expend billions of dollars trying to integrate eastern Germany with the rest of the newly unified country. EU leaders were deterred by the potential price tag for providing direct investment in infrastructure for Russia and decided that EU assistance efforts would focus on the provision of technical assistance. This choice played into the assumption at the time that Russia, although misdeveloped by years of communism, also enjoyed the benefits of a large industrial base, an educated population, and abundant natural resources. The EU believed that a large program with several hundred targeted, short-term projects would help train Russians in how to revitalize their economy, integrate Russia into the global market, and contribute to overall political stabilization in the region. In July 1991, the EU adopted a regulation establishing the legal authority for the European Commission[2]2 to implement a technical assistance program, later named the Technical Assistance for the Commonwealth of Independent States. Since that time, the Commission has been responsible for implementing the program. The EU has reauthorized TACIS three times since its creation, through regulations issued by the

---

[1] The European Council is composed of representatives from the 15 member states of the European Union. Its decisions reflect the consensus political will of the EU member states and provide overall political guidance to the activities of the EU.

[2] The European Commission is responsible for, among other things, the implementation of political decisions made by the institutions of the EU

Council of the EU in 1993, 1996, and 1999.[3] These regulations, combined with periodic policy resolutions issued by the EU Council, provide the Commission with overall political guidance for the program. In addition, implementation decisions such as issuing tenders (bids) for contractors and developing the objectives and scope of work for specific projects are overseen by representatives from the 15 member states of the EU, with input from the Russian government.

Overall Objective and Initial Assumptions

Since its inception, the overall objective of the TACIS program in Russia has been to assist and accelerate market economic reforms in Russia. Other objectives pertaining to democracy and rule of law were added in 1993 and 1999. The program has been guided by a common series of assumptions about how TACIS projects would help bring reform to Russia. From the outset, the EU recognized that its ability to influence change in Russia through TACIS was limited. The European Council resolution that created TACIS in 1991 explicitly noted that the resources available for the program were minuscule relative to the size of Russia and the problems it would face during the transition. Successful individual projects could have little impact in such a large country. As a consequence, TACIS strategies and plans stressed the importance of focusing efforts in a few key sectors and tried to cluster projects in reform-minded localities and regions to help achieve broader impact.

EU leaders also believed the transition in Russia would take some time and be very expensive. A TACIS document from 1992 speaks openly of the challenges the program faced in starting operations in Russia. These included the rapidly changing political situation and the magnitude of the problems to be addressed, as well as TACIS' own institutional constraints, especially a critical shortage of staff.

Implicit in TACIS' design is the EU's belief that technical assistance is a relatively inexpensive and cost-efficient way to promote reform. Rather than providing large sums of money to enhance restructuring of enterprises or to finance the social safety net while reforms were being implemented, the EU focused on encouraging the transfer of know-how about market systems to Russia. Related to this assumption was the belief that TACIS' technical assistance would help bring about market reforms. These reforms would attract the foreign direct investment Russia needed to help share the high costs of modernizing and restructuring the Russian economy.

The TACIS program has also stressed the importance of close cooperation with Russian counterparts on strategies, project design, and evaluation. By working alongside its Russian counterparts, the EU hoped to ensure that the resulting TACIS projects would be closely tied to Russian priorities and would reflect the realities on the ground in Russia. This would enhance the program's impact.

---

[3] The Council of the European Union adopts resolutions, which are legally binding on the institutions that comprise the EU, such as the European Commission, and the EU member states. In this instance, the regulation creating TACIS is roughly equivalent to congressional authorizing legislation.

TACIS also recognized that Russian buy-in to an individual project might not be enough to ensure success. Broad progress in making appropriate reforms and providing stability in the macroeconomy creates a stable foundation for technical assistance efforts that are important for overall program success. This assumption recognized that projects were not being conducted in a vacuum. The EU assumed that the support of government officials, an enabling environment of sound economic policies, and progress toward an open and democratic society were necessary for individual TACIS projects and the program as a whole to achieve its goals.

TACIS' INSTRUMENTS

Since its inception in 1991, the TACIS program has relied almost exclusively on six different forms of technical assistance to meet its objectives.[4]

- Policy advisers to government agencies: This has been the primary instrument for the program since its inception. TACIS hires European contractors to work with Russian government officials—sometimes at the federal level, but more frequently at the regional or local level. Policy advisers are supposed to work closely with their counterparts and assist them in pursuing their reform agenda. For example, TACIS is providing policy advisers to assist the Russian government in drafting and implementing tax laws.
- Training and advice to the private sector: Although used less frequently in recent years, many of TACIS' early projects involved training people in various aspects of the operation of the market economy. For example, the largest single project for 1991 provided management education and training for Russian business people in cooperation with the Academy of National Economy. Recently, TACIS has relied less on this instrument due to (1) growing knowledge among Russians about the market and (2) the realization that mass training programs may not be effective if there are no opportunities to use the training outside the classroom. For example, an internal evaluation of TACIS programs in Russia found that training Russians in bank standards based on western practice was not necessarily relevant to the way banks actually operated in Russia.
- Internships: TACIS finances internships that allow Russians to work at EU companies. For example, the managers' training program gives Russian managers from the manufacturing sector a 2- to 3- month internship working at a European firm.
- Funding studies, including pre-investment plans, market research, and feasibility studies: TACIS has provided funding for a wide variety of studies and plans, especially in the early years of the program. The rationale for this instrument is that the Russians may need basic information about the particular problem or issue they

[4] Since 1996, the TACIS regulation has allowed limited use of funds for investment projects. So far, the TACIS program has rarely used this instrument in Russia.

hope to address. Studies also sometimes helped form the foundation for much larger financing from the World Bank or the European Bank for Reconstruction and Development. For example, TACIS recently completed a 2-year study of the feasibility of a gas distribution network extension for the Russian Ministry of Energy. This effort is being used as preparatory work to support a World Bank loan.

- Developing and reforming legal and regulatory frameworks, institutions, and organizations: The EU has also provided technical assistance to help the Russians establish key institutions and processes vital for a market economy. Much of this work involves drafting legislation, training government workers in necessary skills, and offering advice on changing operations. For example, since 1997, TACIS has been supporting efforts to improve the federal-level management of the public health care system in Russia by working with the Ministry of Health to improve its ability to develop and monitor activities to address health concerns.

Linking EU and Russian institutions: In recent years, the EU has placed more emphasis on developing permanent links between EU and Russian institutions, a process the EU calls "twinning." Rather than hiring consultants who may not be around in 12 months' time, the EU will use a European institution, such as a hospital, to implement a program in a Russian hospital. Twinning helps ensure that the Russian counterparts will have a consistent EU partner for follow-up after the conclusion of the program. Ideally, the EU institution would begin to operate its programs in Russia without further EU funding. For example, TACIS' Tempus program promotes links between Russian and EU academic institutions in the areas of economics, business administration, and law.

FUNDING HISTORY FOR RUSSIA

Since 1991, TACIS has committed \$2.7 billion for programs in Russia and disbursed \$1.6 billion (see fig. 25). For most of this period, commitments ranged from \$250 million to \$300 million annually, although commitments for 1999 and 2000 dropped considerably.[5]

[5] Part of the reason for this drop is the introduction of an incentive scheme within the program. About 10 percent of total program funding for 2000 has been taken from country budgets and set aside to finance the best project proposals from all TACIS countries.

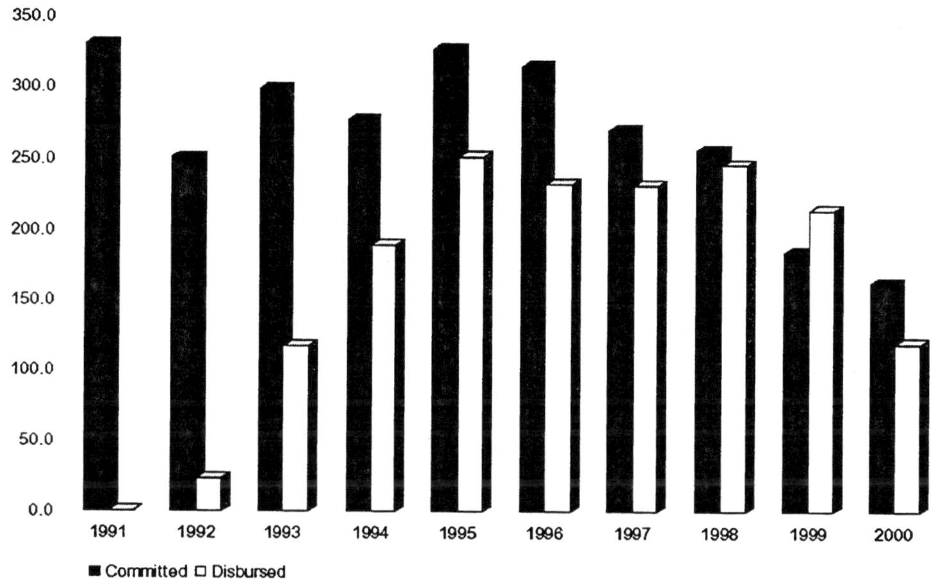

Figure 25: TACIS Commitments and Disbursements for Russia, 1991-2000
Note: Data for 2000 is through August 31. Source: European Commission.

TACIS assistance has been spread across seven major sectors since 1991 (see fig. 26). Energy and enterprise support account for about half of total disbursements to date.[6] Human resources development and agriculture spending are also important sectors. In fact, TACIS has devoted a larger share of its funding—about 9 percent— for agriculture than any of the other donors in our study. Although the 2000 program for Russia emphasizes human rights and civic society, funding for democratic reform has been only a minor portion of the program to date.

6 Energy programs include nuclear reactor safety efforts, as well as technical assistance to rationalize Russia's delivery of all forms of energy within the economy.

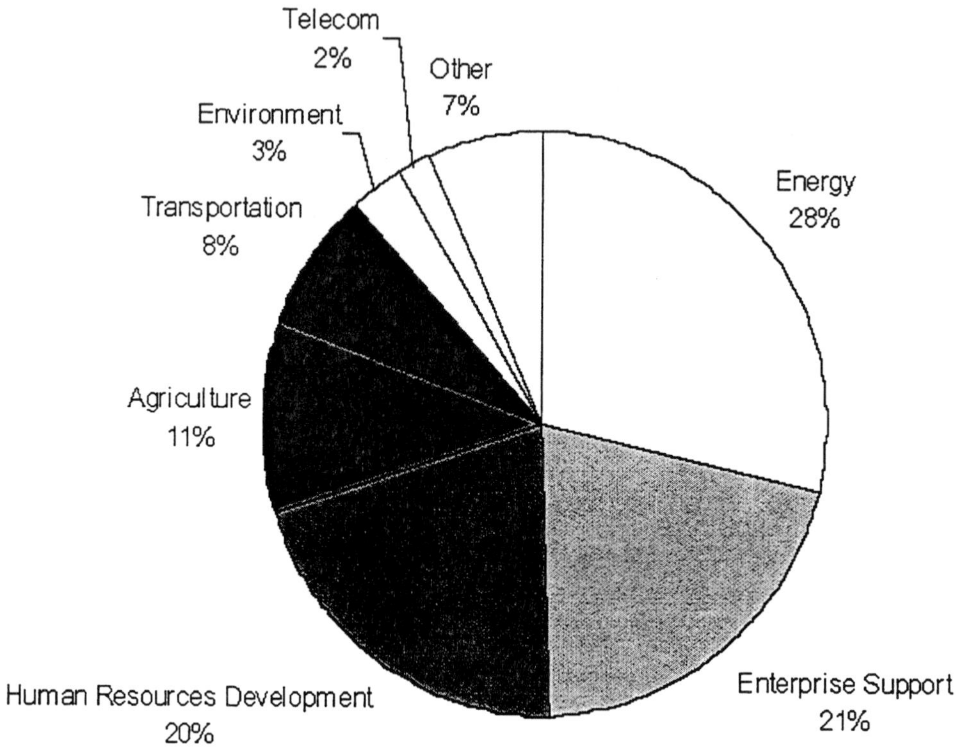

Figure 26: TACIS Commitments by Sector, 1991-1999

Source: European Commission.

STRATEGY

Drawing generalizations about strategy with such a broad and diverse program is difficult. Since 1991, TACIS has implemented more than 500 projects in Russia and as of August 2000 had about 100 projects underway

Although the TACIS strategy for Russia has evolved over time away from having a quick impact toward placing more emphasis on laying the foundations for reform and paying greater attention to democratic reform, some central tenets have remained consistent. TACIS remains largely a technical assistance program that has delivered help to essentially the same sectors since 1991. The EU presents its strategy for TACIS assistance to Russia in a series of publicly available documents, including multiyear indicative plans and annual action plans.

Early Efforts in 1991-94 Focused on Quick Impact

TACIS projects during the early years of the transition focused on having a quick impact, with special attention devoted to training Russians in market economics. Democracy building was not initially a significant part of the program. Although democracy was included as an overarching objective in 1993, the projects TACIS implemented during this period were almost exclusively related to various aspects of economic reform including human resource development, enterprise support, energy, transportation, financial services, and food distribution.

The specific projects implemented to pursue these goals emphasized quickly identifying problems and putting consultants in the field to meet specific Russian needs. Many of the early projects were small, with a focus on diagnosing a problem, and often involved study tours, conferences, or writing reports. There was also an emphasis on training as many people as possible in a variety of areas including banking, finance, and economics. Most of this training was conducted in Russia because TACIS also attempted to support or create permanent institutions to carry out the training after TACIS funding stopped.

From the beginning of the program, TACIS frequently implemented projects at the regional and local levels. In fact, it prepared action plans specifically for ten regions of Russia from 1992-1995, in addition to plans for Russia as a whole. The rationale for focusing on the regions, later echoed by other donors such as the United States and the European Bank for Reconstruction and Development, included a desire to reward more reform-minded regional governments in an effort to show other regions that reforms were both preferable and possible.

Greater Emphasis on Attaining Systemic Change, 1995-98

During this period, support for economic reform and for democracy were the dual goals of the TACIS program in Russia. However, TACIS implementation continued to focus mainly on economic reform, with greater emphasis on attaining systemic change at the federal level. The change in TACIS' approach was driven by the changing conditions in Russia. The EU realized the challenges of transition in Russia proved to be much harder than expected in terms of complexity and the length of time the process would take. From working in the regions, TACIS learned that the success of projects often depended on the overall reform environment. Without a strong base of reform and market-oriented institutions, it proved difficult to have lasting impacts. Thus, TACIS shifted its focus in an attempt to have greater influence on systemic reforms. TACIS implemented larger projects and worked more frequently with partners at the federal level, but projects with federal institutions generally had activities in pilot regions. Although TACIS changed its relative focus from the regions to the federal level, it continued to operate in essentially the same sectors as it always had. For example, the only change in priority sectors between 1994 and 1998 was the addition of environment to the list of sectors that were the focus of technical assistance.

The political context for the TACIS program changed after 1994, when the Partnership and Cooperation Agreement between the EU, EU member states, and the Russian government was signed.[7] This document was an effort to delineate and tighten the links between Russia and the EU. For TACIS, the Partnership and Cooperation Agreement provided clear political guidelines for the program, something that had been lacking in the past. By 1996, TACIS' plans included specific references to the agreement, although the selection of specific projects remained more closely linked to the annual action and multiyear indicative plans.

Some of TACIS' initial assumptions changed during this period. Like other donors, TACIS realized the challenges of promoting reform in Russia were more complicated than initially expected. As an interim EU Commission evaluation of the program reported in 1997, "With hindsight, it is clear that the complexity of societal change in the NIS [new independent states of the former Soviet Union] was grossly underestimated." As a result, project selection began to include more grassroots efforts related to improving civil society and developing small- and medium-sized enterprises.

Post-crisis Reflection Leads to Modified Approach

The Russian financial crisis in late 1998 reinforced TACIS' earlier assumption that Russia's transition to a market economy would be a long-term process. TACIS officials told us that it was clear the transition had not gone as well as initially expected, in part because (1) the institutional underpinnings for a market economy and democratic society were lacking and (2) the necessary political consensus within Russia on how to proceed was not developed. The EU in general revisited its overall approach to helping Russia with the transition process. The increased focus on the institutions necessary for a market economy and democratic society led the EU to add a third objective to the program: support for the development of the rule of law. By 2000, the TACIS' annual program made democracy building the central focus for the first time. TACIS also placed greater emphasis on building institutions, working at the grassroots level, and developing more linkages—"twinning"—between Russian and EU institutions.

During this period, TACIS also changed the way in which it consulted with the Russians about plans and projects. Until the end of 1999, the Russian government had to initiate project proposals before TACIS could develop and implement them. In practice, relying exclusively on Russian project proposals limited TACIS' ability to play a role in several key areas of the transition, especially the democracy building and social service sector. Consequently, the 1999 regulation for TACIS moved to a so-called "dialogue-driven" approach in which project ideas can be initiated by the EU or the Russian government. Project approval remains a mutual EURussian decision.

TACIS' strategy in Russia was also placed more firmly within the framework of broader EU political goals in Russia. The Partnership and Cooperation Agreement was

[7] The Agreement entered into force in December 1997.

supplemented by the development of a common EU strategy for relations with Russia.[8] The main finding in the strategy was that a stable, democratic Russia closely tied to a united Europe was essential for maintaining lasting peace in Europe. To achieve this goal, the EU would focus on achieving two aims: (1) a stable, open, and pluralistic democracy in Russia underpinned by a market economy; and (2) intensified cooperation with Russia on global security goals. Technical assistance to Russia was now more explicitly tied to supporting broader EU goals. In practice, this meant development of projects like improving transportation links, upgrading border controls, and addressing environmental concerns in northwest Russia. Projects like these supported the dual EU goals of backing the transition in Russia to a market economy and democratic society for its own sake and increasing Russia's integration within Europe as a whole.

New Assistance Slowed in 2000

The year 2000 has been unusual for the TACIS program in Russia. First, the introduction of a new regulation for the entire program caused some shifts in priorities, tactics, and instruments. Second, Russia's ongoing war in Chechnya and the EU's concern about the human rights situation there led to a political decision by the EU Council in December 1999 to suspend most work on new TACIS assistance to Russia. Previously approved projects could continue to function, and work began on developing $32.3 million in new projects to bolster civil society and human rights.[9] However, work on new economic assistance projects for Russia was halted. The EU lifted this ban in July 2000 and currently plans to devote $53.3 million for economic assistance to support the implementation of Russia's economic reform package.

TACIS has the legal authorization to continue assistance to Russia through the end of 2006. Given the EU's political commitment to support reform in Russia and increase its integration with the rest of Europe, the nature of the help may change. EU officials told us that future programs may place increasing emphasis on supporting EU-Russia bilateral goals such as complying with Partnership and Cooperation Agreement requirements, approximating EU standards, and removing technical barriers to additional trade, in addition to promoting democratic development and the growth of civil society.

LESSONS LEARNED

TACIS does not have a systematic process for collecting lessons learned about its projects. TACIS officials stressed that such a system would be difficult to implement, given the large number of projects it carries out across Russia and the rest of the former

[8] Under the terms of the treaty obligations that form the legal basis for the EU, the Commission is allowed to act on behalf of the joint interests of the 15 member states on certain foreign policy matters. EU member states negotiated the common goals set out in the common strategy, which were later approved by the Council of the EU after consultation with the Russian government.

[9] The EU approved the plan for these projects in June 2000.

Soviet Union. However, TACIS officials and TACIS reports and evaluations provide some lessons learned from experience in Russia.

- Achieving an impact in Russia is difficult, given the challenges of the operating environment. Russia is a large country with complex problems that are not easily addressed by technical assistance, unless there is clear commitment to reform. Such commitment and consensus are hard to build during a period of economic decline and continued political crisis. Sustainability of results is also difficult and requires follow-through on recommendations. For example, contractors cannot expect to have much influence from writing a report, then leaving.
- Successful projects have support from Russian counterparts and generally require contractors to have a close, long-term presence.
- The lack of political will and the difficulty in obtaining political consensus have been significant impediments to reform in Russia.
- The transition to a market economy and democratic society will take a long time—much longer than initially envisioned. In part this is because a sustainable transition to a market economy and democratic society requires broad, grassroots support; effective and stable institutions; and adequate laws and enforcement.
- The quality of individual consultants is central to project effectiveness.
- Russians are now more familiar with "how it is done" in the West. They need help in developing solutions that work within the Russian context. Within this context, the previous emphasis on knowledge transfer may require modification. Instead, TACIS implementers and their Russian partners should expect to share knowledge and information to develop joint solutions more frequently. For example, according to one EU official, about half of TACIS' ongoing projects in Russia use local experts.
- There is a clear understanding that TACIS could further improve the delivery of its assistance, both in terms of timeliness and impact. Many reports noted the lengthy delays between project approval and project implementation and found that these delays were rooted in (1) the complex EU tendering process, (2) critical understaffing of the program, and (3) political complications stemming from the requirement to obtain approval from 15 member states and the Russian government. The new regulation approved in December 1999 was designed to address some of these problems.

Appendix VI

TIME LINE OF KEY ECONOMIC AND POLITICAL EVENTS IN THE RUSSIAN FEDERATION, 1990-2000

YEAR ECONOMIC EVENTS, POLITICAL AND SOCIAL EVENTS

1990

- G7 asks for joint study of the Soviet economy
- Soviet output declines
- System of state orders begins to break down in face of growing strikes, interethnic strife, and creation of local and republic trade barriers follows
- Competitive local and republic level democratic elections held; anti-Communist parties do well
- Soviet constitution amended to remove Communist supremacy in political matters; new parties emerge
- Presidential guideline issued giving republics considerable freedom over pace of reform

1991

- Gorbachev issues new economic anticrisis program
- Trade bloc with former East bloc dissolved; volume of trade quickly declines
- Yeltsin granted emergency powers to reform the Russian economy; calls for rapid, ambitious reform including privatization, ending most wage and price controls, and removing government controls on trade and foreign currency transactions
- Inflation surges, output falls, deficit quickly grows due to low taxes and continued high government transfers to households and enterprises
- Boris Yeltsin popularly elected Russian President
- Communist hard-liners' attempted coup fails, but episode undermines the political authority of the Soviet Union and Gorbachev

- Yeltsin issues decrees declaring Russia's economic sovereignty and takes control of Soviet government agencies
- Yeltsin appoints pro-reform government and appeals for donor assistance; Yegor Gaider named Deputy Prime Minister
- Accord between Russia, Ukraine, and Belarus dissolves the Soviet Union; Gorbachev resigns and the Soviet Union is formally dissolved

1992

- Ruble allowed to float freely
- Most prices liberalized leading to increases five to sixteen fold in retail prices
- State trading monopoly abolished
- Mass privatization program adopted
- Exchange rate unified
- Voucher privatization begins
- Russian legislature tries to halt Yeltsin's reform efforts
- Western nations announce $24 billion aid package
- Acting Prime Minister Gaidar ousted and replaced by Viktor Chernomyrdin
- Gereschenko becomes head of the Central Bank of Russia, and proceeds to lend money directly to enterprises
- Russia joins the IMF and World Bank

1993

- Treasury bills market started
- New ruble introduced
- Ruble zone collapses
- Legislature narrowly fails to impeach Yeltsin; passes resolution limiting powers of government to implement reforms
- President dissolves the Russian parliament and calls for elections
- Parliamentary forces attack a TV station and the mayor's office; government forces storm the parliament building
- Yeltsin introduces special presidential rule
- Federal elections for the new Duma result in victory for Communist and nationalist parties
- New constitution giving President greater power, approved in referendum

1994

- Voucher privatization completed
- Cash-based privatization begins

- Speculators attack the ruble, causing a 20 percent drop in value in one day
- New federal Duma attempts to block the government's reform plans; Yeltsin responds by issuing decrees
- Reformers brought back into government
- Russian troops invade Chechnya

1995

- Currency bonds introduced
- Federal Assembly bans loans from Central Bank to the government without Assembly approval
- Loans for shares auction begins
- Communist Party dominates Duma elections
- Yeltsin's popularity rating falls below 10 percent
- Duma tries to impeach Yeltsin and fails
- Russian oligarchs agree to suspend their differences and unite to back Yeltsin's presidential campaign

1996

- Foreign trade liberalized
- Full current account convertibility introduced
- Federal Eurobond sale begins
- Yeltsin wins Presidential election, but is stricken with poor health for much of the year
- Russian troops withdraw from Chechnya

1997

- Regional Eurobond sale begins
- Paris Club admission
- London Club debt rescheduling
- Russia's first year of (barely) positive economic growth
- Financial crisis in Asia places pressure on the ruble
- Key reformers brought back into the government in March
- Scandal over book royalties proves politically damaging to some key reformers
- Duma tries to impeach Yeltsin and fails

1998

- Interest rates on Russian bonds, securities rises as government attempts to finance growing deficit and defend ruble • $22.6 billion Western financial assistance package announced
- Financial crisis: Russia defaults on government bonds, places moratorium on external debt service, widened exchange rate bands—ruble plunges, stocks plunge, GDP falls, prices soar
- Reformers removed from key positions in government
- Yeltsin fires Chernomyrdin, and Sergei Kiriyenko is confirmed as Prime Minister
- Yeltsin dismisses entire cabinet, and Yuri Primakov becomes Prime Minister

1999

- New government fails to enact meaningful reform in response to crisis; but also does not turn back past reforms
- New tax code enacted
- Exchange rate reunified after a brief dual exchange rate regime
- New $4.6-billion IMF program announced; only $600 million disbursed to date
- Economic growth, led by increased domestic production, resumes sooner than expected
- Yeltsin dismisses cabinet again, including Primakov; Sergei Stepashin named new Prime Minister
- Duma tries to impeach Yeltsin and fails
- Vladimir Putin named prime minister after Stepashin is dismissed
- Russian troops enter Chechnya, launching second war there
- Duma elections result in pro-government majority for the first time
- Yeltsin resigns and names Putin acting President

2000

- Oil price increase, leads to large trade and balance of payments surpluses
- Economic growth accelerates
- Russian government releases outlines of economic reform package
- Duma approves changes to tax laws
- Putin is elected president
- New laws reduce political autonomy of the regions
- Government cracks down on opposition media

Appendix VII

ADDITIONAL INFORMATION ON ECONOMIC TRENDS

In this appendix, we sketch the key economic trends that have prevailed during Russia's economic transition. We have limited the discussion to trends in Russian output, poverty, debt, trade, foreign investment, and capital flight.

Since the early 1990s, Russia has been described as having an "economy in transition;" that is, it is in the process of transforming the institutions, incentive systems, and economic structures of central planning into those appropriate to a market system of decentralized decision-making. Russia's economic transition faces the challenge of transforming the rigid production and social structures handed down to Russia by the former Soviet Union. Although Russia still has a long way to go to create a market economy, it has seen some success in overcoming the vestiges of the Soviet command economy. However, the transition has been, at times, accompanied by a substantial degree of macroeconomic instability in the form of declining economic output, soaring inflation, large government deficits, unsustainable debt, capital flight, and deteriorating living standards.

ASPECTS OF THE DECLINE OF RUSSIAN OUTPUT

The fall of the former Soviet Union led to the collapse of Russia's trade with traditional partners as well as reduced flows of goods and services among the former republics. The Russian output began to slip as supply and distribution problems idled enterprises and as the economy deteriorated into barter. Also, as the government removed production subsidies, much of the capital capacity went out of use. Reductions in military expenditures further accelerated the fall in production.

Figure 27 shows the severe drop in gross domestic production experienced by Russia since 1990, together with the even sharper contraction in investment and industrial output. The decline in consumption was less drastic, reflecting a correction in Soviet-era policies that discouraged consumption.

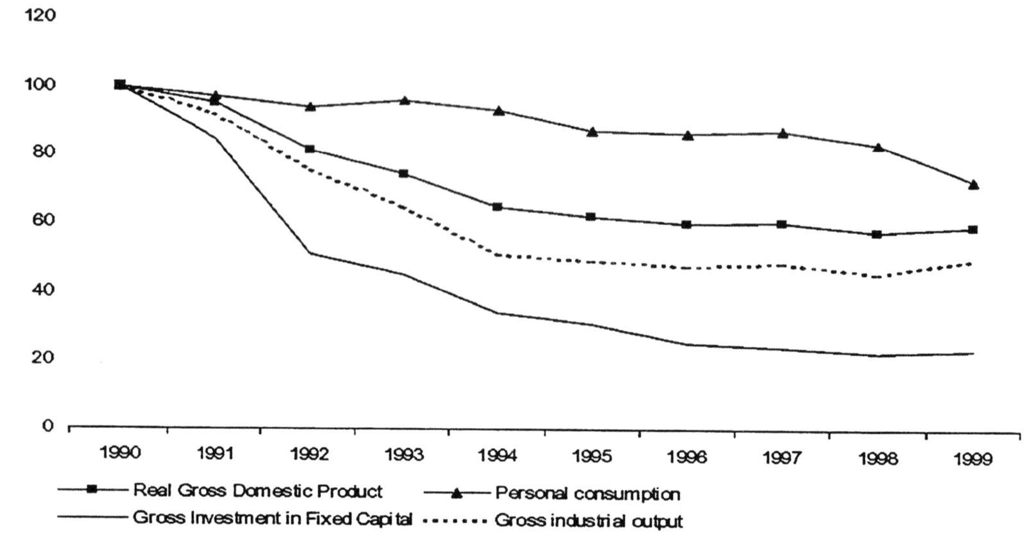

Figure 27: Index of Russian Production, Consumption, Industrial Output, and Investment, 1990-1999, 1990 = 100

Source: PlanEcon.

Measured economic output, however, may not accurately reflect Russian production, because many economic activities have been drawn away from the formal sector to the informal sector. Also, official statistics may have exaggerated the decline to some degree.[1] Furthermore, how the decline in output affected the welfare of Russian citizens is complex. The elimination of expensive military investments, downsizing of energy-intensive polluting industries, and closure of some industries that produced little actual value - added had some beneficial effects.

Russia achieved a positive nominal GDP growth in 1999, as industrial production grew by 8 percent. GDP grew by 3.2 percent in 1999, exceeding western forecasts. This recovery was primarily attributable to the import substitution effect after the ruble devaluation of August 1998, the increase in prices of Russia's oil exports, and some industrial restructuring. As of September 2000,the IMF forecast GDP growth of 7.0 percent in 2000 and 4.0 percent in 2001.

POVERTY AND LIVING STANDARDS

Russia has seen a surge in poverty and a deterioration of living standards for a large number of its citizens. Most social indicators show significant worsening since the collapse of the Soviet Union in 1991. According to the latest United Nations human development report, Russia in 1999 ranked 71st among 173 countries. In 1991 based on data for 1985-90, the United Nations had ranked the Soviet Union as 31st out of 160 countries. One measure for the extent of poverty in Russia is the trend of real GDP per capita and real average wages, which shows that by 1999 the average Russian citizen lost nearly 40 percent of his or her 1990 income. During the first quarter of 2000, 59.9 million Russians, or 41.2 percent of the population, lived below the poverty line or subsistence level of 1,138 rubles ($40.21) a month. The average life expectancy in Russia has reflected the trend in poverty and living conditions (see fig. 28).

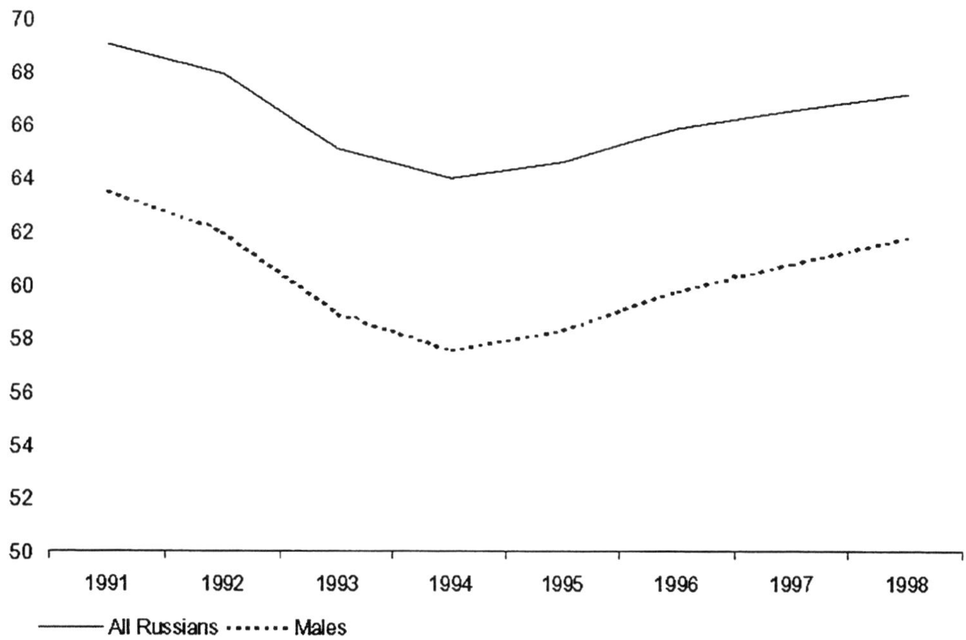

Figure 28: Average Russian Life Expectancy at Birth, in Years
Source: IMF, Russian Federation: Recent Economic Developments.

Much of the increase in poverty can be linked to the collapse of output and income, coinciding with very high rates of inflation early in the transition process. As a result of the increase in income inequality, the share of the population below the subsistence level does not necessarily improve with output growth. Other causes of the increase in poverty include reductions in state subsidies, and nonpayment and erratic payment of wages and pensions.[2]

As can be seen from figure 29, after an initial surge during the early years of high inflation, the share of population below the subsistence level was relatively stable at around 20 percent from the end of 1995 to July 1998. In September 1998, the share of

[1] The extent of the decline in output in official statistics may be exaggerated, because expenditure data indicated a less severe downturn, and also because electricity consumption by industry had fallen far less than the reported decline in industrial production.

population below the subsistence level surged due to the financial crisis and subsequent reduction in real wages. The traditional social support system has been severely affected by the budget crises of local, regional, and central governments; with health services, housing, and recreational and cultural facilities becoming increasingly inaccessible to those who are poor.

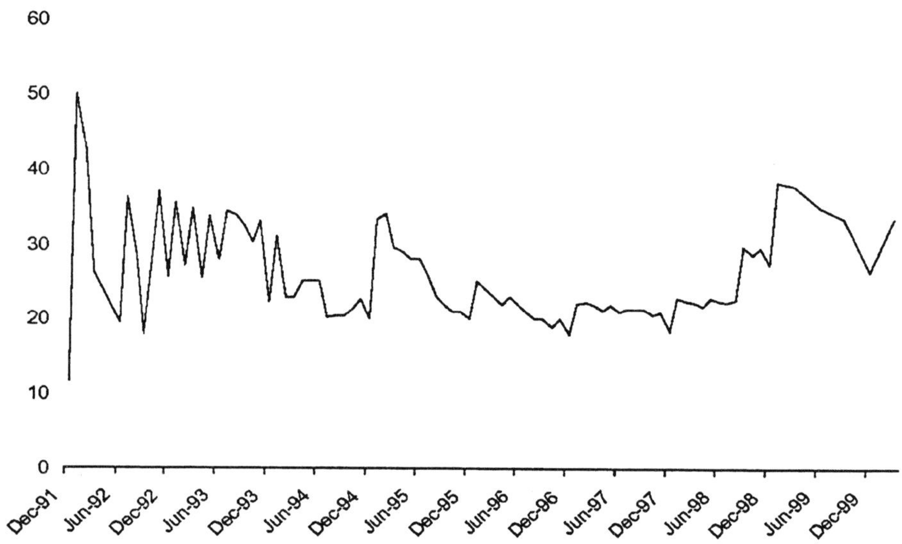

Figure 29: Share of Russian Population Below Subsistence Level, December 1991-June 2000
Source: Russian Economic Trends database, 2000.

FOREIGN TRADE

The supply and distribution linkages within Russia and the former union fell apart when the former Soviet Union dissolved. In the absence of these linkages, the region lacked an effective payments system to facilitate trade. Russia, therefore, faced a collapsed demand for its traditional industrial exports and uncertain input supplies from domestic and former Soviet Union sources to produce its exports. Russia's exports have been concentrated in energy and raw materials, making export revenues highly sensitive to changes in commodity prices. Its imports were primarily consumer goods, foodstuffs, and machinery and equipment.

Russia has generated a persistent trade surplus despite a very low level of trade for the size of the Russian economy. In mid 1993, both imports and exports began to increase, when higher oil and gas export prices prevailed and a depreciated ruble made exports more competitive. Imports of western goods and services were boosted by eased foreign exchange constraints. In 1998, oil prices fell and the Russian financial crisis

[2] In 1997, overdue wages were estimated at 63 trillion rubles (equivalent to 5 weeks' wages in the whole economy).

caused a devaluation of the ruble and imports dropped sharply. In 1999, a further drop in imports helped to raise the merchandise trade surplus to a record $35 billion (see fig. 30).

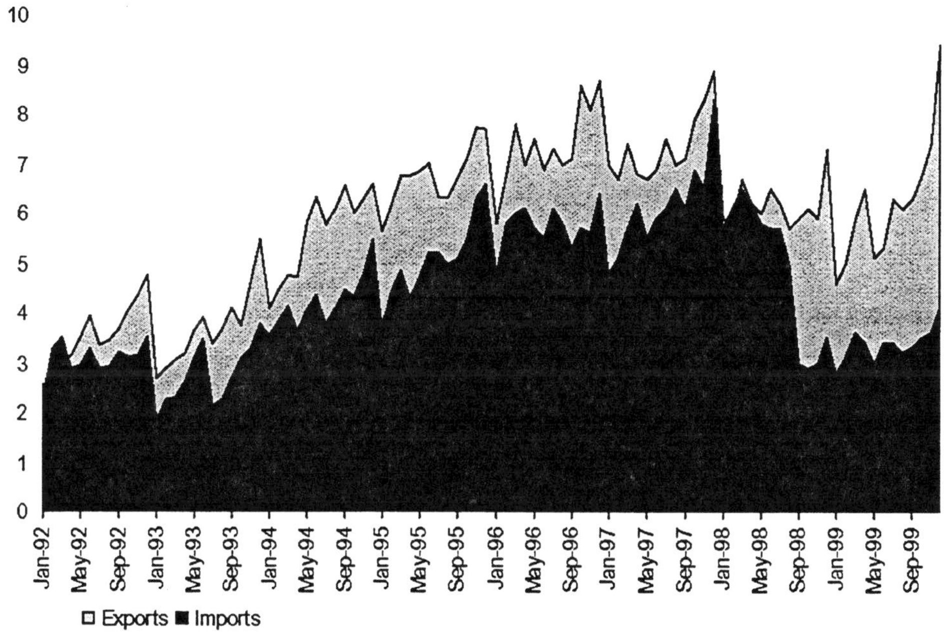

Figure 30: Merchandise Trade of Russia, January 1992-December 1999 (Billions of U.S. dollars)
Source: Russian Economic Trends database, 2000.

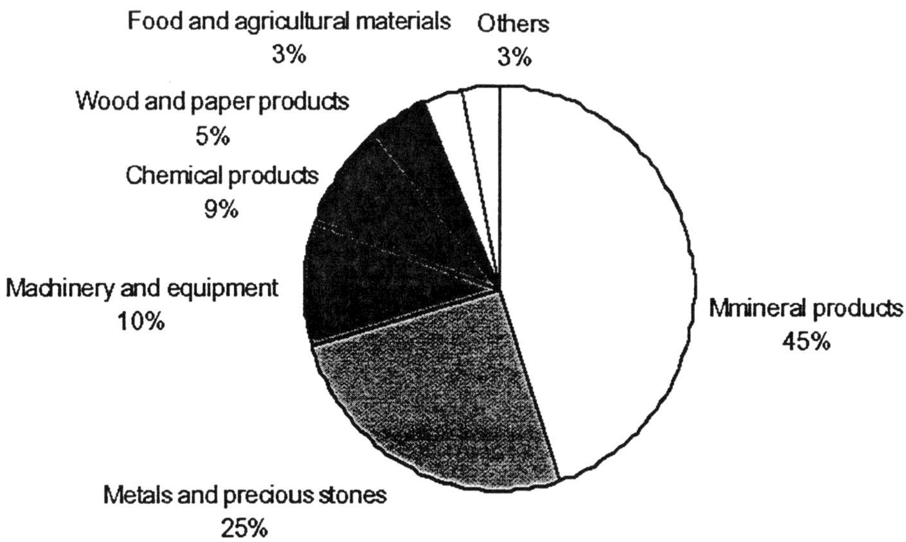

Figure 31: Composition of Russian Exports, 1994-98
Note: "others" includes textiles, footwear, leather, and fur.
Sources: Goskomstat: Russian Economic Trends, 1999.

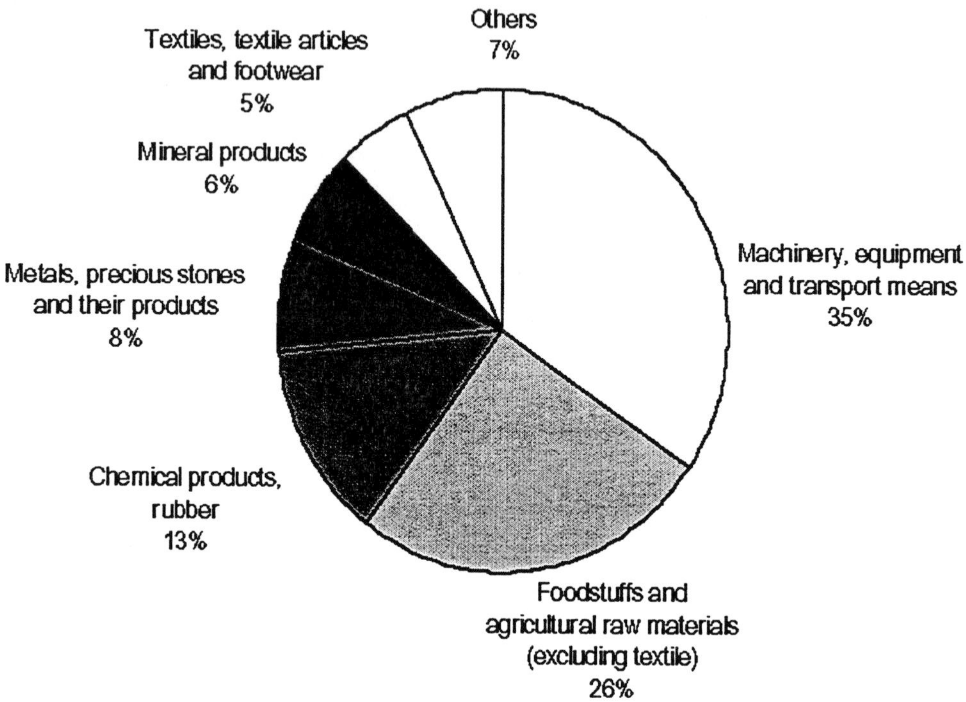

Figure 32: Composition of Russian Imports, 1994-98
Note: "others" includes wood and paper products, leather, and fur.
Source: Goskomstat: Russian Economic Trends, 1999.

Debt of the Government of Russian Federation

The Russian government has substantial foreign debt, estimated at $146 billion (see fig. 33) at the end of 1999. Approximately $100 billion of Russia's foreign debt was inherited from the former Soviet Union. Russia assumed all the debt of the former Soviet Union in exchange for the Soviet Union's foreign assets. The Russian government also has domestic debt, which was approximately $33 billion as of the end of 1999.[3]

Russia's current payment obligations to creditors represent a significant expense in the federal budget. Debt service obligations in 1999 were $17.9 billion, or 29 percent of federal expenditures. In addition, servicing domestic debt amounted to another 11 percent of federal expenditures. Table 8 shows the amount of external debt service due and paid in 1999. Russia paid all the debt service due on debt obligations incurred by the Russian federation, the majority of which was payments to multilateral institutions. In contrast, in

[3] A portion of the domestic debt is valued in foreign currency, which makes servicing the debt particularly burdensome to the federal budget when the ruble exchange rate depreciates, as was the case in 1998.

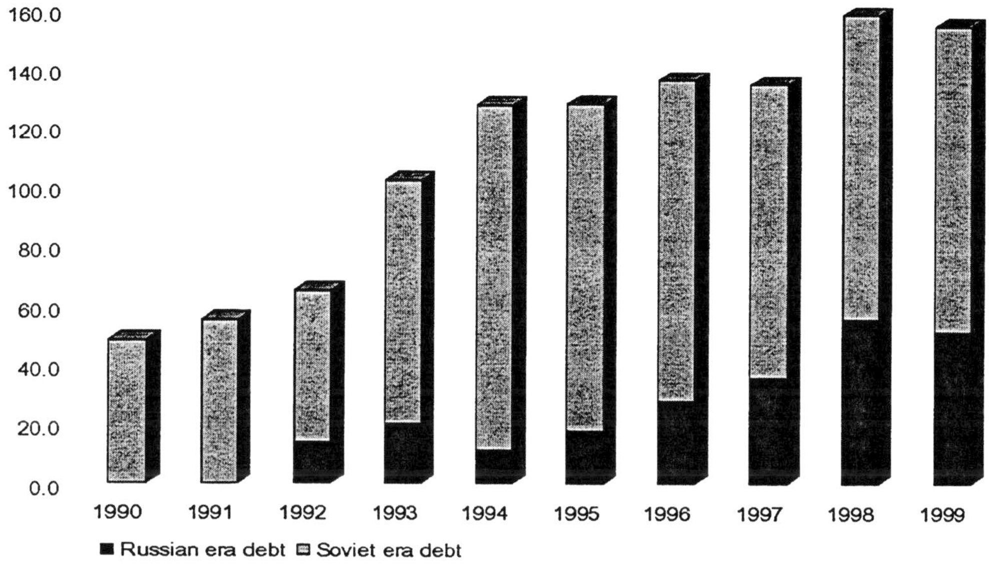

Figure 33: Russia's Foreign Debt, 1990-99 (Billions of U.S. dollars)
Note: Soviet era debt = Debt inherited from the former Soviet Union Russian era debt = Debt of the Russian Federation contracted after January 1, 1992 Source: 1990-93 figures were calculated by GAO using World Bank, Global Development Finance, 1994-99 figures are from IMF, Russian Federation: Recent Economic Developments.

1999 Russia paid about $600 million on the $8.9 billion debt service due on Soviet era debt owed primarily to Paris Club bilateral creditors. Furthermore, its payments on the debt of the former Soviet Union have been rescheduled several times. The rescheduling of the debt has generally postponed payments of interest. In February 2000, Russia's commercial creditors agreed to write off $11.6 billion in debt and to restructure the remaining debt over 30 years. Russia has argued that the high costs of market reforms call for lower debt repayments and has requested additional debt relief on its Soviet era debt from its official bilateral creditors.

Between 1994 and 1999, Russia paid interest and principal of about $12 billion on loans it had received from international financial organizations. Russia expects to pay roughly $10 billion in foreign debt payments in 2000. Also, from 2001 on, it will have to retire the Eurobonds it placed in 1997 and 1998. In addition, the grace period on debt repayment to the London and Paris clubs ends in 2002, boosting significantly annual foreign debt repayments. According to the World Bank, it is estimated that between 2001 and 2008, a total of $117 billion in debt service will be due.

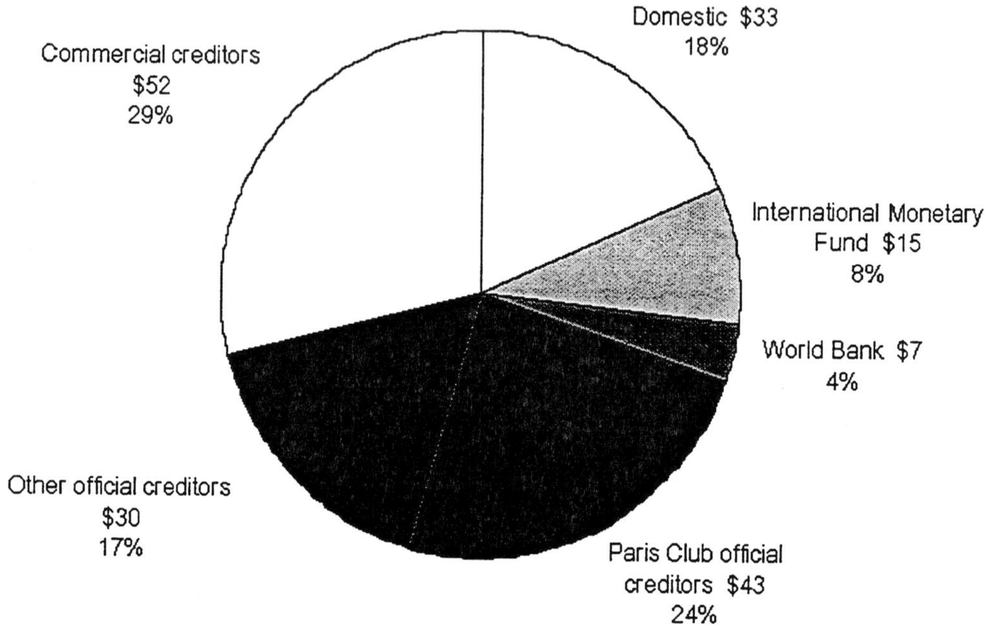

Figure 34: Debt Components of the Russian Government, End 1999 (Billions of U.S. Dollars)
Source: Institute for Economies in Transition, 1999.

Table 8: Foreign Currency Debt Service of the Russian Federation in 1999

Billions of U.S. dollars				
	Soviet era[a]		Russian era[b]	
	Due	Paid	Due	Paid
Principal	3.06	0.18	5.72	5.72
Interest	5.83	0.45	3.31	3.31
Total debt service	**8.89**	**0.63**	**9.03**	**9.03**
of which				
Multilateral	0.00	0.00	5.54	5.54
Official bilateral	8.39	0.40	1.56	1.56
Bonds	0.00	0.00	1.64	1.64
Other commercial	**	0.23	0.29	0.29
Interest on arrears	0.50	0.00	0.00	0.00

[a]Debt service on debt of the former Soviet Union for which Russia has accepted responsibility.
[b]Debt service on debt of the Russian Federation contracted after January 1, 1992.
** Data included in official bilateral creditors. Source: International Monetary Fund

FOREIGN INVESTMENT

The Russian federation presents a potentially lucrative opportunity for foreign investment due to its large domestic market, skilled and educated labor force, and valuable natural resources. Most foreign investment in Russia has been concentrated in the energy, food, and trade sectors with the United States and Germany as the leading foreign investors in Russia. Russia has, however, attracted little foreign investment compared to most other transition countries. Taxes, corruption, changing regulatory environments, bureaucratic processes, and underdeveloped property right and contract laws have been cited as deterrents to foreign investment to Russia.

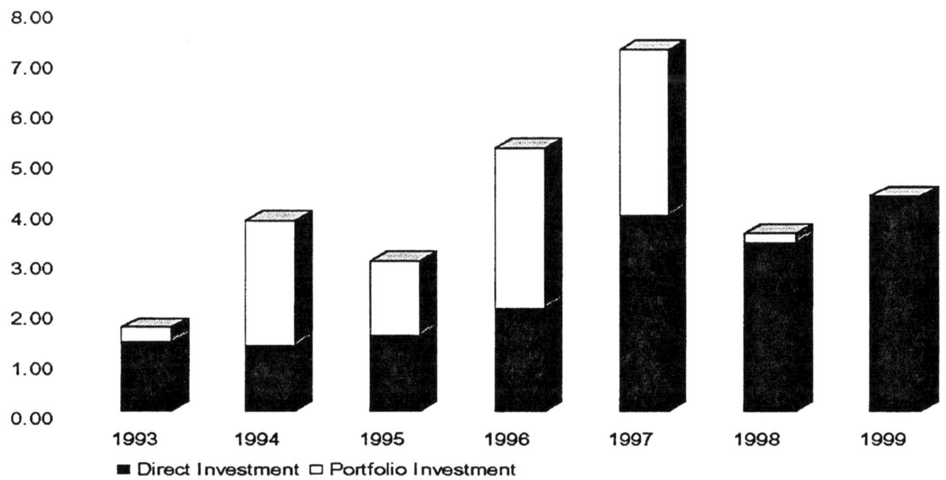

Figure 35: Gross Foreign Investment in Russia, 1993-99 (Billions of U.S. dollars)
Source: Business Information Service for the Newly Independent States (BISNIS), U.S. Department of Commerce, Washington, DC.

According to the United Nations Economic Commission for Europe, cumulative net foreign direct investment in Russia from 1988 to1999 had amounted to $19.9 billion. On per capita basis, this is approximately $135 per capita (see fig. 36), far less than the Czech republic ($1612 per capita) and Poland ($527 per capita). Net foreign direct investment in Russia in 1999 amounted to about $2 billion, out of a global total of $827 billion. Meanwhile, the average age of Russian manufacturing plant and equipment is on average three times older than that of countries in the Organization for Economic Cooperation and Development, implying that updating or replacing these items will take plenty of foreign investment.

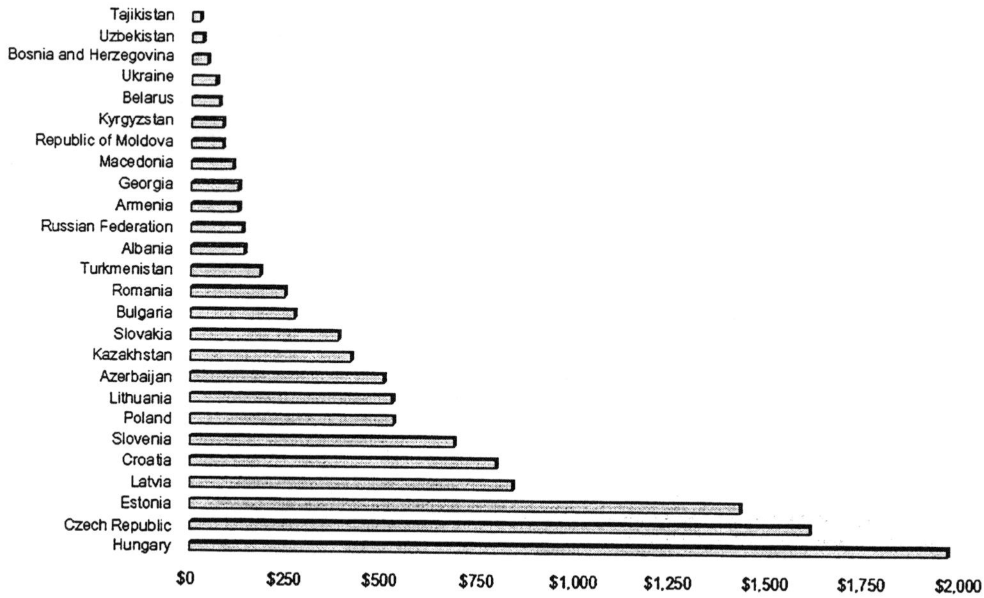

Figure 36: Per Capita Cumulative Foreign Direct Investment in Transition Economies (1988-99)
Source: U.N. Economic Commission for Europe: Transition Report, 2000.

CAPITAL FLIGHT

Capital flight is broadly defined as all outflows of funds that occur in excess of those that would normally be expected as part of an international portfolio diversification strategy. Outflows of funds originating from truly criminal activities, outflows of legally earned funds that breach capital controls and taxes, and fully legal outflows that comply with existing regulations but are motivated by a desire on the part of the investor to flee the country owing to political uncertainty are regarded as capital flight. The economic consequences of capital flight are reduced investment in the economy, loss of productive capacity, lower government revenue for easing the less desirable aspects of economic adjustment, and loss of control of monetary policy.

The transition process has caused Russia to confront a variety of problems that make it risky for its citizens to hold financial assets within Russia's borders. These problems include macroeconomic instability, unsettled political environments, corruption, poorly defined property rights, a fragile banking system, high and unevenly enforced taxes, and fraudulent managerial practices. As a result, capital flight has depleted financial resources needed for economic reform and revitalization. The main forms of capital flight from Russia include (1) understated export earnings, (2) smuggling or unreported exports of goods, (3) over-invoicing of imports, (4) advance payments for import contracts without subsequent deliveries, and (4) capital account transactions with nonresident (offshore) banks that are not regulated by Russian authorities. The channels of capital flight in Russia are mainly the foreign trade sector and the banking sector. In the export sector, revenues from the energy sector are the primary source of capital flight. Over-invoiced imports of foodstuffs are also alleged to be a channel for capital flight.

Estimates of capital flight are limited by the inability to distinguish between legal and illegal capital flows. The Central Bank of Russia estimated that capital flight during 1994-98 averaged $11 billion a year, or approximately $75 per capita (see fig. 38). Other estimates of capital flight from Russia range between $10 billion and $20 billion per year. According to the IMF, Russian authorities have sought to decrease capital flight through intensification of exchange controls, tightened tax administration and financial sector supervision.

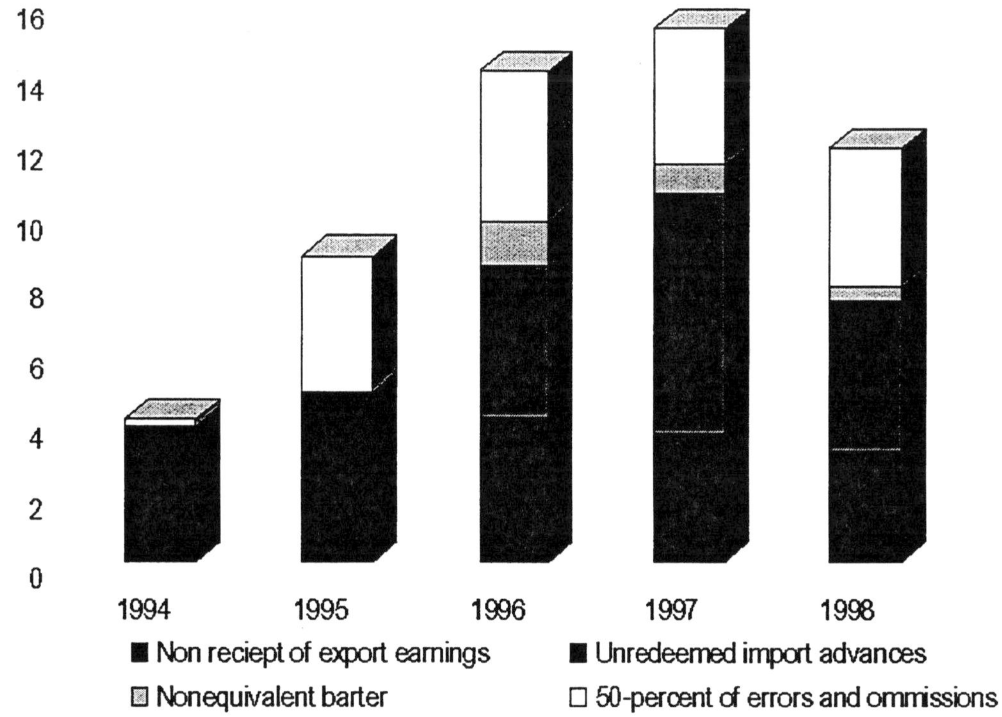

Figure 37: Estimate of Capital Flight From Russia, 1994-98 (Billions of U.S. dollars)
Source: Central Bank of Russia

INDEX

R

S

T

U

V

W

Corporate Governance in Context
Corporations, States, and Markets in Europe, Japan, and the US

Edited by

Klaus J. Hopt, Eddy Wymeersch, Hideki Kanda, and Harald Baum

OXFORD
UNIVERSITY PRESS

OXFORD
UNIVERSITY PRESS
Great Clarendon Street, Oxford OX2 6DP
Oxford University Press is a department of the University of Oxford.
It furthers the University's objective of excellence in research, scholarship,
and education by publishing worldwide in
Oxford New York
Auckland Cape Town Dar es Salaam Hong Kong Karachi
Kuala Lumpur Madrid Melbourne Mexico City Nairobi
New Delhi Shanghai Taipei Toronto
with offices in
Argentina Austria Brazil Chile Czech Republic France Greece
Guatemala Hungary Italy Japan Poland Portugal Singapore
South Korea Switzerland Thailand Turkey Ukraine Vietnam
Oxford is a registered trade mark of Oxford University Press
in the UK and in certain other countries
Published in the United States
by Oxford University Press Inc., New York

First published 2005

British Library Cataloguing in Publication Data
Data available
Library of Congress Cataloging in Publication Data
Data available
Printed in Great Britain
on acid-free paper by
Antony Rowe Ltd, Chippenham
ISBN 0-19-929070-9 978-0-19-929070-3
1 3 5 7 9 10 8 6 4 2

Preface

Over the past two decades, the consequences of globalization have been the topic of intense discussion. One positive outcome is a significant increase in regulatory competition. This in turn has sharpened the comparative awareness of advantages or disadvantages of different national models of political economy and economic organization, of governance and regulation. As a result of the exposure to competition from other jurisdictions, national rules are showing a tendency to bend, either toward greater flexibility or toward solutions that have already been adopted elsewhere. However, although it has been controversially debated, no persuasive model of political and corporate governance has yet been developed. In addition, a comprehensive and generally agreed-upon theory of legal regulation is still lacking. Because institutional change is path-dependent and subject to functional complementarities as well as to social and cultural embeddedness, recognizable patterns of national differences persist. The often-proclaimed convergence of systems remains elusive, and institutional diversity continues to show surprising resilience.

These observations notwithstanding, *some* features of successful modern market economies have been in the process of converging over the last decades, even if the changes have many facets and the speed and scope of their transformation vary in the different economies. The most important – and central – change is a shift in governance from the state to the market. In the case of natural monopolies, this comes as a shift from public to private ownership. When rules intended to protect investors are challenged by new practices in places where protection is derived from the efficient functioning of the market, we see a shift from bureaucratic ex-ante control to judicial ex-post control. Administrative discretion is increasingly being replaced by the rule of law as guidelines for the economy. And, at least to some extent, public enforcement is being reduced in favor of private enforcement by way of disclosure, enhanced liability, and correspondent litigation for damages.

With respect to the players in the market and their relationship toward each other, a significant loss of trust appears to be another consequence of the transnational growth of the markets. Partners of transactions have become increasingly anonymous; thus, detailed and enforceable contracts along with rules and institutions that actually allow an easy enforcement of these contractual rights have replaced informal and short agreements not meant to be presented in court.

The present and still ongoing legal, judicial, and administrative reforms in Japan are a striking example of many of these changes. However, the regulatory burden continues to be significant there and in the other jurisdictions mentioned. This may be so because specific pieces of previously tight regulation providing protection to special interests of the electorate are hard to overcome, or because after deregulation – especially in the wake of the numerous scandals that have beset all of these jurisdictions at one time or another – repeated and sometimes hasty re-regulation has emerged.

These changes are posing daunting challenges to regulators and academics trying to redefine the fundamental governance and regulatory setting. They are confronted with the task of making or keeping the national regulatory structure attractive to investors in the face of competitive pressures from other jurisdictions to adopt state-of-the-art solutions. But, at the same time, they must establish a coherent institutional framework that accommodates the efficient (modern) rules with the existing and hard-to-change (path-dependent) institutional setting. Only by avoiding these easily exploited frictions can scandals and the corresponding economic loss caused by reduced investor confidence be kept at bay.

These challenges – put in a comparative and interdisciplinary perspective – are the subject of this book. It intends to forward the international discussion and search for answers to these pressing questions. As a reflection of the complexity and transnationality of the problems to be solved, the only viable approach for such an undertaking is to include participants from all three of the economies that form the world's leading economies: the EU, the US, and Japan. The first will be largely but not exclusively represented by Germany as a representative example. Japan was selected because of its position as Asia's most successful economy to date.

The general theme has been divided into five parts. First, changes of governance in the 20th century are analyzed from a historical point of view in Germany, Japan, and the US (part I). This provides a general background for the more specific topics that follow. These begin in the second section with corporations as the major economic players in the markets. In all three economies and jurisdictions mentioned above, issues of corporate governance are subject to far-reaching reforms. Some are caused by outright scandals, while other reforms are prompted by the previously legitimate but unwanted exploitation of some stakeholders by others – namely management – as well as a general loss of economic competitiveness and performance. Again, no optimal and pervasive model of corporate governance has yet been found (part II).

Next, the state in its role as regulator comes into the picture. The proper scope of government depends on the institutional choice between corporatist and market models. A related aspect is the desirable level of regulation. Additionally, the proper role of the bureaucracy in a modern market economy will be discussed. The answers to these questions enlarge or reduce the spectrum within which the economic players in the markets can operate (part III).

The fourth part focuses on the market. Three aspects have been selected: financial markets, the market for corporate control, and subsidies and anti-trust. In the financial markets the change in governance from the state to the market can be clearly seen. Examples are the shift of ownership of stock exchanges – formerly perceived as natural monopolies – from public to private ownership, or the shift from bureaucratic ex-ante control to judicial ex-post control. The market for corporate control and its function as well as its efficient regulation